ACCEPT NO MEDIOCRE LIFE

ACCEPT NO MEDIOCRE LIFE

Living Beyond Labels,
Libels, and Limitations

David Foster

WARNER
Faith®

NEW YORK BOSTON NASHVILLE

Scriptures noted NIV are taken from the HOLY BIBLE: NEW
INTERNATIONAL VERSION®. Copyright © 1973, 1978, 1984 by International
Bible Society. Used by permission of Zondervan Publishing House. All rights reserved.
Scriptures noted KJV are taken from the King James Version of the Bible.
Scriptures noted TLB are taken from *The Living Bible,* copyright © 1971.
Used by permission of Tyndale House Publishers, Inc., Wheaton,
Illinios 60189. All rights reserved.
Scriptures noted THE MESSAGE are taken from *The Message: The New Testament in
Contemporary English.* Copyright © 1993 by Eugene H. Peterson.
Scriptures noted NRSV are taken from the NEW REVISED STANDARD VERSION
of the Bible. Copyright © 1989 by the Division of Christian Education of the
National Council of The Churches of Christ in the U.S.A. All rights reserved.
Scriptures noted TEV are taken from TODAY'S ENGLISH VERSION.
Copyright © American Bible Society 1966, 1971, 1976, 1992.
Scriptures noted NLT are from the *Holy Bible,* New Living Translation, copyright ©
1996. Used by permission of Tyndale House Publishers, Inc., Wheaton, Illinois 60189.
All rights reserved.

Warner Faith

Time Warner Book Group
1271 Avenue of the Americas, New York, NY 10020
Visit our website at www.twbookmark.com
The Warner Faith name and logo are registered trademarks of
Time Warner Book Group Inc.

Printed in the United States of America
First Edition: February 2005
10 9 8 7 6 5 4 3 2 1

Library of Congress Cataloging-in-Publication Data
Foster, David
    Accept no mediocre life : living beyond labels, libels, and limitations / David Foster.
        p. cm.
    ISBN 0-446-57686-7
    1. Success—Religious aspects—Christianity. 2. Self-realization—Religious aspects—
Christianity. I. Title.
    BV4598.3.F66 2005
    248.4—dc22
                                                            2004017359

THIS BOOK IS DEDICATED TO THE WOMEN IN MY LIFE:

To Paula, for having relentless belief in me, which
rescued me from a mediocre life.

To Erin, for introducing me to the joys
of fatherhood.

To Lindsey, for showing me a compassionate
heart can be strong.

To Paige, for reminding me to "keep it real."

Contents

INTRODUCTION

Born to Be Mild? No Way!

*So, then, to every man his chance—to every man, regardless of
his birth, his shining golden opportunity—to every man his
right to live, to work, to be himself, to become whatever his
manhood and his vision can combine to make him.*
—THOMAS WOLFE

One minute after birth you were given an Apgar test.
Your heart rate, respiration, muscle tone, reflex response, and color were monitored and measured. If you
scored between 7 and 10, you were declared born in excellent
condition. Anything less and you were categorized as "at risk."
After the doctors and nurses finished with you, they handed you
to your parents, who continued the process by identifying your
family resemblance or lack thereof. "She looks like my side of the
family," or "He looks like my father—pudgy, bald-headed, and
toothless." Before you were aware of what was going on, people
started hanging labels on you. Most of them were good-natured
and harmless, but some stuck to your soul. Like masking tape left
on a wall too long, they've left a faint, dingy scar even after they
were removed.

How many times have you felt the stinging reprimand of a
question or comment like the following? "Why can't you be
more like your brother?" "Why can't you be more like the neighbor kid?" "Why can't you be smart like Sam?" "Why can't you
be pretty like Paula?" "You're just like your father!" Even well-

intentioned parents, who love their kids more than life itself, can hang labels around their children's necks libeling them for a lifetime.

Mitch Albom says, "All parents damage their children. It cannot be helped. Youth, like pristine glass, absorbs the prints of its handlers. Some parents smudge, others crack, a few shatter."[1] Since we almost always come out on the short end of the comparison stick, we spend too much of our lives trying to find ways to conform to other people's criticism of us so that we won't attract more of it. But surely by now you know you can't get small enough for some people to miss sticking a label on you.

The art of labeling, libeling, and limiting isn't just a weird family thing; it's a worldwide, lifelong, everyday thing. What started at the hospital and in the home gets handed off to the hallowed halls of learning. Instead of being in a place where we learn to love learning, we find that school often becomes society's official labeling factory. Parents may become incensed because their "child prodigy" fails to meet requirements for admission to an elite, high-priced kindergarten. We held our daughters out of school for an extra year for the very reason that we wanted them to be emotionally, intellectually, and spiritually prepared for the rigors of repeated testing and labeling. We didn't want their self-worth reduced to a letter grade, good or bad!

What makes being pigeonholed at school traumatic is that these people are professionals. Up to that point only amateurs labeled us. So, in elementary school we learned that others measured our intelligence by letters. The best got A's. The worst got F's. The majority got C's. That was me; I excelled at C's. And they told me if I was a C student, I was *average*. That was where most of us landed, so it didn't seem so bad at the time.

Some words give a hint to their meaning just by the way they sound. Words like *boring, lackluster, mediocre,* and certainly *average*. I wondered what it really meant to be average. I wasn't the worst kid in the class, but I wasn't the best either. I thought average meant you're either the worst of the best or the best of the worst. What an awful thing to discover early in life. I overheard one of my ninth grade teachers describe me as *mild-mannered*. I didn't know what it meant to be *mild*, but I didn't want any part of it. Was I born to be mild?

It was 1968 and a group named Steppenwolf expressed my soul's suffocation with the song "Born to Be Wild." When I heard the lyrics, laid on top of a driving rock beat, I remember screaming out, "Yea, that's what I want, an adventure out on the highway of possibilities." And when the last refrain exploded, I wanted to climb high, never die, and reject for all time the small-minded notion that I was born to be Milquetoast or mediocre. While my peers were telling me I was "born to be mild," what I heard in my heart was *born to be wild!*

High school brings even more divisions among the "will be's" and the "will never be's," when college-bound kids are separated from those who have name tags and hair nets in their future. The labeling expands from academics to the social scene as all the cool kids sit on one side of the cafeteria, the rebels on the other side, and all the mediocre kids in the middle.

From the hospital to the home to the halls of higher learning, we've been labeled so long, we feel libeled and stifled. Too many splendid, gifted men and women have accepted mediocre as their lot in life. It gets pounded into us so much, by so many, after a while it's almost as though there's a conspiracy going on. It is a spiritual conspiracy to get us to accept mediocre as a standard of life. It is a war for control of our hearts, minds, and souls. The Bible states, "For we wrestle not against flesh and blood, but against principalities, against powers, against the rulers of the darkness of this world, against spiritual wickedness in high places" (Eph. 6:12 KJV). What is Satan's ploy? He's fixed on our spiritual destruction. He's a "liar and the father of lies" (John 8:44 NIV). But his tactics are exceedingly subtle. He bombards us with feelings of inadequacy. He seeks to clothe our hearts and minds with a drab coat of beige. He delights when we are labeled average and mediocre, for he knows most labels are libels that limit our capacity to dream, aspire to greatness, or even feel worthy to know God or accept His love. The result? We live well within our perceived limitations and grade-point averages.

This book is for those who refuse to accept mediocre as the standard by which they live their lives. If you're ready to rip off the labels sown to your heart by a lifetime of comparisons and expert opinion, and you're ready to live beyond the limitations others have set for you, then read on.

In a speech given in Washington, D.C., on January 20, 1961, President John F. Kennedy said, "The American, by nature, is optimistic. He is experimental, an inventor and a builder who builds best when called upon to build greatly." It is the goal of this book to urge you to make your life a masterpiece by calling you to a lifelong commitment to excellence in everything you do. It will equip you to *excel at being who you are, where you are, with what you have, while you can.* If you excel in these four areas, you will never have to worry about being mild. To me, *mild* means being "mediocre in life and death." The truth is, if you're mediocre in one, you'll be mediocre in both.

God created you *uniquely* you as an act of joy. He placed within you the design and desire for greatness. But greatness does not grow well in the soil of mediocrity. It is a sad truth that excellence makes people nervous, especially people who settle for second-rate reality. Throw off mild and mediocre just as you would a cheap suit. To help you do this, I'll expose two myths you've put up with long enough.

Myth number one is, "you're mediocre, and there's not much you can do about it." Reject the judgments of experts who label, libel, and limit you by their curt and coy comparison. While some label you accidentally, others know exactly what they are doing. Their insistence that you belong in the middle is often motivated by the mediocrity they tolerate in themselves. You are meant for far more than joining the mainstream and the middle class. After all, everything we know about the postmodern world tells us the bell curve doesn't apply anymore, if it ever did.

Myth number two is, "you're the best." This myth sounds solid at first blush because it's a much-welcomed cure for the mediocre middle. The problem is, there is no such thing as "the best." The best sports team this year is often next year's cellar dweller. The best salesman this month will be outdone the next. The record set by today's achievement will be broken by tomorrow's accomplishment. Striving to be the best at anything is a high-speed chase to disappointment and discouragement. The goal is not to be *the* best, but to be *my* best. To be my best means I've jumped off the fence and stepped over the line. I've pulled out all the stops, and I'm holding nothing of the best back. There's no turning back, slowing down, or backing away. It's life outside the box for me. I've stopped trying to make life work, and I've started trying to make life sing. I reject secondhand faith, third-rate dreams, and low-risk crusades. By God's grace and with His help, I will grow up into the greatness He had in mind when He made me.

Achieving your full potential tomorrow means learning to fully appreciate your life today. I like the truth of the old Burmese proverb, "He who aims at excellence will be above mediocrity; he who aims at mediocrity will be far short of it." Aiming high is essential, and there's no other way to aim at reaching the awesome possibilities ahead of you and me without being creatively and fully alive today. I come alive creatively when I dare to live in the moment with a view of what is possible in the future. I can see what is possible only when I am free from other people's labels, libels, and limitations. Reaching my full potential by appreciating who I am, where I am, and what I have, empowers me to reject the most odious label of them all. It's the one label that has libeled more hearts and stolen more dreams than all the other labels combined. It's the two-word label—*not enough*.

Enough is a word I've come to both love and hate. I love it when I have enough. It's like a holiday when I know I've done enough. Thank God for the days of enough love, enough health, enough food, and enough money. But too often I despise the word *enough*. Too often I've felt I don't do enough, earn enough, or get enough credit. It's a word used to whip us into shape and keep us chasing after that elusive state of *enough*.

If everything inside you cries out to "accept no mediocre life" and if you're ready to go beyond the labels, libels, and limitations, then read on. You're about to go on an adventure that will force you to break out of the sameness around you and free you to be, do, and have everything that God has in mind for you. If you want to be remembered as a person of quality and excellence who made the absolute most of who he was, where he was, with what he was given, then this book will show the way.

During the first stop of this journey into excellence, you will learn how to excel at *being who you are*. Excelling at being you is the key to your uniqueness, being real is the key to gaining respect, and demanding the best of yourself is the key to quality and lifelong achievement.

At the second stop on your quest, you will learn how to excel *where you are*. You'll discover that being deliberate, unafraid, and undaunted are the keys to being different, unshakable, and unstoppable under less-than-perfect conditions. Perfect conditions do not exist. You will learn how to win in common moments and adverse circumstances.

On the third leg of your excellent adventure, you will stop to take stock of the power, passion, and boldness to attract the right kinds of people into your life. People with passion and a bias for bold action attract other people on the same quest. Here you will learn that while resources make things possible, energetic, excellent people make things *happen*.

The fourth and final segment of the journey will help you understand that all things excellent have a sense of urgency to them. Excelling at being who you are, where you are, with what you have, is to do it now *while you can*. Here you will commit to being ruthless with time, patient with the process, and determined to finish well.

Before you start on your adventure into excellence, let me say, "Congratulations!" You are a member of a rare breed. You live with a sense of inner obligation to act as if the fate of the world depended on your actions. You and I see the pursuit of excellence as not just a good thing, but also a God thing. We live with the conviction that doing our best glorifies God, not ourselves. We label this quest for excellence a mark of maturity, not madness. For us the quest for power is childish, but the pursuit of God's pleasure is pure joy. We take seriously the biblical admonition to "eagerly desire the greater gifts. And now I will show you the most excellent way" (1 Cor. 12:31 NIV). We will not be denied because we refuse to live within the limits of man-made labels and libels. We will not accept a mediocre life, and we will not disappear quietly into the middle. We gladly accept the proverb, "Those who hear not the music, think the dancer's mad." We hear the music, it's in our hearts and souls, and we must dance.

ACCEPT NO MEDIOCRE LIFE

Commitment #1

EXCELLING AT
BEING WHO I AM

Not in the clamor of the crowded street,
Not in the shouts and plaudits of the throng,
But in ourselves, are triumph and defeat.
—HENRY WADSWORTH LONGFELLOW

1

I Will Embrace My Uniqueness

It takes courage to grow up and turn out to be who you really are.
—E. E. CUMMINGS

What we have to be is what we are.
—THOMAS MERTON

The first time I was told to be ashamed of myself was at home. The first time I actually felt ashamed of myself was at church on Senior Day. This rite of passage awaited every high school senior in my childhood church. We seniors lined up behind the ornate white pulpit and, one by one, shuffled to the microphone to announce the universities to which we would be matriculating in the fall. Just as cruel fate would have it, the kid just before me announced he was going to Harvard on a full ride, no less. Then I stepped to the microphone with a sick feeling in the pit of my stomach. I didn't want to be there. It was silly. It was no one's business but my own what I was going to do with my life. I wanted to run, but since I couldn't, I did the next best thing; I lied. I thought about announcing I was going to Harvard, but my teachers in the audience knew my grades. In the heat of the moment I stepped to the microphone and blurted out, "While they're all going to school, I'm going to work!" Ha, ha, not really?

No one laughed, seemed shocked, or disappointed. The reaction was nil. I guess it sounded like the right thing for an average kid from an average family to do. I was the only one surprised or wounded by my words. Everything within me wanted someone to stand up in protest. I wanted my coach, one of my teachers, my parents, my pastor, or anyone to stand up and say, "You're a smart kid, David. You're destined for great things!" I shuffled off the stage in a hurry to get anywhere but there. I ran down the hall-way, wanting more than anything to hear the sound of someone running after me. I needed someone to tell me I was important, I was special, and I could do anything I set my mind to do. But no one came, no one called, and no one seemed to notice or care. It wasn't just okay for me to be ordinary; it was expected. It was okay with my parents and my school, and now I had the mis-guided opinion it was even okay with God. But it wasn't okay with me. I already hated my life and dreaded my future. I decided from that day on, I would show the world just how common and ordinary my behavior could be.

I didn't know why or how, but as I lit up a Marlboro in my souped-up, flaming orange '66 Chevy Impala Super Sport that morning, I vowed to break loose from the labels and limitations that were suffocating me even before I had the chance to succeed, or fail for that matter. I set out on a quest that day to find some-one to believe in me. There had to be someone in this world who could see beyond my rough, tough-guy exterior and discover something of greatness, but where was this person, and how could I find him? That day I rejected the mind-set that said, "Get a job, get a wife, get a mortgage, and then get burial insurance!"

By the time I was seventeen, I had accepted the idea that rules are more important than relationships, fitting in is more desirable than standing out, and you'll never amount to anything without trying to be like someone else. I had already learned not to like myself. I didn't know then that I'd tend to live according to other people's expectations of me. The Scriptures put it this way: "For as he thinketh in his heart, so is he" (Prov. 23:7 KJV).

Labels affix themselves to your heart and possess your think-ing. I realize now this cycle of low expectation and lower desire is not limited to my town, my home, or even my church. It is epidemic because most people have accepted mediocre as the measuring stick of their lives. Why? We've been labeled, and those labels libel and limit us. We don't believe in ourselves because we're taught to look at our lives through the lens of labels.

Looking Through Labels

I'm an escapee from a small town located in a county in Kentucky called Barren. As a teenager, I felt barren. How bad is it when the pioneers who, after forging through forests and crossing the rivers, came upon a place so unimpressive they called it Barren? Can anything good come out of this? When Jesus was reared in Nazareth, the saying was, "Can anything, anyone of significance, come out of a little hick place like that?" At least I was in good company.

I grew up in the typical county seat town. Life revolved around ritual and routine. Monday through Friday centered on school, sports, and after-school jobs. Saturday was for sleeping late and watching afternoon movies, and Sunday was for going to church. Every Sunday I asked my mother, "Why do we have to go to church today?" And every Sunday morning she said, "You're going so you'll grow up to be a good person." I went to church, and I saw people who I knew weren't very good. I knew some of the stuff they were into during the week. When I heard, "Be good," I translated that to mean, "Be nice; be neuter." Don't make noise. Don't do anything that might be construed as bold or controversial.

A young boy longs for adventure, so the admonition to be good isn't appealing. I wanted to be dangerous. I wanted to be interesting and mysterious. I wanted to be Roy Rogers, John Wayne, and Superman all rolled up into one. Young boys run around the house in their red underwear, with a towel around their necks, wanting to be Superman. And young girls play dress up, not dress down.

A young businessman asked Jesus one day, "Teacher, what

good thing must I do to get eternal life?" Jesus replied, "Why do you ask me about what is good? There is only One who is good. If you want to enter life, obey the commandments" (Matt. 19:16–17 NIV). Whether the young man was taken off guard or just plain arrogant, he assured Jesus that he had obeyed all of the commandments his entire life. When I heard this story as a kid, I knew I had already blown it big time. I wasn't good, and I didn't know anyone who was. So, if the God thing depended on good behavior, I was out before I ever got in.

My Sunday school teacher assured me that God loved me, but he warned me that His love was conditional upon my being good. The pastor cemented this teaching from the pulpit. My parents reinforced the virtue of goodness for goodness' sake during the week. I suppose it seemed to be a good way to motivate a mischievous boy to behave, but the result is, church kids grow up plagued with shame, guilt, remorse, and self-loathing because they've been raised believing in a God who is in a foul mood looking for someone to rain down judgment upon.

With our lips we proclaim God loves us, but our lives betray our confession. We live as though God's love for us is in some vague, abstract religious theory trapped in the words of an arcane hymnal. Yet God has demonstrated His great love for us in the story of the gospel. This is a love not of feelings but of action. It is a scandalous love in which our God sent His Son to die for people who couldn't be good without His love. British author G. K. Chesterton called the Christian life a "furious love affair."

It took me a while to rip off the self-righteous label and embrace the transforming truth that God loves me in the morning sun and in the evening rain, without caution, regret, boundary, or breaking point. No matter what may come, He can't stop loving me. This is our hope and passion that we don't have to be good to be worthy of His grace, just open to embracing it.

Every six weeks my school sent a little card home to my parents to remind them of how average I was. They, in turn, displayed their displeasure by threatening me with all kinds of dreadful punishment. Mostly they explained that if I didn't work hard in school, it would be placed on my permanent record and follow me for the rest of my life. I wondered whether there was a government agency that followed you around wherever you went, recording everything you did onto your supersecret, superbad permanent record. That was also how I grew up thinking of God. He had angels keeping every sin listed on your permanent record in heaven.

Sometimes my parents would tag-team in their effort to scare me onto the honor roll. They demanded A's and B's out loud, but I knew in their hearts they hoped for C's. The pressure to please was so strong that if I got C's and D's, I changed the D to a C before the grade card got home. My parents' excitement bordered on the hysteria of hitting the lottery. They were relieved their son was at least average. They were elated, but I was humiliated. Changing the grade on the card couldn't erase the disappointment I felt deep within. I knew I could do better, but motivation is hard to find when you're beige and bad. I wanted to do better, but I've never responded well to threats, name-calling, and humiliation. I've discovered nobody else does either.

I don't know if you've ever felt beige, bad, or boring. For me it's the feeling I don't fit in and I'm never going to be good at anything. What brand of life can an average, good-for-nothing, beige person expect? Who ever wooed and won a wife by saying, "Hey, baby, I'm a mediocre man, I've been looking for a mediocre woman, and you're the most mediocre woman I've seen so far. How about you and me get together? We'll have a mediocre marriage and a mediocre life. We'll live in a mediocre house and raise mediocre kids. We'll send 'em to mediocre schools so they, too, can be mediocre"? Not on your life! No one says that! But a lot of us feel trapped by it because of the old labels and lenses we were handed as kids.

Labels make you feel afraid of almost everything. If you feel weak, you're afraid of the strong. Those labeled average are often afraid and intimidated by the gifted and exceptional. That fear shrinks the soul and slumps the body. Shrinking is the way to be safe. If you get small enough, people won't be able to notice you even exist, and they'll stop comparing, critiquing, and criticizing you. The number one value in a post–9/11 world is, it seems to me, safety. People we don't know in places we can't pronounce are plotting to kill us. We're terrified of terrorists, yet there are already enough nuclear weapons in the hands of lunatics to destroy the world fifteen times over. There is no such thing as a fail-safe world or a small enough place to hide. You can't escape urban problems by fleeing to the suburbs, you can't drown domestic difficulty at the bottom of a bottle, and you can't defeat your inner demons by isolating yourself from God or the rest of the world.

Labels make us afraid because they not only obscure the truth about us, but also obscure the truth about God. The truth is, although there are lots of lunatics out there, there's a sovereign, good, and powerful God in control of the affairs of human beings. He will never let us destroy ourselves. As Stonewall Jackson was noted for saying, "I am as safe on the battlefield as I am in my own bed." But even if you could hide in a deep bunker underground, you would have succeeded only in digging your own grave if the world blows up.

God created you to live large with your face toward the sun. He gave you two legs and a backbone so you could stand erect and tall. Stanley Hauerwas of Duke University said, "It's hard to remember Jesus did not come to make us safe, but rather to make us disciples, citizens of God's new age, a kingdom of surprise."[1] God is aware of the dangers, and He is at the controls. He is big, bold, bodacious, and hot on your trail. Not to fry you, stamp you, or label you, but to love you, lift you, and liberate you.

My mother's favorite tactical complaint of me was, "Why can't you be more like your brother?" It seemed clear to me because I was not him! I got the feeling very early from home, school, and church, I was not enough now, and it was very likely I was never going to be enough in the future. And the cure for my unlucky lack of native talent and good looks was to do more, to achieve more, and to get more, so I would be more. I call it the tyranny of more. Someone asked Howard Hughes, the eccentric billionaire of a past generation, "How much is enough?" He said, "Just a little more!" This idea can be found even in Greek mythology. Sisyphus, the son of Aeolus, was founder of Corinth. He betrayed the secrets of the gods and was condemned to roll, for eternity, a huge boulder up a steep hill, only to have it roll back down to the bottom again just as it reached the top. The gods could think of no more dreadful punishment than that of futile and hopeless labor.

Hopeless is not an option because of two facts only you can face. You are today what your choices have made you. Not your mama, not your daddy, not your brother. You did not choose your labels, but only you can choose to remove the old lenses and look at your life from God's perspective. You are not responsible for all the "stuff" done to you. You shouldn't feel ashamed of what some halfhearted, small-minded person in your past said or did. But only you control what happens to what happened to you. The second bit of good news is, you can be better the moment you decide to be. The first declaration to make is, "I am loved right now as I am, and that is enough." That's freedom. God knows everything about you and loves you anyway. He will never love you more than He does right now, and He will never love you any less. That's grace.

Learning how to live in God's love, I think, is spending the rest of your life just saying, "God, how can I be the best at being me?" Instead of trying to be someone else, be the best you can be, but be that! Be yourself! Stop being ashamed of being who you are. Embracing your uniqueness starts with exchanging the lens of labels for the lens of love.

Looking Through Love

In Thornton Wilder's play *Our Town*, there is a scene in which a family is asleep in a cottage in the forest at dawn. The chimney smoke is having a conversation with the morning mist rising from the glade: "Do you think these people really know who they are?" And the smoke answers, "They wouldn't believe us if we told them." We have difficulty wrapping our minds around some things. The cross of Christ is one of these things. But it is God's loving and ultimate statement of His idea of your worth.

An intriguing insight to Christ's attitude toward the Cross is revealed in these words: "He was willing to die a shameful death on the cross because of the joy he knew would be his afterwards"(Heb. 12:2 TLB). Max Lucado said it this way: "You aren't an accident. You weren't mass-produced. You aren't an assembly-line product. You were deliberately planned, specifically gifted, and lovingly positioned on this earth by the Master Craftsman."[2] If that is true, then what do we see when we look through a lens of God's love?

Jesus told stories to help us grasp God's opinion of us. While teaching a large crowd, He said, "The kingdom of heaven is like treasure hidden in a field. When a man found it, he hid it again, and then in his joy went and sold all he had and bought that field" (Matt. 13:44 NIV). Banks didn't exist in the first century. People buried their most valuable articles in the ground. To protect those valuables, the law stipulated that if you found a treasure scattered in a field, you could gather it up and keep it. If you dug up a container or chest with valuables in it, then it belonged to the land. In this story a man finds a treasure so great, he liquidates everything he has in order to buy the field.

He's interested not in the field, but in what's in the field. He wants the treasure, and he's willing to pay for it. Jesus held up this story as a lens through which we see a clearer picture of God's love for us. It is a sacrificial love. God loves you enough that He was willing to pay an awful price for the privilege. This is a far cry from the picture painted by those highlighting your lack of perfection. You are a treasure to be sought and bought. To God, your Creator and Savior, you are worth whatever He had to pay to love you. This is a far cry from what I heard in Sunday school or church.

Jesus continued the story by saying, "Again, the kingdom of heaven is like a merchant looking for fine pearls. When he found one of great value, he went away and sold everything he had and bought it" (Matt. 13:45–46 NIV). Here God is the jewel merchant.

I've often wondered why Jesus used pearls in this story. Is there something in the nature of a pearl that parallels our nature? A pearl begins as a single grain of sand, which makes its way into an oyster shell. Once there, it penetrates the membrane, causing irritation. The oyster secretes a milky white substance, which coats the grain of sand. Over time, this process is repeated until a pearl is produced. Even then, a diver has to go down and retrieve the oyster, open it up, and through trial and error, search until he finds the pearl. A pearl is hard to make and hard to find. Given the fact we tend to hide from God, I can see the parallels in the pearl story and my own. God seeks me and finds me. And when He finds me, I'm the winner.

This understanding was a real breakthrough as well as hangup for me. Nobody pursued me. Nobody thought me worthy of praise. Yet here is God seeking me, paying a price to love me. This was and remains the greatest thought I've ever had. When Karl Barth, the famous German theologian, was asked what was the greatest theological concept he'd ever entertained, he said, "Jesus loves me this I know, for the Bible tells me so."

Jesus' third story was a fisherman's tale: "Once again, the kingdom of heaven is like a net that was let down into the lake and caught all kinds of fish. When it was full, the fishermen pulled it up on the shore. Then they sat down and collected the good fish in baskets, but threw the bad away" (Matt. 13:47–48 NIV). This story reminds me of a summer spent on my uncle Henry's farm. It was the summer I learned how to chop tobacco, drive a tractor, and use a fishing net. Early one evening, with the daily chores behind us, Uncle Henry, several hired hands, and I gathered at the big pond. We stretched a wide net with wooden poles across the surface of the water. As the net was dragged across the bottom, it became heavy. All six of us worked to drag the net over to the bank. I saw all kinds of little creatures hopping and flopping around in the net. There were small snakes, turtles, and slithery reptilian creatures I had never seen before. My uncle knew the ones to be kept from the ones to be thrown back. When Jesus said the fishermen collected the good and threw away the bad, I can still remember putting on gloves and trying to grab hold of the fish in the net.

God views us as a catch to be caught and kept. In these three stories, Jesus reveals God's new way of looking at us. It is the lens of love. Through this lens, each of us is a treasure, a prize, and a catch. This lens is a far cry from the labels that others stick on us. This information is new to some. Others of you know God loves you unconditionally, but you've allowed time and circumstance to cover the truth with a coat of beige indifference.

Former boxing writer Harold Conrad visited a women's prison with heavyweight fighter Muhammad Ali. "All the inmates lined up," wrote Conrad. "They were ooh-ing and aah-ing as Ali went along. There were some good-looking ones. But he kissed only the ugly ones." After they left the prison, Conrad asked the fighter to explain why he chose to kiss only those women. "Because no one ever kisses the ugly girls," he replied.[3] What a graphic illustration of what Christ has done for us! He came to kiss the ugly and the unloved. Straight-A students get compliments, good athletes receive cheers, but average people don't attract much attention. They just tend to blend in with the woodwork. Everybody craves affirmation and affection. You were created in God's image to receive love and to give it away. Performance aside, people need to be noticed. They need pats on the back, smiles, and hugs. It's how we tell one another, "Hey, you're not alone!" It's how God uses other people to help us realize it's okay to be who we are without apology or compromise.

Remember Not to Forget

Recently my daughter Lindsey called to activate her new credit card. The operator told her she wasn't the person identified by the social security number she gave. Lindsey insisted she was indeed who she said she was. The credit card operator insisted, with an air of superiority, "I assure you, miss, you are not Lindsey Foster. Our records are impeccable."

Lindsey was shaken by being told that she was not who she thought she was. I suggested she call the social security office. The social security operator asked her a series of questions and then asked for her social security number. After a long pause, she came back on the line and said, "After checking our records, I am glad to say you are who you thought you were." What a relief! I could've been putting the wrong person through college!

A few days later I related the story to a friend, who said, "I have one that can top that. We had some friends over for dinner. The father introduced his seventeen-year-old son by saying, 'His real name is John, but I call him Harley because he came along while I was trying to save up for a Harley-Davidson motorcycle and so I had to put all my money into him. I've called him Harley ever since.' My friend said, 'I bet you've been hearing that story all your life, huh?' " The boy just nodded. How sad when parents label their children as objects rather than the good, gifted, and loved people they are.

E. E. Cummings wisely said, "To be nobody but yourself in a world which is doing its best to make you everybody else— means to fight the hardest battle which any human being can fight and never stop fighting." If you allow other people to tell you who you are, two things happen. On the one hand, people will underestimate your worth and value; on the other, they will overestimate what you can actually do. Neither is healthy. Therefore, neither is acceptable.

Lily Tomlin commented, "I always wanted to be somebody, but I should have been more specific." I agree, but when you're told for so long, by so many, that trying to be someone is sinful pride, you begin to believe it. David asked,

> When I consider your heavens, the work of your fingers,
> the moon and the stars, which you have set in place,
> what is man that you are mindful of him,
> the son of man that you care for him?
> You made him a little lower than the heavenly beings
> and crowned him with glory and honor. (Ps. 8:3–5 NIV)

I was raised in a church whose fatal sin was pride and whose favorite solution was shame. Every Sunday my pride was attacked, but I didn't feel prideful at all. I was trying to figure out if I had anything in me to be proud of. In contrast to what I heard growing up, experience has taught me that most people feel not too *good* about themselves, but too *bad*. I've worked with people for more than thirty years, and the vast majority feel absolutely rotten about themselves, no matter how good they try to be or how much they try to do. We work ourselves to death trying to be the good little boy or good little girl so we can gain approval. From childhood to adulthood we are taught to feel bad about who we are. But when you're sick and tired of being yourself, you are in deep trouble because that's all you can ever be. Remember, the opposite of pride is shame, not humility.

The simple instruction of Scripture is to "be honest in your estimate of yourselves, measuring your value by how much faith God has given you" (Rom. 12:3 TLB). If it is wrong to overestimate yourself, isn't it at least equally wrong to underestimate yourself? Because we haven't learned to balance pride and humility, the paradox of our time in history is that we can buy more, but enjoy it less. We have more conveniences, but less time; more degrees, but less sense; more knowledge, but less judgment; more medicine, but less wellness. We have multiplied our possessions without adding to our worth. We're obsessed with making a living, but not a life. Medical breakthroughs have added years to life, but not life to those years. We've done bigger things, but not better things. We eat fast food; we suffer slow digestion and shallow relationships. In our quest to get "the good life" we have two incomes, but more debt; fancier houses, but broken homes. We take quick trips, use disposable diapers, possess a throwaway morality, have overweight bodies, and buy pills that do everything from cheer to quiet to kill. All in a futile quest to get what we already have—love.

John, the disciple loved by Jesus, said, "How great is the love the Father has lavished on us, that we should be called children of God! And that is what we are!" (1 John 3:1 NIV).

If I'm not who you think I am, either good or bad, and I'm too often not who I think I am, either good or bad, then who am I? I'm who God says I am. Paul proclaimed, "I'm just as happy with little as with much, with much as with little. I've found the recipe for being happy whether full or hungry, hands full or hands empty. Whatever I have, wherever I am, I can make it through anything in the One who makes me who I am" (Phil. 4:11–12 THE MESSAGE). Jesus Christ is God's statement of your worth. You are worth His love, His death, His sacrifice! Listen to the description:

It was you who formed my inward parts;
   you knit me together in my mother's womb.
I praise you, for I am fearfully and wonderfully made.
Wonderful are your works; that I know very well.
My frame was not hidden from you when I was being
   made in secret,
   intricately woven in the depths of the earth.
Your eyes beheld my informed substance.
In your book were written all the days that were formed
   for me,
   when none of them as yet existed. (Ps. 139:13–16 NRSV)

I read a story about Michelangelo chipping away with his chisel at a huge, shapeless piece of rock. The sculptor was asked what he was doing. "I am releasing the angel imprisoned in this marble," he answered. Jesus is the One who seeks to release the hidden hero in you. Saint Augustine said, "People travel to wonder at the height of mountains, at the huge waves of the sea, at the long courses of the rivers, at the vast compass of the ocean, at the circular motion of the stars—and they pass by themselves without wondering."

I sign every e-mail I send to my three daughters the same way. At the bottom of the e-mail I type "I-L-B-Y-D!!" The letters stand for "I love being your dad." It's like a secret code between us, a constant reminder of our relationship. God wants you to under-

stand, "I-L-B-Y-D!! I love being your Dad!!" Each dime or dollar
I've spent on my kids has been a privilege. As a matter of fact, my
kids have never asked me, have never come close to asking me, for
as much as I'm willing to give them. How much do you have
when you consider this declaration, "He who did not spare his
own Son, but gave him up for us all—how will he not also, along
with him, graciously give us all things?" (Rom. 8:32 NIV)?

Think about how different Christianity would be if Jesus
chose His twelve disciples using the lens of a consulting firm.
Here is how the advice to Him might read:

To: Jesus, Son of Joseph
Woodcrafter's Carpenter Shop, Nazareth
From: Jordan Management Consultants, Jerusalem
RE: Staff Team Evaluation

Thank You for submitting the resumes of the twelve
men You've picked for management positions in Your
new organization. All of them have now taken our battery of tests, and we have not only run the results
through our computer, we have also arranged and conducted personal interviews for each of them, with our
psychologist and vocational aptitude consultants.

It is the staff's opinion that most of Your nominees
lack the background, education and vocational aptitude
for the type of enterprise You're undertaking. For example: Simon Peter is emotionally unstable and given
to fits of temper. Andrew has no qualities of leadership
whatsoever. The two brothers, James and John, sons of
Zebedee, place personal interests above company loyalty. Thomas demonstrates a questionable attitude that
would tend to undermine morale.

We feel it our duty to tell You that Matthew has
been blacklisted by the Greater Jerusalem Better Business Bureau. James, the son of Alphaeus, and Thaddeus

definitely have radical leanings, and they both registered high on the manic depressive scale.

However, one of Your candidates shows great potential. He's a man of great ability and resourcefulness. He meets people well. He has a keen sense of business, has contacts in high places. He is highly motivated, ambitious and responsible. We recommend that Judas Iscariot be the comptroller and right-hand man of your new organization.[4]

God can do extraordinary things through you. If you're willing to be the one and only unique you, that is all that God requires. The Bible gives this assurance: "God who began the good work within you will keep right on helping you grow in his grace until his task within you is finally finished" (Phil. 1:6 TLB).

Never forget these three important truths. First, you are today what you have decided to become. Second, you can be more than you are right now. Third, you will never be happy until you engage in the effort to excel at being the best you that you can be as an act of worship to God. Don't be afraid to express yourself.

Express Yourself

Remember, you are a unique person created as an expression of the Father's love, and you have the assurance that "God's gifts and his call can never be withdrawn; he will never go back on his promises" (Rom. 11:29 TLB). You are created in His image to express the nobility of His love and goodness. You can only be the best at being you; therefore, embrace your uniqueness every day without apology. You have incredible worth for just having been born. You have worth before you think a thought, lift a finger, or earn a dime. Because of God's love, you have everything to be thankful for, but nothing to be proud of that hasn't come from Him. Robert H. Schuller cleverly noted, "Anyone can count the number of seeds in an apple, but only God can count the number of apples in a seed." Use this image as a memory device when you're tempted to doubt your worth to God.

Brennan Manning illustrates the reach of God's love with this simple story:

Four years ago in a large city in the far West, rumors spread that a certain Catholic woman was having visions of Jesus. The reports reached the archbishop. He decided to check her out. There is always a fine line between the authentic mystic and the lunatic fringe. "Is it true ma'am, that you have visions of Jesus?" asked the cleric. "Yes," the woman replied simply. "Well, the next time you have a vision, I want you to ask Jesus to tell you the sins that I confessed in my last confession." The woman was stunned. "Did I hear you right, bishop? You actually want me to ask Jesus to tell me the sins of your past?" "Exactly. Please call me if anything happens." Ten days later the woman notified her spiritual leader of a recent apparition. "Please come," she said. Within the hour the archbishop arrived. He trusted eye-to-eye contact. "You just told me on the phone that you actually had a vision of Jesus. Did you do what I asked?" "Yes, bishop, I asked Jesus to tell me the sins you confessed in your last confession." The bishop leaned forward with anticipation. His eyes narrowed. "What did Jesus say?" She took his hand and gazed deep into his eyes. "Bishop," she said, "these are his exact words: 'I can't remember.'"[5]

Instead of holding your past sins and failures over your head, God will turn your past into a beautiful story of grace and redemption worth sharing with the world. One of the real dangers when you talk about God to other people is to sound as if you are trafficking in truths you've not experienced. It's like talking about a picture of Mona Lisa you've seen in an art book as opposed to sharing what it's like to stand in front of the actual painting in the Louvre. It is one thing to say God is faithful; it is entirely a different thing to join David in shouting, "I was young and now I am old, yet I have never seen the righteous forsaken or their children begging bread" (Ps. 37:25 NIV).

You're not one in a million; you're more like one in several billion. Embrace your uniqueness and don't apologize for it. You have unique experiences, insights, strengths, and passions. Pursue them! Cultivate what motivates your mind and makes you come alive. Pursue a noble cause. You are created an original, so you need never live a carbon copy of anyone else. Forget about who others think you are and become who you really are.

While living in East Tennessee, I heard the story of a young boy born to an unwed mother. He had a hard time growing up because everywhere he went people asked, "Who's your daddy?" Whether he was at school, in the grocery store or drugstore, people asked the same question. He started hiding at recess and lunchtime from other kids. He avoided people because the question caused shame.

When he was about twelve years old, a new preacher came to his church. He always went in late and slipped out early to avoid hearing the question, "Who's your daddy?" But one day, the new preacher said the benediction so fast, he got caught and had to walk out with the crowd. Just about the time he got to the back door, the new preacher, not knowing his past, put his hand on his shoulder and asked him, "Son, who's your daddy?" The whole church got deathly quiet. The boy could feel every eye in the church looking at him. Now everyone would finally know the answer to the question, "Who's your daddy?"

The preacher sensed the situation of the scared little boy. "Wait a minute!" he said. "I know who you are. I see the family resemblance now. You are a child of God." He patted the boy on his shoulder and said, "Boy, you've got a great inheritance. Go and claim it." With that, the boy smiled for the first time in a long time and walked out the door a changed person. He was never the same again. Whenever anybody asked him, "Who's your daddy?" he'd just reply, "I'm a child of God." The little boy in this story turned out to be Ben W. Hooper, who grew up to be the Republican governor of Tennessee from 1911 to 1915. Never forget you are loved, like you are, as you are. You don't have to be good to be loved, but because you are loved by God, you have the potential for greatness if you will embrace your uniqueness and express yourself.

Be yourself; never be ashamed of who you are, what you look like, how you're put together, how tall you are, how short you are, or how pudgy you are. You could take some Oreos out of your diet, but forget trying to look like those anorexic, sad-sack, Adobe Photoshop–altered people on the front of magazines who glorify image over substance, glamour over grace. Reject those facades, trust God's opinion of you, and then trust yourself. Create the kind of self that you will be happy to live with all your life. Make the most of your life by fanning the tiny, inner sparks of possibility into the flames of achievement. Heed the words of Thomas à Kempis, who said, "First keep the peace within yourself, then you can also bring peace to others."

2

I Will Be the Real Deal

*The most fatiguing activity in the world is the drive to
seem other than you are.*
—SYDNEY J. HARRIS

Born the son of an Arizona copper miner in 1909, Ettore
"Ted" DeGrazia is remembered and revered as one of
America's foremost artists. Using the terrain of the American Southwest as his backdrop, he became an extraordinary
painter of the relationship between color and sound. His favorite
subjects were the children of the desert. One of his most memorable works portrays a little pigtailed girl at play in the glittering
colors of a yellow desert afternoon, while a donkey is wandering
off in the pearlescent hues of a desert sunset. Although DeGrazia
painted children with faces of innocence and honesty, most of his
adults are faceless. When asked the reason, he explained that children are happy, smiling, effervescent, and expressive, but by the
time they've reached adulthood, they slowly lose their identity
and start looking alike. I reluctantly agree with DeGrazia's observation. Children laugh, smile, snicker, and make funny faces. Adult
faces seem to express sadness that the act of growing up has replaced delight with disappointment. And yet every person I've
met believed deep down inside there was some reason she or he
was placed on this small planet we call earth, having this exhilarating experience we call life.

Early on in life we learn how to gain approval by playacting.

Over time we become good at faking sincerity. Unless we rip off the labels that threaten to bury our authenticity, we can spend our lives as phonies. Authenticity and originality can't grow in the soil of deception and duplicity. That's why excelling at being who I am requires acceptance, embracing my God-created uniqueness and authenticity, which give me courage to be the real deal. Showing your true colors to a world that likes its people beige and benign can be daunting, but it is well worth the effort.

The centerpiece of Disney World is the beautiful Sleeping Beauty's castle. Its tall towers, fluttering banners, imposing size, and fairy-tale perfection make it one of the most photographed images in the world. From a distance it is majestic, but the truth is, the castle is a fake. It is as hollow as a drum. I had imagined exploring the magical nooks and crannies, secret staircases, and vast ballrooms, but Sleeping Beauty's castle is no castle at all. Its only function is to be a glorified archway. What a bummer!

Sleeping Beauty's castle has no inner life and that's disappointing, but when the same thing can be said of a person, it is tragic. Outward appearances can be deceiving. Jesus offers to transform you from the inside out, not from the outside in. Whatever the hollowed-out areas of your life, He can fill them with His presence and power. He alone holds the power to give you a new heart of faith, hope, and love. All of us have had encounters with phonies and hypocrites. It's hard to stomach people who fake their affection and even harder to erase the scar that some people can scrape across your soul.

People who fake their way through life are fearful. They fear being exposed for what they really are. They're like Sleeping Beauty's castle; they look good from a distance, but up close they are as hollow as a gourd. Everyone wants to be viewed as a person of substance. No matter who you are or what your background, you want people to believe you're the genuine article. Authenticity is the inner strength to be what you are and who you are at all times without apology or regret.

Fakers accuse others of being phony, but they lack the capacity to see their own duplicity. Jesus asked, "Why do you look at the speck of sawdust in your brother's eye and pay no attention to the plank in your own eye?" (Matt. 7:3 NIV). And the Scripture warns, "The wicked man flees though no one pursues, but the righteous are as bold as a lion" (Prov. 28:1 NIV). Honestly, who cares if other people get bent out of shape as long as God judges me whole and worthy? If I'm right with God, if God has promised to line up on my side, nothing can be all that wrong with the rest of the world.

A fearful and small-minded person will always be easily offended. His is the cry of the victim: "I didn't do it! It's my mother's fault! It's my father's fault!" Listen long enough and you'll think we live in a no-fault society, a victimized world. It's never anyone's fault.

Fakers aren't always faking to deceive; sometimes they're trying to please or appease to gain approval. People pleasing is a sure way to be miserable and bent out of shape. To even attempt it is to compromise your identity and self-respect. The antidote to people pleasing is in this promise: "If God is for us, who can be against us?" (Rom. 8:31 NIV). With this iron rod of faith driven down my back it matters little what other people think. If God is for me, no one can take from me or keep from me what God wants for me, except me. And trust me, that's a huge distinction.

How can you ever be the very best "you" until you have the courage to declare: "Here I am. It's me. Warts and all, this is how I look. This is the real me. This is my personality. This is my energy level. This is what I can and can't, will and won't, do. Deal with it!" If your identity is intact, you can say no and mean it, and you can say yes and back it up.

Authentic people also refuse to pose. A Polish athlete named Stella Walsh won the women's 100-meter dash at the 1932 Olympics in Los Angeles, becoming the first woman to break the 12-second barrier. When she was killed in 1980 as an innocent victim of a robbery, an autopsy declared her to be a male. In other words, "Stella was a fella." Real people are not imposters. A poser is someone who is trying to be what other people expect. As a kid, I was told, "Now we're going to Aunt Vera's house. Be good for a change." Play like you're a good kid. Could you pose like an actor in *Leave It to Beaver* for about an hour and a half? I never thought I was all that bad. I just wanted to have fun. And I knew we weren't going to have any fun visiting people we didn't like and pretending to enjoy the visit just because the people were family. Even as a kid, I didn't like pretending to like people I didn't know. And I hated trying to please people by shutting down my personality.

Some people have learned how to make a good living posing as famous people, but everyone knows it's all in good fun. Some people pose in order to exploit others. Listen to the warning: "After I leave you, false teachers, like vicious wolves, will appear among you, not sparing the flock. Some of you yourselves will distort the truth in order to draw a following. Watch out!" (Acts 20:29–31 TLB).

Posing's agenda arises out of fear, shame, and pain, especially the pain that comes from being ashamed of who you are and how you're wired. Trying to be what you're not so that you may achieve fame or notoriety is a shallow, sorrowful way to live. Fame is fleeting, popularity is temporary, and riches run away. Those who cheer you today will curse you tomorrow. Only one thing endures—genuine, authentic integrity.

Real people say no to posturing. Posing is hiding behind a mask mainly for approval or advantage, while posturing is trying to position yourself in a place of power. A great example of this was a request from the mother of two of Jesus' disciples: "Then the mother of James and John, the sons of Zebedee, brought them to Jesus and respectfully asked a favor. 'What is your request?' he asked. She replied, 'In your Kingdom, will you let my two sons sit on two thrones next to yours?'" (Matt. 20:20–21 TLB). Jesus responded to her with a question: "Can they drink from the cup?"

He basically said, "You have no idea what you're asking. Do you want your boys to die with Me? Is that what you're really asking? Do you want those boys to be crucified? Is that what you want?" They were posturing for a preferred position. Jesus used her posturing as an opportunity to teach about real power. He taught that authority comes through the pathways of service and sacrifice. Real power is not in lording it over other people, but in serving them. Greatness is attained through service and sacrifice, not power and position. The truth is, "If God is for us, who can be against us?" Or said another way, "If God is for us, who cares who's against us?" Posing and posturing are techniques used by the love-starved and the powerless. Neither description fits you and me. If God is for us, posturing is not necessary.

We've all snickered at the clear contradictions in terms such as *jumbo shrimp, freezer burn, genuine imitation, legally drunk, plastic glasses, pretty ugly,* and *working vacation.* But these oxymorons can't hold a candle to one of the weirdest trends today—reality TV. This is the name given to the new genre of TV that places people in situations guaranteed to bring out the weirdness in them. TV itself is fantasy peddled as reality. In a world of cosmetic surgery, we long for something more substantial and someone less pretentious.

When it hurts, it hurts. When you're upset, you're upset. When you're mad, you can go to God and unload. When you're frustrated, you can express it, and He responds as a patient, loving, gracious Savior, who knows you need to be loved most when you deserve it least. Get it in your head and heart that you are loved. You never need to pose, posture, or pretend. God is for you, good or bad, happy or sad, and that's all you'll ever really need.

The Path to Self-Respect

God created you a victor, not a victim. He wants you to grow up, not grovel; to soar high, not sink; to overcome, not be overwhelmed. But because you've been good at posing, posturing, and pretending, it's often frightening to let the real you rise to the surface. You have looked through the lens of labels, libels, and limitations for so long that changing glasses is difficult. The fact of your worth may be settled in heaven, but you have to work it out here on earth. That's why a life committed to excellence starts with the commitment to excel at being fully and unapologetically who you are. You embrace your uniqueness with all your limits and possibilities. You also commit to be the real deal. You are a child of God by birth and by rebirth.

God's love for you is a reality, which needs translating from theory to practice, from silk to denim, and from the church world to the real world. Doing that means to "continue to work out your salvation with fear and trembling" (Phil. 2:12 NIV). Working out what God has already worked into your heart requires working smart. Understand the progression of an authentic life. God's love sets your self-worth. Your self-worth sets your self-image. Your self-image sets your self-discipline, and your self-discipline produces self-respect.

Jimmy Carter, the thirty-ninth president of the United States, came from the small, rural town of Plains, Georgia. Rising from humble beginnings to national prominence is no small feat, no matter where you come from. President Carter had one brother whose only claim to fame was running a service station back in Plains and drinking lots of beer.

He drank so much, they named a beer after him—Billy Beer. On the day of Jimmy Carter's inauguration his mother, affectionately known as "Miss Lillian," was asked by reporters, "Mrs. Carter, are you proud of your son today?" She replied, "Which one?" A mother loves her gas-station-running, beer-drinking son just as much as her president-elect son. A mother's love is about as close as we're going to get to understanding God's love for us—unconditional, impartial, and unashamed.

God's love for you goes beyond all human reason and rationale. Think of the wonderful pronouncement: "This is love: not that we loved God, but that he loved us and sent his Son as an atoning sacrifice for our sins" (1 John 4:10 NIV). This is God's attitude toward you. Despite your sin and sadness, your pride and prejudices, God "showed his great love for us by sending Christ to die for us while we were still sinners. . . . And since, when we were his enemies, we were brought back to God by the death of his Son, what blessings he must have for us now that we are his friends, and he is living within us! Now we rejoice in our wonderful new relationship with God—all because of what our Lord Jesus Christ has done in dying for our sins—making us friends of God" (Rom. 5:8–11 TLB).

Author and pastor of Moody Church in Chicago Erwin W. Lutzer said, "If the value of an article is dependent upon the price paid for it, Christ's death made our value skyrocket." Let no one say, "I am worthless." God is not a foolish speculator; He would never invest in worthless property.

It seems we know how be to be passionate about everything but the right thing. We get excited over everything from soap to sports. I admit to getting downright giddy over a good-looking muscle car. I learned to drive during the days when Detroit turned out cars with such legendary names as the GTO, the Camaro Super Sport, and the Road Runner. And who could forget the Shelby GT version of the Ford Mustang? We are giddy over cars, but we lose sight of our uniqueness. In 1995, Ford celebrated the thirtieth anniversary of the Ford Mustang. This ad appeared in the December 16, 1994, edition of *USA Today*:

It was the horse that carried away a nation and an untamed spirit captured in chrome. It took the whole country for a spin. And we never came back.

It was the key that put a generation in motion. At first we lined up to see it, an internal combustion celebrity, like Elvis in overdrive. We dreamed of possessing it and became possessed by it. Our heart doing the Watusi as we touched the wheel. Quicker than a thousand road crews, it remade every stretch of asphalt it rolled over, taking us places we'd never been, on roads we'd traveled all our lives. We never got over it. We didn't want to.

It is a time machine, launching the past into the future. An idea nurtured by a handful of believers obsessed with turning history into current events. Fueled on pure adrenaline, it travels places beyond the reach of roads, a sheet metal smile stretching from coast to coast. Strapped into steel shaped by the power of a dream, your pulse stampedes in your chest, keeping time with distant hoofbeats. You'll never get over it. You'll never want to.

If we can feel that jazzed and juiced by a car, why can't we feel good enough to be truly and unapologetically the original that God made each of us to be in light of His unbridled, unabridged promise: If God is for me, who can be against me? The love of God poured out on Calvary's cross is the key, which carried away the world on untamed spirit captured in the Garden of Gethsemane and crucified in a garbage dump. Once you experience this love, you'll never get over it, and you'll never want to.

Swiss poet and philosopher Henri F. Amiel wrote, "It is not what he has, nor even what he does which directly expresses the worth of a man, but what he is." This truth reminds me of one of my favorite childhood stories, Hans Christian Andersen's fable "The Ugly Duckling." The story revolves around a young swan that, as an egg, got mixed up with some duck eggs. When he was hatched, the baby swan looked nothing like the other ducklings. Therefore, he was labeled ugly, odd, and awkward, and consequently, he was marked for mistreatment. It wasn't until the swan grew up and saw his first group of swans that he discovered he wasn't ugly at all. He was actually a beautiful, graceful swan. Feeling overwhelmed by the joy of discovering his true self, the swan said, "I never dreamed of so much happiness when I was the Ugly Duckling!" The moral of the story is this: "It matters nothing if one is born in a duck-yard, if one has only lain in a swan's egg."

Sacred Scriptures teach me I'm created in the image of God: "God said, 'Let us make man in our image, in our likeness, and let them rule over the fish of the sea and the birds of the air, over the livestock, over all the earth, and over all the creatures that move along the ground.' So God created man in his own image, in the image of God he created him; male and female he created them" (Gen. 1:26–27 NIV). Since I am created in the image of God as a thinking, feeling, acting, living soul, I am the highest form of

God's creation. And not only am I an image bearer, but I have been given the right to "rule."

Scottish author and lecturer Oswald Chambers noted, "Confidence in the natural world is self-reliance, in the spiritual world it is God-reliance." Therefore, the pursuit of excellence is never a push for power. The desire for excellence is a gift of God characterized by a yearning to use God's gifts in a way that pleases Him. Antonio Stradivari, the seventeenth-century violin maker whose name in Latin, *Stradivarius*, is synonymous with excellence, said, "When any master holds 'twixt chin and hand a violin of mine, he will be glad Stradivari lived, made violins and made them of the best. If my hand slacked I should rob God, since he is the fullest good, but he could not make Antonio Stradivari's violins without Antonio."

How do you truly see yourself? Are you looking through the lens of labels or love? Do you find it all too easy to look at the labels and listen to the old tapes from the past? Maybe you still hear your father's voice, "We really didn't want you," or "You're so stupid, I don't know why I put up with you." I can still hear my teachers' voices, "You're just not smart enough to go to college." If you hear a voice and see images, let them be from God, saying, "I created you in My image and gave you a destiny. You are Mine. I gave you dignity at birth. You are not a loser. You're more than a conqueror through My love and My power. You are a member of a royal family. Act like it. Think like it. Love like it. Live like it!"

Abraham Lincoln framed the value of self-respect this way: "I desire so to conduct the affairs of this administration that if at the end, when I come to lay down the reins of power, I have lost every other friend on earth, I shall at least have one friend left, and that friend shall be down inside of me." Self-worth is a gift of God, but self-respect is a gift you give yourself. It is earned when you live the life that is consistent with the real you. God gave the Ten Commandments not to restrict you from freedom, but to help you remember who you are. These commandments have been turned into something negative and restrictive. But the truth is, they are the rules for an intimate relationship with God. Today, they remain the benchmark of all human dignity. I seek to live by them not to earn God's love, but as the fruit of the love of God I'm already enjoying.

To be real, I accept God's opinion of me. The life, death, and resurrection of my Savior, Jesus Christ, are proof positive I am worthy of receiving and giving love. If God loves me and is for me, what does it matter if others withhold their approval? My self-worth sets my self-image. I am a saint and son of God, and my self-image motivates me to live with integrity. My behavior is informed by love, not conformed by fear. And when my belief and behavior match, I feel good about myself. I have a healthy pride fueled by gratitude.

The Tests of Authenticity

Authenticity is easier to detect than it is to define. And where it is present, it is a beautiful, powerful thing. It's not unlike the impressive presence I felt as a kid in Kentucky, whenever I was around a thoroughbred racehorse; power under control and quiet confidence ready for action at a moment's notice. It is not an easy quality to dissect, but I think there are some sure signs to look for. The qualities of an authentic life can be seen in four simple tests.

1. The Test of Honesty

Honesty is the heart of authenticity. The Bible assures us that "perfect love drives out fear" (1 John 4:18 NIV). The heart filled with fear cannot be honest, and the heart assured of love need not be afraid of the truth. Being real with God means being honest about myself. It was William Shakespeare who wrote, "No legacy is so rich as honesty." I am a deeply wounded and flawed person whom God loves and on whom His favor rests. If God knows me as I am and loves me anyway, what else do I have to fear or prove?

Marcus Tullius Cicero asked, "Where is there dignity unless there is honesty?" Authentic people live transparent lives; therefore, they have a quiet confidence about them. They need not impress others because their needs are met. Having the assurance of the abundant life that God's grace provides, they do not lie to impress or hide to confuse. Their words are vibrant, clear, and peaceable. There is no guile in their hearts or gossip on their tongues. They are open to all who love truth and beauty, and closed to all who wear a facade of friendliness hiding an agenda to manipulate.

2. The Test of Honor

A Greek proverb asserts, "Goodness is not tied to greatness, but greatness is tied to goodness." An example of this occurred at the 2001 Tour de France. The 1997 German winner, Jan Ullrich, was pursuing Lance Armstrong. In the thirteenth stage of the race, Ullrich had a bad crash. He was run off the road and thrown over his handlebars. Armstrong saw it, stopped, and waited while Ullrich recovered. Armstrong was ultimately victorious, and Ullrich took the runner-up trophy.

Two years later in the 2003 Tour de France, as Armstrong sought a fifth consecutive victory, with Ullrich trailing him by a razor-thin 15 seconds, Armstrong hooked his handlebars on the bag of a fan leaning across the barrier. Ullrich stopped and waited while Armstrong picked himself up and remounted. At the end of the fifteenth stage, Lance Armstrong had extended his lead to 67 seconds. Waiting for a fallen competitor is part of road-racing etiquette. But remember, etiquette is a matter of honor, not rule. Ullrich would have been well within his rights to sprint ahead and take advantage of Armstrong's fall. Armstrong went on to win the 2003 Tour de France. These men have honor, strength of character written in the heart. Honor is more than an ideal; it is a commitment. Paul wrote that we should give "honor to whom honor is due" (Rom. 13:7 NRSV).

3. The Test of Humility

A well-known incident in the life of Robert E. Lee occurred while he was riding on a train to Richmond. The general was seated at the rear, and all the other places were filled with officers and soldiers. An elderly woman, poorly dressed, entered the coach at one station. Having no seat offered to her, she trudged down the aisle to the back of the car. Immediately, Lee stood up and gave her his place. One man after another then arose to give the general his seat. "No, gentlemen," he said, "if there is none for this lady, there can be none for me!" General Lee demonstrated that good manners and humility demand consideration for people in all walks of life, not merely for those of high social ranking like himself.

Humility is easier to detect than define. Dennis the Menace, one of my favorite TV characters, gave his best friend a good definition of *humility*: "The secret, Joey, is to know you're somebody without thinking you're somebody." The skeptical German poet Heinrich Heine said to Christians, "You show me your redeemed life and I might be inclined to believe in your Redeemer." The authentic life, which speaks the gospel with a spirit of loving sacrifice, will be eminently convincing.

Author Addison Walker rightly noted, "It's not true that nice guys finish last. Nice guys are winners before the game even starts." This is true because authentic people claim to serve an audience of One. The One we serve with all our hearts was the first to show us love with all of His. Humility is gratitude for being loved so lavishly that all we can do in response is to live a life committed to excellence as an offering of worship and adoration.

4. The Test of Humanity

Authenticity is seen in honesty, honor, and humility, but it is also easily detectable in those who have the quality I call humanity. It was exemplified during a segment of the 2004 Grammy Awards when "Dance with My Father," nominated for the Song of the Year, was about to be performed. The song's recording artist, Luther Vandross, had suffered a stroke just before its release and was still recovering from the effects. Celine Dion was chosen to stand in for Luther. Poised at the piano to accompany her was cowriter and producer Richard Marx. Everything was ready but the sound technicians.

The problems started when the vocal mike failed. Dion, the

consummate professional, struggled to regain her bearings. A stagehand dressed in black quickly appeared to change the faulty mike. Then Dion's ear monitors failed, and a back channel was opened so that all that could be heard was the panic of the sound crew. A painful uneasiness covered her face until she glanced into the eyes of her accompanist, Richard Marx. He looked at her and gave her a nod of confidence that said, "Don't worry; it's going to be okay." With that, her composure returned, resulting in a brilliant performance.

When "Dance with My Father" was awarded Song of the Year, Vandross was not there, and it was up to Marx to make the acceptance speech. His words were praise for the artistry and strength of Vandross. Not one reference was made to his contribution, except to lavish praise on his wife and sons. As I watched, I thought, *What class!* That's true humanity when you can help another as the walls of his world are caving in and at the same time shift the spotlight onto him as the awards are handed out without taking credit for either.

Keeping It Real

I overheard two teenagers greet each other this way: "Hey, man, whatcha been doin'?" "Keepin' it real" was the response. Not bad advice for any of us. Living authentically in a world of artificial intelligence, fast food, quick fixes, and microwavable relationships is no easy task, but there are some whispers of how to get it done along the way.

It was Nietzsche who said, "The most common lie is the lie one tells to oneself." Keeping it real starts with no secrets from God. King David's cry to God was,

Search me, O God, and know my heart;
     test me and know my anxious thoughts.
See if there is any offensive way in me,
     and lead me in the way everlasting. (Ps. 139:23–24 NIV)

I can feel the pathos in those honest words: "Search me, O God, and know my heart." Confession is essential on the path to spiritual authenticity and maturity. God promises, "If we confess our sins, he is faithful and just to forgive us our sins, and to cleanse us" (1 John 1:9 KJV). Confession is a good thing, a cleansing thing, a healing thing; it's like cleaning out all the closets of your soul. It's saying, "God, here are all the things I've been hiding because I was afraid to come clean. Here is the dirt I've been hiding because I didn't want You to see how dark my heart has become." It feels good to keep current your accounts with God.

How refreshing and liberating to live openly and honestly before God! What a dehumanizing burden to pretend to be strong and in control when you know you're not. But what freedom to admit when you're wrong and be forgiven. Paul's confession was, "I've tried everything and nothing helps. I'm at the end of my rope. Is there no one who can do anything for me?" (Rom. 7:24–25 THE MESSAGE). Isn't that the real question? The answer, thank God, is that Jesus Christ can and does. He acted to set things right in this life of contradictions where I want to serve God with all my heart and mind, but am pulled by the influence of sin to do something totally different.

Keeping it real means having no secrets and holding no grudges. James, the half brother of Jesus, advised, "Everyone should be quick to listen, slow to speak and slow to become angry, for man's anger does not bring about the righteous life that God desires" (James 1:19–20 NIV). I have heard angry condemnation and pontificating come out of the mouths of so-called religious people. We grieve God when we refuse to extend to others what we so freely accept from Him. People say things such as, "You made your bed; now lie in it," "The chickens are coming home to roost," or worse yet, "God is judging you for your secret sins." Is that really what it means to be real? To sit on a high and lofty place, looking down our spiritual noses at the broken, bruised, and battered, and say, "See there? You got exactly what you deserve. In the name of God, suffer!"

A real person holds no grudge because he knows, "but for the grace of God, there go I." Jesus said, "Love your enemies. Do good to those who hate you. Pray for the happiness of those who curse you; implore God's blessing on those who hurt you" (Luke 6:27–28 TLB). You know you're free when you can pray for someone who has hurt you or let you down and say, "God, I hold no grudge. I hold no debt. I release him. But for the grace of God, there go I." Real people are free from the habit of holding others hostage.

No Limits

Real people say no to secrets, grudges, and artificial limits laid on them by labels. They focus their energy forward in the process of dreaming, planning, and preparing to do something great with their lives. They turn a deaf ear to those who say, "Who do you think you are?" or "Where do you come from?" or "Who qualified you to show up and be somebody?" Real people refuse to hand over their future to the critics and know-it-alls.

Night after night we watch shows such as *Joe Millionaire, American Idol, The Apprentice,* and *Nashville Star.* We take solace in laughing at these people who obviously have less singing talent than the moon has cheese. And yet these people have more guts, albeit misdirected, than those of us sitting safe and snug on our sofas. At least they're out there taking their shot.

Where are the people who are "livin' large" and unafraid of what other people say or think? Real people don't place limits on God. They don't pose, posture, or pretend. They do not diminish their lives by harboring secret sins. When the day of accounting comes, they want to say, "I loved much, I dreamed much, and I dared much." And they want to see Him smile and hear Him say, "Welcome home. You are a good, faithful son or daughter, and I take great pleasure in you."

Who's going to change this sad world? Ordinary people who trust God to do extraordinary things through them are our hope. Gifted novelist Frederick Buechner well said:

People are prepared for everything except for the fact that
beyond the darkness of their blindness there is a great
light. They are prepared to go on breaking their backs
plowing the same old field until the cows come home
without seeing, until they stub their toes on it, that there
is a treasure buried in that field rich enough to buy Texas.
They are prepared for a God who strikes hard bargains
but not for a God who gives as much for an hour's work
as for a day's. They are prepared for a mustard-seed
kingdom of God no bigger than the eye of a newt but
not for the great banyan it becomes with birds in its
branches singing Mozart. They are prepared for the
potluck supper at First Presbyterian but not for the
marriage supper of the lamb.[1]

One of my favorite characters in the Bible is a guy by the
name of Gideon. He lived in a time when a nomadic tribe, the
Midianites, was ravaging Israel. They rode in from the desert on
camels and clouds of dust. They pounced on the people and stole
their crops. It had gotten so bad, the Israelites had moved to the
mountains to live.

Gideon was trying to scrape up enough food to fill his empty
stomach. The Bible describes the scene:

When the angel of the LORD appeared to Gideon, he said,
"The LORD is with you, mighty warrior." "But sir," Gideon
replied, "if the LORD is with us, why has all this happened
to us? Where are all his wonders that our fathers told us
about when they said, 'Did not the LORD bring us up out
of Egypt?' But now the LORD has abandoned us and put us
into the hand of Midian." The LORD turned to him and
said, "Go in the strength you have and save Israel out of
Midian's hand. Am I not sending you?" "But Lord," Gideon
asked, "how can I save Israel? My clan is the weakest in
Manasseh, and I am the least in my family." The LORD

answered, "I will be with you, and you will strike down all the Midianites together." (Judg. 6:12–16 NIV)

Gideon's response was a cynical, "If the Lord is with us, why has all this happened to us? Where are all the wonders our fathers told us about? Didn't He bring us up out of Egypt, but now the Lord has abandoned us and put us into the hands of the Midianites?" God answered, "Go in the strength you have and save your country."

When you say, "O God, why do babies die? Why are kids abused and abandoned? Why do bad things happen to good people? O God, explain why good people can't keep their marriages together. Why do good people, when they get everything just as they want it, wind up with cancer or lose their jobs? Lord, explain it all to me!" He'll tell you, "Go in your own strength and save your country. I'm with you. Take the limits off. Be a part of the solution. Trust Me for great things."

God is for you, and it doesn't matter who tries to label, libel, or limit you. It doesn't matter whether you come from a broken home, have less than a stellar past, or lack the resources and training. If God is for you, what else do you actually need?

God gives you the courage to be real enough to stop playing games, to stop being phony. God gives you the courage to be honest, open, and unafraid to let the light into dark places. He helps you to open all of the windows and say, "God, look into every room of my heart." G. K. Chesterton wrote, "You say grace before meals. All right. But I say grace before the play and the opera, and grace before the concert and pantomime, and grace before I open a book, and grace before sketching, painting, swimming, fencing, boxing, walking, playing, dancing; and grace before I dip the pen in the ink."

When you get what you want in your struggle for pelf,
    And the world makes you King for a day,
    Then go to the mirror and look at yourself,
    And see what that guy has to say.

For it isn't your Father, or Mother, or Wife,
Who judgement upon you must pass.
The feller whose verdict counts most in your life
Is the guy staring back from the glass.

He's the feller to please, never mind all the rest,
For he's with you clear up to the end,
And you've passed your most dangerous, difficult test
If the guy in the glass is your friend.

You may be like Jack Horner and "chisel" a plum,
And think you're a wonderful guy,
But the man in the glass says you're only a bum
If you can't look him straight in the eye.

You can fool the whole world down the pathway of years,
And get pats on the back as you pass,
But your final reward will be heartaches and tears
If you've cheated the guy in the glass.

—Peter "Dale" Wimbrow

3

I Will Go the Extra Mile

*Now it is a funny thing about life. If you refuse to accept
anything but the best you very often get it. If you utterly
decline to make do with what you can get, then somehow or
other you are likely to get what you want.*
—SOMERSET MAUGHAM

The songs I learned to sing in church are fond memories
from my childhood. They seem too elementary for the
sophistication of adulthood until you pause to revisit
the profound simplicity of their words, for example, "Jesus loves
the little children, all the children of the world. Red and yellow,
black and white, they are precious in His sight. Jesus loves the little children of the world." How the prejudices of adulthood could
use the enlightenment of such simple truths! Or how about the
song "He's Got the Whole World in His Hands"? Yet none is
more profound to me now than the simple song "Deep and
Wide." The lyrics, along with hand motions to keep a kid's energy engaged, say, "Deep and wide, deep and wide, there's a foun-
tain flowing deep and wide."

When I remember that song, I'm reminded that life goes
deep before it gets wide because *doing* comes out of *being*. In other
words, it is important to *do* good things, but it is more important
to *be* because doing flows out of being eventually. And any doing
that does not result from being will be found out. That is why to
excel at being who I am requires me to embrace my uniqueness,

be the real deal, and show the real me through a commitment to go the extra mile, even though I'm surrounded by a culture that applauds slick deals and shortcuts.

A visitor was admiring St. Paul's Cathedral in London. He saw monuments erected to the great heroes of the British Empire but none to the architect who had dreamed and designed the grand edifice. Feeling the architect had been forgotten, he asked the guide, "Where is the monument to the architect?" The guide led him to a dimly lit crypt beside a slab in the floor and told him the body of the architect, Sir Christopher Wren, lay beneath that slab. A tablet contained this inscription, *Lector, si monumentum requiris circumspice.* It means, "Reader, if you would see his monument, look about you."

You, too, are building a monument to the quality of your life every day you live. You do it in the way you do your job, treat a stranger, a neighbor, or a colleague. You do it the way you keep your promises, care for your possessions, and groom your body. In a thousand small ways during a million mundane moments you are building a reputation for excellence or mediocrity. How you build is up to you, but how you will be remembered is determined by that choice. Make it well. You and you alone will choose whether your life will be a testament to integrity or a cautionary tale.

You are at one of three places right now as you read these words. You are stuck or stagnated, feeling more trapped and frustrated with each passing day. You are in decline and disengaging. Or you are entering a period of unprecedented growth and change.

Stagnation occurs when you do what you've always done, expecting what you've always expected. This is the "if it ain't broke, don't fix it" approach to life, which really means you are content to recycle old assumptions. Someone has defined *crazy* as doing the same things again and again, still expecting a different result. If that is you, then you are in for a long, boring life dotted with repeated periods of regret.

Decline begins when you surrender to your assumptions. You

assume there will always be a tomorrow to get serious and get started. You assume your spouse will always be around to pick you up or catch you when you fall. You assume your kids will understand why you can't come to their games. After all, you're working late just for them. You're in decline when you give up, quit trying, and go with the flow.

The choice to change for the better means you're ready to go on to the next level with God. You've been given the gifts, talents, and abilities you'll need to execute the purpose for which you were created. But not even God can make the choice to use them. It's like the farmer who replied to a friend's question about how his crop was doing by saying, "Great! The best I've ever had." The man said, "Well, I know you give the credit to God." The farmer said, "I do, but you should have seen the field when God had it by Himself."

Growing and maturing require understanding the balance between God's part and your part. You can't do God's part, and He won't do yours. The choice to grow smarter and stronger is yours and yours alone. The commitment to excel and go the extra mile starts within you. You're the one who decides to reject mediocrity as the standard by which you measure your performance. Trying to control circumstances, market forces, or world events is like trying to predict the lightning pattern of a coming storm. But external forces cannot set the standard of excellence with which you will live your one and only life. Excellence is not a set of obligations or rules that can be superimposed from one person to another. You are the only one who can commit to excel at who you are, where you are, with what you have, while you can. Only you can find something you love to do and do it the best way you can, for as long as you can.

Excellence Isn't

What is excellence? Sometimes the best way to begin to understand what something is, is to understand what it isn't.

For some, excellence is about being a perfectionist. But perfection isn't possible for anyone, anywhere, at any time. Winston Churchill observed, "Perfectionism spells paralysis." Perfectionism makes you neurotic and condescending. Instead of attracting the best people, the arrogance of anyone who pretends to be perfect repels them. It has been said, "A perfectionist is someone who takes infinite pains and gives them to others," and "The closest thing to perfection a person ever comes is when he fills out a job application." Perfectionism is more an ego pathology than it is a path to excellence.

Excellence is not status seeking. It is not a ploy to gain advantage over another person. Status seeking is for people who need a position of power or prominence to validate their worth. Truly authentic people don't need undue attention, and they are often downright uncomfortable in the spotlight. As Harry S. Truman, the man who had to take the place of the beloved wartime president Franklin D. Roosevelt after only ninety days as vice president, said, "It's amazing what you can accomplish if you do not care who gets the credit."

Excellence is not trying to outdo, outshine, and outperform everyone else. As a matter of fact, if you're committed to excellence, you're going to be too busy to bother with the other guy, except to figure out how you can help him to success. And if you really understand the power of excellence, you'll discover that no one excels at anything alone. Genuine excellence seeks to draw people in and up. Excellence is not a solo sport because true excellence is selfless. It seeks only the highest good for everyone concerned.

Some people have the idea that excellence is only for the elite few. Excellence is for the "beautiful" people with native abilities (to whom everything comes easily) or for child prodigies who were born with a silver spoon in their mouths. This is a silly set of assumptions, used most often as excuses to hide behind. There are no perfect people for whom all things noble and excellent come easily.

Excellence Is

As a person for whom faith is a core value and lifelong passion, I am alarmed at the number of people who claim the same commitment and yet object to the call to excellence as nonbiblical, nonspiritual, and therefore not important. They are quick to cite the abuses of those who teach a name-it-and-claim-it religion. And I concede there are hucksters hawking a half-baked theology. Some teach that excellence is the lust for money, power, and prestige. And some go as far as to make the possession of health, wealth, and fame the primary signs of God's blessing. I acknowledge the excesses, and I try to punch holes in them too. But I refuse to jettison a principle as central to authentic spirituality as excellence just because some people abuse it.

I believe a passion to go deep into my faith is also an obligation to go wide with my life. So I ask, Does quality matter at work? Doesn't quality matter on the playing field and in the marketplace as well as in the boardroom? Doesn't my spouse deserve a quality home life? And don't my kids long for a quality set of parents who love them so completely that the fear of abandonment never enters their minds?

The amount of money, time, and effort spent on something is relative to the object's importance. For example, if I believe God is worthy of my best effort, then that belief is reflected in my behavior. When this happens, I am living a quality life as a matter of my inner integrity. Integrity occurs when I integrate what I say I believe in how I behave. Character is the fruit of being, then doing. Integrity and character guarantee that my actions truly reflect my inner commitment to God.

Excellence is a standard set by God. Look around at this amazing planet on which we live. Think of the majesty of the mountains and the delicate balance between all living things. Take the time to enjoy a sunset, and the result will be awe. Isn't our God, who does all things well, worthy of our best efforts? Paul calls us to "live a life worthy of the Lord and . . . please him in every way: bearing fruit in every good work, growing in the knowledge of God" (Col. 1:10 NIV).

Excellence is the currency of influence in our culture. People who work with quality and serve with quality are the people we listen to. Why shouldn't we? People of quality are the people we admire because they march to a Divine Drummer. Paul wrote, "I urge you, brothers, in view of God's mercy, to offer your bodies as living sacrifices, holy and pleasing to God—this is your spiritual act of worship" (Rom. 12:1 NIV).

A commitment to everyday excellence is a powerful act of worship. It's not only a powerful statement about whom I worship; it *is* worship in and of itself. Worship isn't just something we do in a room one day a week. It is something we do with our lives. We ascribe worth to God on the basis of how we live in His presence. Quality pleases God. If we sense God and express that through serving Him, then we have truly worshiped. We are then not guilty of being all head with no heart or all heart with no head. To sense God without serving Him is a mockery, but to serve Him without sensing Him is drudgery. Only the best possible is good enough for God! To serve God out of love is to serve Him with quality.

My commitment to living deep and wide is a mirror of my spiritual maturity. The Scriptures admonish us, "Let us leave the elementary teachings about Christ and go on to maturity" (Heb. 6:1 NIV). Max Lucado said, "There is a canyon of difference between doing your best to glorify God and doing whatever it takes to glorify yourself. The quest for excellence is a mark of maturity. The quest for power is childish."[1]

The Habits of Excellence

The Bible is filled with quality people. Let me illustrate with one person; his name is Daniel. He was stolen while still a youth, taken to a foreign country, and forced to live among his captors. He could have justified adopting the attitude of a victim. He could have refused to do anything but sulk and feel sorry for himself. But that was not the kind of man he was. He chose to make the best of a bad situation by blooming where he had been force-planted. He chose excellence as his defense against despair. By his choice, he gained a reputation for excellence: "Now Daniel so distinguished himself . . . by his exceptional qualities that the king planned to set him over the whole kingdom" (Dan. 6:3 NIV). Daniel, a captive in a foreign land, fought back against the injustices he faced by going the extra mile. He proved what Aristotle said, "Quality is not an act; it is a habit." So let's talk about the habits of excellence.

Give Everything You've Got to Everything You Do

F. Scott Fitzgerald, the great American novelist, declared, "I never blame fortune—there are too many complicated situations in life. But, I am absolutely merciless toward lack of effort." The first habit of excellence is giving everything you've got to everything you do. Because I first live *deep*, finding my acceptance and authenticity in Christ, I am able to live *wide*, which means I bring all of everything I am to everything I do. Listen to this: "Whatever you do, work at it with all your heart, as working for the Lord, not for men" (Col. 3:23 NIV). Everything you do, you do it from the heart for God. You see, if you work for the Lord and you work like the Lord, you can expect your reward to come from the Lord.

Mother Teresa said, "It doesn't matter what you do. It only matters how much love you put into what you do." Martin Luther King Jr. stated, "If a man is called to be a street sweeper, he should sweep streets as Michelangelo painted, or Beethoven composed music, or Shakespeare wrote poetry. He should sweep streets so well all the hosts of heaven and earth will pause to say, 'Here lived a great street sweeper, who did his job well.'" Don't wait for a stage on which to perform. Perform every day before an audience of One who applauds every effort and appreciates every gesture done in His name, even the giving of a "cup of cold water" (Matt. 10:42 NIV).

Giving everything you do, everything you've got, for an audience of One means you can wait on tables to the glory of God. You can dig ditches to the glory of God. Bloom where you're planted, and then God will see to it you get something better.

In high school, Friday nights were for football. I remember one night in particular. We were behind, and our heads were hanging low. We were too far behind to hope for a win. Coach Gilbert grabbed the face mask of one big lineman and screamed, "What's the matter with you?" The guy answered, "Coach, I'm saving myself for the next game." I could have sworn I saw smoke coming out of the coach's ears when he shouted, "Next game, next game, there is no next game! There is only this game here and now." I've never forgotten those words. Many times since then I've wanted to lean across a desk, look into a person's eyes, and ask, "What are you saving yourself for?" This is the game right here, right now.

Your only true competition is with yourself. Are you bringing all you are to bear on all you do right now? Are you using all your God-given creative capacity to solve a problem, right a wrong, help a friend, and win the war with mediocrity? Are you living not to lose, or are you playing to win without regard to the score or the odds, which are supposedly stacked against you? You never would have heard of Theodore Roosevelt if he had only halfheartedly committed himself to his task. The great genius of his career was that he flung all his passion, not a part of it, with all the determination and energy and power he could muster, into everything he undertook. No dillydallying, no fainthearted efforts, no lukewarm purpose for him.

Know Your Business

Satchel Paige threw his first major-league pitch at the age of forty-two. Actually, he was good enough to play in the majors at the age of eighteen, but he couldn't—Satchel Paige was African-American. Seven years after Jackie Robinson broke the color barrier in baseball, Paige, an undisputed superstar everywhere but in the Major Leagues, finally got his chance. Cleveland owner Bill Veeck was criticized for adding such an old man to his roster. Some sportswriters and critics called it a publicity stunt. Others said Paige was getting the break he had deserved for years, though most doubted his ability to compete effectively at his age. Paige silenced the critics when he won his first three games—shutting out Chicago twice in the process.

All along he knew he was good enough to pitch in the Major Leagues, and when he got his chance, he proved it. He approached his major-league pitching debut no differently than he approached any of the 2,500 games he pitched during his career. "It was just another game," he said. "And home plate was where it always was." Though Paige had the ability to make throwing a baseball look effortless, he spent his life perfecting the art. And eventually, he got his chance to show the world he was capable of competing with the best.

The secret habit of excellence is to know your business. Then you will know what it takes to excel. The Scriptures promise, "Do you see a man skilled in his work? He will serve before kings; he will not serve before obscure men" (Prov. 22:29 NIV). Focus on becoming good at the task at hand. If you're a kindergarten teacher, know how the very best kindergarten teachers got that way. Identify the best kindergarten teacher in your town. Meet with him or her. Offer to pay him for his time. Formulate questions ahead of time and take notes. Then find out who is the best kindergarten teacher in your state. Meet with her. How about in the country? Focus on being the best kindergarten teacher you can possibly be. Know what it takes to excel. This is a wise thing because "he who gets wisdom loves his own soul; he who cherishes understanding prospers" (Prov. 19:8 NIV).

Maybe you're in retail. Do you know the very best method to conduct retail sales? Do you know how to do your job the very best it can be done? Find the skills. Be the best at what you do. Go out and find out! God gave you a billion-dollar body and a trillion-dollar brain. Put your brain in gear and make it work for you. Read, ask questions, seek advice, be hungry and humble, and you will gain a wealth of information. Understand this: all leaders are learners, and great leaders are lifelong learners. People who excel at life gather around them other young and not-so-young, hungry people. They love sharing. You have an unlimited capacity for growth and change. God gave you a brilliant brain, two eyes to see and soak up beauty, two ears to listen and process wisdom, and a strong heart to process the information into action. Ralph Waldo Emerson noted, "If a man can write a better book, preach a better sermon, or make a better mouse-trap, than his neighbor, though he build his house in the woods, the world will make a beaten path to his door." How are your job skills? Are you stagnated, in decline, or growing?

Be Enthusiastic

Nothing great is achieved without enthusiasm. Someone has suggested that the sting of a bee is 5 percent stinger and 95 percent enthusiasm. Anybody can be enthusiastic. It costs you nothing, and it can earn you respect. Too many people pretend to be too cool and coy to get excited.

Take the average Monday morning in America. People drag into work tired after a weekend of rest. They tell their war stories about the game of golf they played, the sporting event they attended, or the home improvement project they completed. They share their weekend warrior stories with gusto, but shuffle through the workday like a sad dog spreading gloom. And when they lose their jobs to more energetic, enthusiastic people, they cry out, "O God, what happened? Why did You let this happen to me?" It's not God's fault and I'm not guaranteeing enthusiasm will make you "layoff proof," but it will come closer than anything I know. It's hard to consider doing without someone who brings enthusiasm and positive energy to the workplace, or any place for that matter.

Enthusiasm means "in God" or "God in you." What's the characteristic of God? God is happy, in a great mood, strong, vital, effervescent, and creative. All these things can be a part of you too.

Be the First to Act Intelligently

A man was taking a poll about apathy in the general population. He stopped a guy on the street and asked, "Some say the two greatest problems in America are ignorance and apathy. What do you think?" As the man hurried away, he said, "I don't know and I don't care!" That's the same attitude Solomon so graphically described: "As vinegar to the teeth and smoke to the eyes, so is a sluggard to those who send him" (Prov. 10:26 NIV). It's so destructive, the Bible says, "one who is slack in his work is brother to one who destroys" (Prov. 18:9 NIV).

Be a person who takes thoughtful action aimed at a worthy target. Think. Ponder. Look at all the tools you have available to you: prayer, the Bible, other people who are willing to share their knowledge and the experiences they turned into stepping-stones toward excellence. There are hints and help all around those who have eager eyes open to see them and employ them to make good decisions with an economy of effort.

Years ago, during my daughter's graduation ceremony, one of the commencement speakers said, "Remember, knowledge is power." I thought how strange and somehow wrong that was. If knowledge were power, then the makers of Tide detergent should put a panel of scientists across the front of their commercials telling people that Tide is made of superior chemical combinations that have been proven in double-blind studies to get your clothes cleaner than any other detergent. Nike shoes shouldn't have to pay high-priced athletes to hype their shoes. They'd just tell you how superior they are scientifically. There wouldn't be any teenage smoking in America because you'd just have to send out a brochure outlining the ills of smoking and teenage smoking would be wiped out in a week! Giving people more information is not the key to change. It is certainly no guarantee of wisdom.

Knowledge is only potential power. It's what you do with knowledge that makes it powerful and life changing. The acquisition and the application of wisdom give you a powerful advantage. Be the person who gathers the available information, collates it quickly, makes decisions promptly, and puts it into action. Don't hesitate. Do investigate. Then act with deliberation.

Earn a Reputation for Reliability

Earning a reputation for reliability can set you apart from the army of also-rans. Showing up at work on time—or showing up at all—can set you apart from everyone else who drags in with the same lame excuses. Let this soak in: "Many a man claims to have unfailing love, but a faithful man who can find?" (Prov. 20:6 NIV), or "Like a bad tooth or a lame foot is reliance on the unfaithful in times of trouble" (Prov. 25:19 NIV). A good friend of mine started a remodeling company. I asked him how he was doing, and he said, "Dave, all I have to do is show up when I say I will, and I'm already ahead of the game. Because I show up, I have more work than I can do, and I have never spent a dime on advertising."

Mark Twain said it this way: "Few things are harder to put up with than the annoyance of a good example." It's like the kid who applied for a job. The ad said, "Wanted, responsible worker." The interviewer asked him, "What about you makes you think you are a responsible worker?" He replied, "Everywhere I've worked, when something went wrong, they'd point at me and say, 'You're responsible.'" I'm not quite sure that's what I'm talking about here.

I lived in Huntsville, Alabama, for a couple of years, and everywhere I went I heard the legend of Wernher von Braun. Von Braun is considered the father of the modern space age and the creator of the Redstone engine, which powered the Saturn rocket and made the Apollo moon missions possible. After the *Apollo IV* mission, von Braun gave a speech in which he revealed these statistics: "The *Saturn V* has 5,600,000 parts. Even if we had 99.9 percent reliability, there would still be 5,600 defective parts. Yet the *Apollo IV* mission flew a 'text-book' flight with only two anomalies occurring resulting in a reliability of 99.9999 percent." If an average automobile with 13,000 parts had the same reliability, it would have its first defective part in about 100 years. Who wouldn't love a car like that? Why does Old Faithful in Yellowstone National Park attract so much attention? It's faithful. Faithfulness is a rare quality these days, but it is standard equipment in a commitment to excellence. You don't need a high IQ or the gift of a virtuoso, just the heart of a person who knows that showing up is half the battle won.

Work Smart

Doing life on the extra mile isn't just about working harder; it's about working smarter. Working smart is learning when to load up and go for it (just as I'm doing to get this manuscript in by the due date) and when to limit your labor and enjoy the journey. Dagwood Bumstead, the gregarious gadabout of Sunday comic fame, noted, "You can't teach people to be lazy—either they have it, or they don't." You can't be lazy and expect to excel; neither can you become a feverish blur of endless getting. The Bible teaches, "He who works his land will have abundant food, but the one who chases fantasies will have his fill of poverty" (Prov. 28:19 NIV). Work your land, do your job, then stop. The healthy pattern of labor consists of periods of intense activity punctuated with periods of rest and renewal. Jim Loehr and Tony Schwartz in their best-selling book *The Power of Full Engagement* wrote,

> Most professional athletes . . . enjoy an off-season of four or five months a year. After competing under extraordinary pressure for several months, a long off-season gives athletes the critical time that they need for rest and healing, renewal and growth. By contrast, your "off-season" likely amounts to a few weeks of vacation a year. Even then you probably aren't solely resting and recovering. More likely, you are spending at least some of your vacation time answering mail, checking your voicemail and ruminating about your work.[2]

When Aunt Vera poured us kids our Kool-Aid, she always said, "Tell me when's enough." It's not smart to live without knowing when it's enough. It's not smart to spend your life just getting more stuff. God created you on purpose with all the energy you need to achieve all you need to get done. He has given you enough time to do it so that everything you need to do will fit in your life span. Remember, you're shooting for significance, not just success.

Jesus Christ's human life spanned thirty-three or so years. He used the first thirty to prepare for the last three. He didn't drive a car, own a fax machine, or have a cell phone. There was no Internet, e-mail, or instant messaging. He walked everywhere He went. He gathered a group of only twelve men around Him who were questionable in their ability to ever be more than moderately successful fishermen. And yet He still lives today as the single most influential person who ever lived. As the Scriptures say, "If any man builds on this foundation using gold, silver, costly stones, wood, hay or straw, his work will be shown for what it is, because the Day will bring it to light. It will be revealed with fire, and the fire will test the quality of each man's work" (1 Cor. 3:12–13 NIV). Certainly, the test of time and opposition has revealed the true meddle of the man, Jesus. You could do no better than to adopt His method: prepare well, pick well, rest well, then push to the goal with all due haste.

Take Time to Retool

If you work smart, you know the value of taking the time to recharge, retool, and retrain. Listen to this: "If the ax is dull and its edge unsharpened, more strength is needed but skill will bring success" (Eccles. 10:10 NIV). Think through this analogy carefully. Your goal is to clear some trees or chop wood for the winter, or maybe you need logs to build your home. With a clear picture of your objective, you grab your ax and go to work. Things go well for a while, but soon you find yourself exerting a lot of energy for little return. Someone dares to suggest you stop and sharpen the ax. Your response might be, "I'm far too busy chopping wood to do that." That would be silly, especially since a dull ax is the very thing keeping you from success. The point is, if you're not careful, you'll become too busy to listen to your life or God. If you're too busy to retrain or retool, you're too busy. If you think you're so important and so necessary to the future of the human race you can't slow down long enough to recover what it means to be fully human and creatively alive, you've overestimated how much of the world you own.

If that is how you feel, get a bucket and fill it up with water. Stick your hand in the water, pull it out really fast, and see how much of a hole you leave. That's how big a hole you're going to leave when you die. That's not discouraging, is it? It should be a relief to know the world's going to keep right on ticking after you're done. Does this make you insignificant? No, but it makes you insignificant to the world's spinning. Aren't you glad? One Savior, per person, per lifetime, and you ain't it. Thank God.

Well, who are you significant to? God. Who do you matter to? God. Who has you here for a purpose? You're not here to hold up the universe. You don't have to save me or the world or God, and you can't save yourself. You can take time to breathe, rest, be silly, smile, and have fun. As kids, we laugh three hundred times a day, but by the time we're adults, we laugh only seventeen times. Why? We take on a messiah complex as we get older. We're always in a hurry. But Jesus was never hurried. He was busy; He was engaged. There were plenty of times He took the longest route from point A to point B. There were times when He prayed all night. He rested. He took boat rides. He fished, and He went to parties and dinners. The only events He had trouble with were the funerals He attended. Well, it wasn't exactly trouble. It was the fact that when He showed up, the funeral was over because there was no more corpse. You can't make time, but you can take it. (We'll discuss this in detail in Chapter 10.)

Underpromise and Overdeliver

William Faulkner noted, "Always dream and shoot higher than you know you can do. Don't bother just to be better than your contemporaries or predecessors. Try to be better than yourself." If you make a habit of doing more than you're paid to do, there will come a day when you will be paid more for what you do. Ancient wisdom urges, "Slaves, obey your earthly masters in everything;

and do it, not only when their eye is on you and to win their favor, but with sincerity of heart and reverence for the Lord" (Col. 3:22 NIV). Surprise people with better-than-expected service.

I found this poem several years ago. It describes too many people I've worked around.

> I go for a drink, to sharpen my pencils.
> I search through my desk for forgotten utensils.
> I reset my watch, I adjusted my chair.
> I loosened my tie and I straightened my hair.
> I filled my pen and tested the blotter.
> I've gone for another drink of water.
> I adjusted the calendar; I raised the blinds.
> I sorted through erasers of all different kinds.
> Now down to work I can finally sit.
> Oops, too late. It's time to quit.

Do you play when the boss is away, or do you work diligently without the need to be watched? A farmer in South America was clearing a plantation, and he noticed the laborers worked only when he watched them. He had a glass eye, so he took out the eye and placed it on a stump whenever he had to be away. The laborers saw the eye watching them and continued to work as though the farmer himself was sitting on the stump. People who work with excellence bring their own motivation to the workplace. They are self-starters, and they don't need glass eyes, security cameras, or policy manuals.

Author, speaker Og Mandino said, "The only certain means of success is to render more and better service than is expected of you, no matter what your task may be." Since the beginning of time, all successful people have followed this habit. The surest way to doom yourself to mediocrity is to perform only the work for which you are paid. Helen Keller acknowledged, "I long to accomplish a great and noble task; but it is my chief duty and joy to accomplish humble tasks as though they were great and noble." The world is moved along not only by the mighty shoves of its heroes, but also by the aggregate of the tiny pushes of each honest worker. Remember the ways of the ant:

> Go to the ant, you sluggard;
>   consider its ways and be wise!
> It has no commander, no overseer or ruler,
> yet it stores its provisions in summer
>   and gathers its food at harvest. (Prov. 6:6–7 NIV)

Demonstrate a Positive Attitude

The Bible instructs, "Do everything without complaining or arguing, so that you may become blameless and pure, children of God without fault in a crooked and depraved generation, in which you shine like stars in the universe" (Phil. 2:14–15 NIV). It is easy to sit in the cynics' corner. The great American pastime seems to be the cut-down. In the break room, workroom, or conference room somebody is cutting somebody else down. If you engage in it, what does that say about you? So many do it so much, it's tempting to drift down to their level and engage in the same put-downs. But someone gets angry or hurt, and you wake up. You come to your senses and start raising the course of the conversation around you. In whatever environment you find yourself, refuse to complain, argue, or grumble.

All my life I've been told that Christians are different. But God didn't intend the difference to be our propensity to huddle and hide from the big, bad, negative world. The difference is, we engage in the marketplace of ideas and possibilities. We seek to outlove, not just outperform everyone else. For us, a positive attitude is an act of worship, not a tactic of competition. It's our way of saying, "Thank You, God," for the gift of life. It is only a side benefit that when we build up rather than tear down and when we seek to help rather than hurt, we might just end up writing a better song, playing a better instrument, or creating a better mousetrap. We earn the right to talk about the God who changed our lives after and only after we demonstrate the difference in how we talk to and treat other people.

If you want to be noticed, be positive. We have enough chronic complainers. There is the chronic whiner whose favorite phrase is "it's not fair." He gets up to "rise and whine." Then there's the martyr who believes, "nobody appreciates me." The cynic says, "Nothing will ever change." The perfectionist asks, "Is this the best you can do?" The Scriptures warn, "A hot-tempered man stirs up dissension, but a patient man calms a quarrel" (Prov. 15:18 NIV). Want to be a person of quality and excellence? Then be positive. It will place you in great stead with God and man.

Remember, There Is No Traffic Jam on the Extra Mile

Henry Ford stated, "There is not a man living who cannot do more than he thinks he can." Jesus told us, "If someone forces you to go one mile, go with him two miles" (Matt. 5:41 NIV). In the ancient world, when a Roman soldier was on his way to a battle, any person, by law, could be conscripted immediately to carry his armor one mile. The reason is obvious. If the soldier carried his armor from battlefield to battlefield, he wouldn't have strength for the fight. Jesus said, "Go the one mile the law requires, and then go two." It's the extra mile, the one you don't have to do, that will draw people's attention to you. Quit praying, "O God, expand my territory," if you can't handle what you've got now! But when you do handle it, God says, "Here is a faithful, reliable, quality person."

Some of the best memories of my childhood come from the summers on Uncle Henry's farm. I remember one particular long, hot summer afternoon spent hauling hay. I walked up and down the hayfield pitching bales of hay onto a wagon. After loading it in the field, we had to unload it in the barn. At the end of the day I was hot, gritty, and nasty! Rings of grime, grit, and sweat were caked around the creases of my neck and under my armpits. Two things happened I've never forgotten. First, we drank milk so cold, it made my teeth hurt. Second, we lay on the linoleum-covered living room floor in front of two giant window fans. Man, it felt good. It didn't matter how hot it was outside, the linoleum floor was always cool. I'm lying there on the linoleum floor with a milk mustache. I have never felt so good and tired. When I'm done on this earth and I stand before God, I hope He has cold milk and a linoleum floor. I want to lie down on it and hear Him say, "Well done, thou good and faithful servant . . . enter thou into the joy of thy lord" (Matt. 25:21 KJV).

Willie Mays observed, "Almost anybody can be good at what they do once in a while. It's being good every day that separates the good from the great." When everyone else around you is taking the shortcut to success, stay on the extra mile. It's the mediocre person who says, "Do the minimum work for the maximum pay."

Turn a deaf ear to those who call you to compromise your everyday commitment to personal excellence. The late pastor, author A. W. Tozer advised, "Let your heart soar as high as it will. Refuse to be average." One person who refuses to live down to the labels, libels, and limitations placed on him or her makes the difference.

A man with some spare cash thought he had found a bargain when he bought for $18,000 a run-down house on the south side of Chicago. He painted it inside and out, fixed the plumbing, added landscaping, and put it on the market. To his surprise, there were no offers. He asked a realtor friend for advice, "What's wrong with this house?" "It's not the house," he replied. "It's the neighborhood." Immediately, the man went to his bank and borrowed the down payment for four additional fixer-uppers on the same block. By the time the last one was painted and the final shrub was in place, something began to happen on that street. Up and down the block people brought out their paintbrushes and garden tools. In a matter of months, home values in the neighborhood climbed dramatically. What happened? One man made a firm commitment to go first-class, and the effect was contagious. Who will dare do life on the extra mile? The road is long and hard, but it's not crowded—and the rewards are limitless.

Commitment #2
EXCELLING AT BEING WHERE I AM

‿

*The lesson which life repeats and constantly
enforces is "look under foot." You are always
nearer the divine and the true sources
of your power than you think. The lure
of the distant and the difficult is
deceptive. The great opportunity
is where you are. Do not despise
your own place and hour. Every
place is under the stars, every
place is the center of the world.*
—JOHN BURROUGHS

4

I Will Seize Opportunities

~

Still round the corner there may wait,
A new road, or a secret gate.
—J. R. R. TOLKIEN

Let your hook be always cast. In the pool where
you least expect it, will be fish.
—OVID

An ancient Persian legend tells the story of a wealthy landowner by the name of Al Haffed. One evening a traveler related to him tales of fabulous amounts of diamonds that could be found in other parts of the world, and of the great riches they could bring him. Even though his land had earned him immense wealth, the romantic idea of discovering greater riches in an exotic land far away made Haffed increasingly unhappy with what he already owned. He grew so dissatisfied with cultivating his land that he sold it and set out to find new treasures. After years of wandering, his search proved fruitless. In despair at winding up penniless, he committed suicide by jumping into the sea.

Meanwhile, the man to whom Al Haffed sold his farm noticed as he was plowing one day the glint of an unusual stone in a shallow stream. He reached into the water, and to his amazement, he pulled out a huge diamond the size of his fist. Later while working in his garden, he uncovered more valuable gems.

Poor Al Haffed had spent his life traveling to distant lands seeking wealth when on the farm he had left behind were all the precious stones his heart could have desired. The moral of the story is simply that opportunities abound right where you are. Stop waiting for a better place with a warmer climate and buried treasure.

Look around you; opportunities are literally everywhere. Solomon's wisdom applies here: "If you wait for perfect conditions, you will never get anything done. . . . Keep on sowing your seed, for you never know which will grow—perhaps it all will. It is a wonderful thing to be alive!" (Eccles. 11:4–7 TLB).

Is this how you feel right now? Are you happy to be alive right now, right where you are reading this book? You may be in your home, on the road, in a hotel, or in a hospital room. No matter where you are or what you're experiencing, the world is confronting you with opportunities to make your life count. Solomon said, "Anyone who is among the living has hope—even a live dog is better off than a dead lion!" (Eccles. 9:4 NIV). What an image to consider! Surely you've got more going for you than a dog does. You're alive, and that's all you need to start. There are acres of diamonds all around you. Can you see them?

I have discovered one of the rarest abilities is to be happy with the life you're living where you are. There is so much to do, so much to see and experience, it's unthinkable that anyone should lack for a meaningful way to invest his or her brief moments on this planet teeming with life and opportunity. The really happy people I've observed are building a boat, composing a symphony, educating a child, discovering a breakthrough drug, writing a song, or looking for dinosaur eggs in the Gobi Desert. They're engaged in living fully and creatively where they are without a thought about searching for happiness as if it were a quarter that rolled under the couch. Happiness is never the goal in itself because it happens while living a life crowded with work worth doing, surrounded by the people you love. George Bernard Shaw wrote about this subject: "Give a man health and a course to steer, and he'll never stop to trouble about whether he's happy or not."

The Four Levels

I've observed four levels of living. The first level is that of *survival*. This is what Abraham Maslow in his groundbreaking work in psychology called "body needs." Maslow noticed while working with monkeys that some needs take precedence over others. If you're hungry and thirsty, you're not too interested in listening to lectures on cooking; you want to eat! In more primitive times just acquiring the basic necessities for survival consumed most of the day. Once physiological needs are secured, you're looking for what's next.

At the second level the need for *safety, stability, and protection* comes into play. This is the level where children look for assurance that mother will nurture them and father will protect them. As they grow, the fear of being abandoned is replaced with structure, healthy limits, and consistent, loving discipline. As we mature, security needs extend to things such as safe neighborhoods, job security, a nest egg for retirement, and health insurance.

The third level of living is the *success* level. This is often the level of achievement, acquisition, and recognition. You've matured to the place where you're separated from your parents and no longer dependent on them for your survival and security. It's the level of maturity that parents hope their children will achieve eventually. We love our children and want them to acquire the skills required to be self-sufficient. The success level is about earning, owning, and having some degree of power. None is bad in itself; they are just never enough.

The highest plateau of human achievement is the level of *significance*. While the success level is about what you are competent enough to collect, the significance level is about character, calling, and contribution. One of the best illustrations of this is in the life of King David. Though he was a deeply flawed person (as are we all), the Bible tells us that he was a man after God's own heart. The summation of his life is given in this insightful statement: "David had served God's purpose in his own generation" (Acts 13:36 NIV). David's life served God's purpose (timeless), and he did it in keeping with his generational milieu (timely). That's a life well lived, isn't it?

I heard an accomplished writer once suggest that a great book requires a great theme. If a book requires a compelling theme, so does a life. Yet too many lives are shadows of what they could be because they are stuck at level three, hoping more money, titles, trophies, or trips will supply what's missing.

God placed a hunger in you for meaning and purpose. You were created not to seek the comfort zone, but to seize a few great moments and turn them into a great life. Having a great theme in life involves taking a risk of moving beyond the narrow limitations of success and discovering your true self where Christ is at the center—nurturing, healing, and empowering you to be a man or woman of significance. If you are committed to excel at character, calling, and contribution, opportunities abound all around you.

You are where you are right now for a purpose greater than paying taxes and dying. Living without a definite, compelling sense of calling is like chopping your way through a thick forest at a maddening pace only to find out at the end that you were in the wrong jungle. Speeding through your days without taking the time to define your contribution is like climbing the ladder of achievement only to find it was leaning against the wrong building. Because we're not sure why we're here (calling) or what we're supposed to be doing (contribution), 95 percent of us have no written goals. And even though research shows that the 5 percent who do have written goals reach their goals 95 percent of the time, it's hard to pour your life into something that you're not sure you'll want once you get it.

Excelling where you are begins with getting intentional about your calling (timely) and your contribution (timeless). When you are clear about these, opportunities will appear in the most unlikely places and situations. This reality came home vividly to me on a crowded flight back to Nashville. I'd been out of town all week in California. I had also been sick most of the week. Since I'm pretty much a homebody, being away from home and sick was a pretty draining combination. The only consolation was that I had my wife, Paula, with me, and she had nursed my flu-like symptoms so I could get through my responsibilities for the week.

I had a radio program early the next morning. We'd been bumped off one flight, another had been canceled, and the airline had lost our luggage. By the time we got on the last flight from Dallas to Nashville, Friday night had become Saturday morning.

As we boarded the plane, I prayed, *Please don't let there be any children on this flight*. It's not that I dislike children, but my head was throbbing, I was tired, and all I wanted to do was get home. There were no children, but right behind us sat a young couple. She was crying in an annoying, whiney pitch that was getting louder and more mournful by the moment. I thought, *Maybe she chipped a nail, or she swallowed her gum*. And I was thinking, *God, help this guy kiss her and make up*. I thought about turning around and saying, *Buddy, tell her you're sorry. Do anything, please!* Then her crying was even more annoying as she went from sobbing to moaning. All I could think about was having to listen to this all the way home. I was not trying to eavesdrop, but I was thinking, *What awful thing has this man done to cause her to cry and irritate me all the way home?* She calmed down a little once we were in the air.

Since they were directly behind me, I could hear most of their conversation. I discovered that she was weeping because she had just received news of her father's death. They were on their way home to confront one of life's worst moments. I felt like such a dope and such an idiot for being so fixated on *me*. In the back of my mind, a little voice said, *This is what you were made for. This is what I put you on the planet for. This is why you're on this flight. So turn around and offer some hope.*

I got excited. I thought, *It's a divine moment*. And then I thought, *Okay, as soon as we take off, I'll turn around and say something*. It would be very easy. She was just a few inches away behind me. And then I thought, *As soon as we reach flying altitude, I'll turn around. She'll be calmed down by then*. I heard them reminiscing about some of the happy times. She let out a little chuckle and snickered here and there.

Halfway through the flight, I was still talking to myself: *Okay, just as soon as we get the beverage tray beyond us, I'm going in. God, give me the right words. Let me be in the moment; seize this opportunity.* Then we hit a little rough area, and I thought, *As soon as we get through the rough stuff, I'm gonna turn around.* Then a bunch of obnoxious guys were talking loud, and I thought, *As soon as they calm down.* By that time we were getting close to Nashville: *Maybe I need to wait until we're on the ground.* Then we were taxiing in and were at the gate: *Maybe when we stand up, I can face them and say something profoundly comforting.* And then, *As soon as we deplane and get into the main area where we wouldn't be conspicuous.* And then I thought, *As soon as we get to baggage claim, and they get their stuff.*

I excused myself all the way out to the shuttle bus and went home. I did nothing. Said nothing. Gave no comfort. Lightened no burden. Should have done something. Was born to have done something! Went to seminary to receive training so I would be prepared to do something. Did nothing. I'm not proud of it, but I'll just add that to a long list of missed opportunities.

The greatest gift that God will ever give you is a problem you were made to solve. You're here only for a little while, and what living you do, you've got to do here and now in this imperfect moment where fathers die and daughters cry and planes are late.

Seize each opportunity because it will come and go, never to return. The doors open, and then they shut. The windows crack, and then they go back down again. Stop waiting for a better moment, better time, more power, more strength, better words, or calmer conditions.

God's best gifts don't come on silver platters. He buries His best gifts at the heart of a big, tough problem. He then invites anyone alert enough and bold enough into the teeth of the problem to discover "the pearl of great price." Everyone who excels in a big way does so by breaking problems apart and finding the prize inside. When I was a kid, my favorite treat was Cracker Jack®, not just for the caramel popcorn, but for the prize inside.

That's how God raises us up to the significance level. He doesn't do everything for us, though He could, but that would only keep us weak. Because He wants us to be strong and free, He plunges us neck deep into problems worth the suffering it takes to solve them.

Without a sense of significance, life is meaningless. Solomon warned, "I have seen all the things that are done under the sun; all of them are meaningless, a chasing after the wind" (Eccles 1:14 NIV). Solomon was an expert at the emptiness of gathering "stuff." A life of success, translated "more stuff" or "more status," isn't worth your life or God's involvement. Life is meaningless unless there's a point, a problem, and a person. The point is to serve God's purpose in your generation, the best you can, for as long as you can. Remember, "many are the plans in a man's heart, but it is the LORD's purpose that prevails" (Prov. 19:21 NIV).

Seeing Opportunities

I read a plaque on an executive's desk that read, "Problems are my business and business is very good." Henry J. Kaiser, the American industrialist who organized the construction of the Hoover Dam and whose shipyards built some 1,460 Liberty ships during World War II, said, "I always view problems as opportunities in work clothes." As odd as that may seem at first glance, there would be no opportunites if there were no problems. But it takes a keen eye to see the possibilities in a problem.

When the new Volkswagen Beetle was introduced, it was said to be burglar proof. To demonstrate that point, Volkswagen hired a professional burglar and called a major news conference. The thief was challenged to break into the car in front of the press to validate the carmaker's claim. With reporters watching and cameras rolling, the burglar looked at the car and circled it for about ten minutes without ever touching it. Then after checking it over from every angle, he went to the front of the car, and with one swift kick, he hammered the bumper. In a split second, the airbags exploded, the door locks popped up, and the doors flew open. Burglar proof? Not to the creative problem solver.

Creative problem solving begins by defining what a problem is. A problem is something I can and want to do something about. If you can't do anything about it, it's just a fact of life. A problem is anything in which you are willing to invest your desire, focus, and time. If you're looking for a big opportunity, you need a big, scary, intimidating problem. Can you tell the difference between a problem and an inconvenience? Are you adroit at distinguishing the difference between a problem and a fact? A fact is something you can do nothing about. A problem is something you were born for. When the right problem comes along, you seize it like gold on the ground.

What's Your Problem?

Problems are plentiful. They're literally everywhere, but there are only a few worth dedicating your life to. Carefully choose the size of your problem because it will determine the size of your contribution. A great example of this principle is found in the story of David and Goliath. The Bible sets the scene for us:

> The Philistines now mustered their army for battle and camped between Socoh in Judah and Azekah in Ephes-dammim. Saul countered with a buildup of forces at Elah Valley. So the Philistines and Israelis faced each other on opposite hills, with the valley between them. Then Goliath, a Philistine champion from Gath, came out of the Philistine ranks to face the forces of Israel. He was a giant of a man, measuring over nine feet tall! He wore a bronze helmet, a two-hundred-pound coat of mail, bronze leggings, and carried a bronze javelin several inches thick, tipped with a twenty-five-pound iron spearhead, and his armor-bearer walked ahead of him with a huge shield. He stood and shouted across to the Israelis, "Do you need a

whole army to settle this? I will represent the Philistines,
and you choose someone to represent you, and we will
settle this in single combat! If your man is able to kill me,
then we will be your slaves. But if I kill him, then you
must be our slaves! I defy the armies of Israel! Send me a
man who will fight with me!" When Saul and the Israeli
army heard this, they were dismayed and frightened.
(1 Sam. 17:1–11 TLB)

The Israelites were facing their archenemy, the Philistines.
The Philistines were on one side of the hill, the Israelites on the
other side of the hill. In the middle was a valley with a giant hurl-
ing insults and drawing lines in the sand. Israel was still in the
Bronze Age, as almost every other nation was. The Philistines
were among the first in the ancient world to use a mixture of
bronze and iron. As a result, the Philistines persisted as a formidable foe that had to be defeated once and for all.

Both sides agreed that instead of massacring each other, they
would send their biggest, baddest warrior to fight to the death.
The Philistines had an ace in the hole—Goliath. He had been
groomed for war. He was more than nine feet tall. His coat alone
weighed two hundred pounds. The head of his spear weighed
twenty-five pounds. This guy invented the concept of "ready to
rumble."

The two nations were at an impasse. No one dared face Goliath in what appeared to be a certain death. Not only was death
involved, but also the guy who lost to Goliath would plunge the
entire nation into captivity. Who in his right mind wants that to
be his legacy?

Enter this grand drama, David, the young shepherd boy who
had recently been chosen as the next king of Israel at a secret ceremony. David was sent to deliver food, but he had a lot more than
figs and fish on his mind. No doubt he was looking for the opportunity that would usher him into the place where he would
be able to ascend the throne of Israel.

David listened to frightened men talk about the reward that

Saul was offering the person who faced Goliath. When he heard that the man who faced Goliath would be given the hand of the princess in marriage, his ears perked up. And even though his brother dismissed him as a cocky brat, David sensed destiny in the moment. What sent other men heading for the hills sent David headed for the moment he had been preparing for all his life.

On the basis of who he understood himself to be, David determined it was his fight. From that point forward he could never be satisfied herding sheep again. Thomas Alva Edison summed up this attitude: "Show me a thoroughly satisfied man and I will show you a failure."

David's life was about to take on a new mission, a mission that would call for courage and send him headlong onto the field of battle to face Goliath. Victor Frankl was a psychiatrist who survived the Nazi concentration camps. While Sigmund Freud said man is driven by the will to pleasure, and Alfred Adler said man is driven for the will to power, Frankl said man is driven by the search for meaning. According to Frankl, man's greatest power is the power to choose his responses. The power to choose a nobler path set David apart, and it was the ability to see the possibilities in the awful problem that helped him make the right choice.

Problems come in three basic varieties. First, there are the problems others create for you. Others make a commitment they fail to keep. You depend on them, they fail to live up to the contract, and you face a problem not of your making. Second, there are the problems you create for yourself. You fail someone who is depending on you, and your lapse has a domino effect, causing major problems. But there are some problems that God allows for your good and His glory. That may sound strange, especially if you listen to the prophets of prosperity who claim life with God to be problem and pain free. But the truth is, God uses problems. He certainly did in David's life.

David knew he was destined for the throne, but not much had happened to place him in line for succession. Facing Goliath and marrying into the royal family were God's green light to David. He saw it and wasted no time moving forward.

God may use a problem to show the state of your character. When external pressure is applied, you discover how solid-state you are. There is no doubt God uses problems to correct you. He says, "Endure hardship as discipline; God is treating you as sons" (Heb. 12:7 NIV). I don't go around trying to discipline other people's children, but I am committed to the firm discipline of my own because I love them.

God uses problems to protect you. It might be a mechanical problem that keeps your plane on the ground. It could be a slight pain in the chest that gets you to the doctor before "the big one" hits. God also uses problems to build your faith, and without question, God uses problems to prepare you for what's up ahead. This is exactly the lesson to be learned in the story of David and Goliath. Goliath was the best thing that ever happened to David.

Your response in the moment of choice is everything. The more you aspire to, the more problems you will attract. A key question that you will want to ask and answer during your decision-making process is, "What's the nature of this problem?" Is it just an annoyance, a part of living in the real world where things seldom go as fast or as well as planned? Maybe the problem is in actuality an open door that God has placed before you.

For example, one morning on my radio talk show Ben called in to respond to the question "How have you turned a problem into a possibility?" Ben said his problem arrived in the form of his daughter's poor health. She had developed a speech problem at a young age. The doctors referred Ben and his wife to a speech therapy clinic in the city. The good news was that with treatment and time, the speech impediment could be overcome. The bad news was, Ben could not afford the clinic, and his insurance didn't cover the treatment. The solution for Ben was to take on an extra job. He found work as a janitor on night shift. Not only was he able to make enough money to cover the speech therapy his daughter needed, but he found he was good at the work.

Ben had an idea one day to start a janitorial service, and the business took off. What made Ben's business plan unique was that he employed only people who needed part-time work to cover unexpected medical expenses. In his first year alone, he had paid out more than a quarter of a million dollars in salaries to parents with sick kids. Ben saw the possibilities in the problem, and he seized the opportunity of a lifetime during the lifetime of the opportunity.

Stop reading for a second and ask these questions: "What big problem am I facing right now that just might be the entrance to the next level? Do I have a big problem that is overwhelming me? Am I facing anything big enough for God to get involved and do a miracle? Do I have a problem with the possibility, if solved, of meeting a great need for humanity? Am I engaged right now in any problem-solving project requiring great faith on my part and divine intervention on God's? Am I engaged in anything doomed for failure unless God shows up?"

What's the Possibility?

Winston Churchill noted, "Most men stumble over great discoveries, most then pick themselves up and walk away." David was definitely not one of those men. The Bible tells us a lot about David. He was a teenager at the time. He was ruddy, which means he was probably redheaded. He had a redneck-type job because as a shepherd, he was classified as a low-skill, low-level, little-potential worker. But he had brothers, all of whom were considered bonus babies.

Samuel, the high priest, was sent to find a new king for Israel because Saul had failed miserably. God sent him to David's home. His dad's name was Jesse, and Jesse had seven sons besides David. Samuel said, "One of your sons is going to be the new king." He added, "Let's trot 'em out and let's see what you've got." After they went through all seven sons, Samuel asked, "Are these all the sons you have?" (1 Sam. 16:11 NIV).

Jesse answered, "There is still the youngest, but he is tending the sheep" (1 Sam. 16:11 NIV). You can almost hear the mumbling in the background: "O Lord! We've got one more brother." "Not him!" "O God, please, anyone but David. Please, not David." You can hear the apology in Jesse's voice: "There's the youngest, but you wouldn't want him. He's kind of a misfit; he's best suited for shepherding." Even David faced the labeling of his family. If someone has labeled you a loser or "not fit" for the job, remember that "God chose the weak things of the world to shame the strong" (1 Cor. 1:27 NIV).

Have you ever felt like the consolation prize? Ever felt like a day late and a dollar short? Ever felt that you just don't measure up? Ever felt that, when you read your résumé, you wouldn't hire yourself? Can you just imagine David coming in from having kept the sheep? How did he smell? Samuel placed this possibility in his brain: "You are a nobody, but God has you slated to be a somebody. It isn't going to happen yet, but be alert because the path will open when you least expect it. You will be king one day. Watch for the defining moment."

How many people sleepwalk right past the opportunity of a lifetime? When they see the problems, they say, "I don't want that. I'm waiting for the good stuff. I'm waiting for something strainless, painless, and most of all, brainless. I'm waiting for my ship to come in." And God is saying, "Help Me out! Do something! Jump into the water and meet it halfway."

David went to battle knowing one day he would be king. With that in mind he heard Saul's incentive for the guy who killed Goliath. Neither he nor his family would ever have to pay taxes again, and he got to marry a princess. How did a redneck get close to the throne? Marry the princess. How did the redneck marry the princess? Face the problem and kill the giant. Don't laugh. This is the way it still works.

Seizing the Moment

Opportunities come and go; they do not come to stay. In the Chinese language two brush strokes are used to write the word *crisis*. One brush stroke stands for danger, and the other for opportu-

nity. In every problem is the seed of an equal or greater benefit.
It takes wisdom to know when action is called for because there
is a time to wait and there is a time to pull the trigger and go for
it with all you have. Blessed is the person who knows the difference. Oswald Chambers said, "God engineers our circumstances
as he did those of his Son; all we have to do is to follow where he
places us." The majority of us are busy trying to place ourselves
in perfect, problem-free circumstances. Even if there were such a
place, we would find no opportunity there.

Think of the power in this amazing promise: " 'For I know
the plans I have for you,' declared the LORD, 'plans to prosper you
and not to harm you, plans to give you hope and a future' " (Jer.
29:11–12 NIV). Don't doubt for a minute that young David had
already been carrying in his heart God's promise for his future. He
had spent endless hours on the back side of the farm tending the
sheep, looking up at the stars and wondering how God was going
to charter his course to greatness. And then, without warning or
fanfare, opportunity appeared, disguised as a picnic lunch carried
to the heart of a hopeless situation.

And while others were running to hide from the present reality, David moved with confident deliberation to find Goliath,
face Goliath, kill Goliath, cut off his head, marry the princess, and
when the time was right, take his rightful place as king.

Just the minute you dare to live beyond the limits of ordinary,
just the moment you dare to dream something big, somebody
from your family will show up and stick a label on you. The Bible
tells us that Jesus Christ could not do many miracles in His hometown. Jesus explained it this way: "Only in his hometown and in
his own house is a prophet without honor" (Matt. 13:57 NIV).

David's brother said, "You are nothing but a cocky brat." He
reminded David, "You're nothing! You're nobody! You're just a
self-serving little brother who's never going to amount to squat.
All you're good for is tending sheep."

Here's the genius. The Bible says that David turned from his
brother to another and asked, "Tell me one more time what you
get for slaying the giant." I wonder if David was a little nervous

after hearing again all the good stuff promised to the one who killed the giant and saved his country. Was David worried the line of the young warriors eager to cash in on this opportunity would be a mile long? Who wouldn't want a tax-free future along with a royal wedding? But to David's utter surprise, there was no one in line to seize the moment of unparalleled possibilities. Don't dare dismiss the story as a cute Bible story for kids. What is true in the ancient retelling of Israel's history and King David's life is still true today—there is no traffic jam on the extra mile. Giant killers have always been in the minority.

David was ushered in to see Saul. Saul looked at him and just laughed, saying, "Right, yeah, do you think for a second we're going to put our entire future on you?"

So David rehearsed to Saul his qualifications. It was the speech of a lifetime. Basically, what he said to Saul was this: "I may look young, I may be redheaded, and I may be a shepherd, but I didn't fall off the turnip truck yesterday. I have experience. God has prepared me for this moment. You think keeping sheep is easy? Number one, sheep are the dumbest animals in the history of the world. No only that; sheep are defenseless." And then he said, "Let me give you an example. There was a tiger who came in. They are stealthy and sly. I trapped it and I killed it." And he said, "On the other end of the spectrum, there was a bear. He was strong, but I killed him too." He said, "I killed them both." Then he added, "This uncircumcised Philistine will be like one of them."

David brought up a very important point; the ability to seize the opportunity of a lifetime must be preceded by the willingness to prepare for it in advance. That's how David used his time with the sheep—training. He didn't come to the battle without a significant training period. Henry Ford observed, "A generation ago there were a thousand men to every opportunity, while today there are a thousand opportunities to every man." That may explain why he believed, "Before everything else, getting ready is the secret of success." You prepare in the quiet for the fight to come in public places.

But preparation is wasted if at the moment of decision, there is not also the courage to show up. The opportunity was available to every soldier in Israel's army, but only David had the courage to show up. When asked to comment on the reason for the successes of his productive life, Theodore Roosevelt said, "I put myself in the way of things happening; and they happened." The character to move in the direction of a fight when you don't even know yet what form it's going to take is bravery. Oliver Wendell Holmes said it well: "The greatest thing in the world is not so much where we stand as in what direction we're moving."

In the movie *The Last Samurai*, Captain Algren (played by Tom Cruise) rescued Lord Katsumoto, the leader of the remaining samurai. As the two men took counsel, Katsumoto asked, "Do you believe a man can change his destiny?" Algren replied, "I think a man does what he can until his destiny is revealed." That's exactly right. That's why the Bible tells us whatever we do, do it with excellence, even if it's a small thing, because it may be the very thing that qualifies us for the big thing.

I have discovered that the difference between the haves and the have-nots can almost always be traced back to the dids and the did-nots.

David went out. He finally got the okay and picked up five smooth stones from a stream. Then he put them in his shepherd's bag. How many stones did he need? Do you know the story? One! Why did he pick up five? Some have suggested that Goliath had four brothers! Who knows?

Goliath looked at him and said, "Am I a dog? This is not a warrior. It's a kid!" So what did David say? "Number one, I'm gonna kill you. Number two, I'm gonna cut off your head, put it on a plate, and take it on tour!"

There is a fine line between arrogance and confidence, I suppose. Most people I meet today aren't anywhere close to being arrogant. Too many feel defeated. They're focused on their failures instead of the possibilities. When God finds a person who is willing to face a problem, able to believe in the possibilities, and willing to prepare in the insignificant moments, great things happen. Ignore the critics who say, "Be like this. Be like that. Wear my armor. Cut your hair. Lose weight. Get taller. Get smaller." Dare to bring the full weight of who you are to all you do. When that happens, powerful things occur.

David had the will to prepare. He had the courage to show up, suit up, and stand up. And then came the moment when everyone saw whether David could perform under the ultimate pressure of a fight to the death. He could talk a good talk, but could he deliver when it mattered? Had he allowed the emotion of the moment and the allure of rewards to draw him into a dead zone from which he had no hope of escaping? Let the story speak for itself:

> [David shouted,] "Today the Lord will conquer you, and I will kill you and cut off your head; and then I will give the dead bodies of your men to the birds and wild animals, and the whole world will know there is a God in Israel! And Israel will learn that the Lord does not depend on weapons to fulfill his plans—he works without regard to human means! He will give you to us!" As Goliath approached, David ran out to meet him and, reaching into his shepherd's bag, took out a stone, hurled it from his sling, and hit the Philistine in the forehead. The stone sank in, and the man fell on his face to the ground. So David conquered the Philistine giant with a sling and a stone. (1 Sam. 17:46–50 TLB)

What an amazing ending to what first appeared an undefeatable foe by the most unlikely hero! But that's how real life works. It's the unlikely hero who at the right moment steps into the strong currents of opportunity and wins the day. Francis Bacon, the great English philosopher, noted, "A wise man will make more opportunities than he finds." God doesn't need your ability; He needs only your availability. How many times have you heard that? But the question is, Are you available today, or are you too busy being beige? Are you too busy listening to the know-it-alls in your life who think they have you figured out? Are you going to believe God's opinion of you?

David wanted to be a prince; God made him a king. What do you want to be? Remember you serve a God who is "able to do immeasurably more than all we ask or imagine, according to his power that is at work within us" (Eph. 3:20 NIV). Ralph Waldo Emerson observed, "We are always getting ready to live, but never living." Never let it be said you wasted your life waiting for the perfect weather that never came.

Refuse to accept mediocre as your response to life's problems. Recognize that wherever you are today, great opportunities are all around you. Al Haffed couldn't see the acres of diamonds he was standing on because he was looking for a fairyland that didn't exist. Look around and ask this question, "Are there any problems around me that are opportunities incognito?" If someone asked you today, "What's your problem?" would you respond by listing all the things that cause you pain, or could you tell a story about a giant you have just slain?

To excel where you are, seize the opportunity to solve a big problem. Look all around you for the sign of a divine appointment. Even though you may feel like David tending the sheep in obscurity, remember the will to prepare for the right moment will determine whether you have the courage to show up and the power to perform once you face the giant. Goliath was the best thing that ever happened to David. There is no greatness without first facing and defeating the giants.

5

I Will Conquer My Fears

Many of our fears are tissue-paper thin, and a single courageous step would carry us clear through them.
—BRENDAN FRANCIS

In her heyday, Ann Landers received more than ten thousand letters a day. Someone asked her, "What is the most common problem people ask about?" She said, "Without a doubt—fear." We have a fear of just about everything. For example, ailurophobia is the fear of cats, while zoophobia is the fear of animals in general. We have amathophobia, which is the dreaded fear of dust; ochlophobia, which is the fear of crowds; and pyrophobia, which is the fear of fire. And I'm sure that we have a name for the fear of the dust that people make while lighting a fire! We are a culture carried away by fear.

Fear adds up your shortcomings, subtracts from strengths, multiplies your worries, and divides your mind. It is powerful enough to blind you to opportunities as well as paralyze your hope and disengage your will. Fear is like a bottomless pit where all things noble go to die and all things beautiful are made ugly. It is the number one plague of humankind and your most formidable foe. By contrast faith is your greatest ally in conquering the fears that would otherwise sterilize your soul and shrink your spirit.

Norman Vincent Peale said, "The cure for fear is faith." I am talking about a real, life-changing, need-meeting, soul-freeing, spirit-lifting, devil-defeating faith. The kind of faith to which I refer makes you shout,

> The LORD is my light and my salvation—
>   whom shall I fear?
> The LORD is the stronghold of my life—
>   of whom shall I be afraid?" (Ps. 27:1 NIV)

God wants you to walk by faith. You're not here to put in your time, avoid your fears, and then punch out. You're here to live well, love well, and leave a legacy. You do that as you walk with Him and trust Him daily. It is in the context of an intimate relationship of trust that He gives us not only what He has, but also who He is. Walking by faith isn't for the faint of heart, but it is the only way to learn that God is indeed your "ever-present help in trouble" (Ps. 46:1 NIV).

Will Rogers wisely stated, "Even if you are on the right track, you're going to be run over if you just sit still." If you're going to live life to the max, as God intended, faith is the key ingredient. The way to please God is to trust Him: "Without faith it is impossible to please God, because anyone who comes to him must believe that he exists and that he rewards those who earnestly seek him" (Heb. 11:6 NIV). If God says, "It's impossible to please Me unless you live by faith," then developing a vibrant, firsthand faith is pretty important to know about. So what is faith? One of the best ways to understand a complex issue is to examine its opposite.

What Fear Is

In the 1978 comedy classic *The 2000 Year Old Man*, Carl Reiner asks, "What was the main mode of transportation two thousand years ago?" Mel Brooks answers, "Fear!" Fear isn't an abstract religious concept. It lives, breathes, mutates, and expands. It attaches itself to the deepest region of the human heart. And once it has its hooks deeply embedded in its host, it feeds without mercy. Nothing is so sacred that fear won't try to drag it into the gutter and shake the life out of it.

Fear loves to leap into the abyss of irrational thought. It hates truth and beauty. It loves paranoia and innuendo. That's why the Bible declares, "The wicked flee when no one is chasing them!" (Prov. 28:1 TLB). Why do they run when no one knows their secrets?

Fear gives birth to all kinds of prejudice. It gives birth to the spirit of division and suspicion. Prejudice measures the worth of a man by the size of his estate, the color of his skin, or the privilege with which he was born. None of these take into account the size of his heart, the strength of his character, or the nobility of his practices. Such is the logic of prejudice. That's what fear is best at, condemning people on the evidence of ignorance and innuendo. It was Emerson who asserted, "Fear always springs from ignorance," which is fertile soil for bigotry and hate.

Fear is father of division and duality. It sires a man who is a "double-minded man, unstable in all he does" (James 1:8 NIV). Fear is as binding and restrictive as a cheap suit when it's wet. It's a shrinking agent that stunts growth and suffocates dreams. It produces clay hearts, puny hopes, and narrow vision. Fear is like a drink of water that at first seems okay, but turns out to be tasteless, odorless poison, which slowly atrophies your attitudes and leaves you blinded by doubt. William Shakespeare wrote, "Our doubts are traitors, and make us lose the good we oft might win by fearing to attempt."

Allowing fear to go unchallenged is like pouring sand into the gears of a finely tuned machine. You may be able to function for a while, but the friction it causes will eventually grind you down. It cannot be conquered by denying it exists, nor is it starved to death by neglect. On the contrary, it grows best when it is allowed to lay submerged just beneath the conscious level. Fear loves free rein to program your subconscious mind with doubt and dread.

Fear cannot be overpowered by a show of false bravado. You

cannot hide from it or avoid it with clichés. You can only conquer it, or it will conquer you. Its only known antidote is firsthand faith. And this kind of faith is possible only when there is someone worth trusting. As a child, I was taught this prayer: "God is good and God is great." And because God is great, He can be trusted, and because He is good He invites us to trust Him. Author and preacher Harry Emerson Fosdick noted the differences between fear and faith: "Fear imprisons, faith liberates; fear paralyzes, faith empowers; fear disheartens, faith encourages; fear sickens, faith heals." Fear fosters helplessness, while faith fosters hope by daring to trust God's promise to act on behalf of anyone who lives by faith.

The Trust Dilemma

A famous tightrope walker once strung a cable across Niagara Falls from the American side all the way to the Canadian side. To the applause of thousands of people, he walked across that tightrope right on the very edge of the falls, the rushing, cascading waters thundering underneath him. He walked back and forth as people applauded wildly. Then to further wow the crowds, he put on a blindfold and went back and forth. Then he rode a bicycle back and forth, and then he pushed a wheelbarrow back and forth. Every day, people came out to watch him. He quite simply was the greatest.

One day while pushing the wheelbarrow back and forth, he called out to the crowd on one end, inquiring whether they thought he could successfully push the wheelbarrow across with a human being riding inside. The crowd went berserk: "Sure you can. You're remarkable. We've watched you for days. We understand and appreciate your skills. We believe in your abilities. You are the greatest." On and on they went until he looked into the wide eyes of a young man chanting his praise. He said, "Do you believe I could transport someone safely across Niagara Falls?" The young man shook his head in affirmation. The tightrope walker looked him straight in the eye and said, "Then, get in."

The young man was stunned by the request, but he shied away and disappeared into the crowd. That's the dilemma of trust. We say we believe with our mouths, but when we're faced with actually placing our full weight behind our trust with our actions, that's a whole different kettle of fish.

I have a question for you to consider. Think before you answer because the knee-jerk response may not be the one that best describes the state of your faith. The question is, "Do you now in this moment trust God with all your heart, mind, soul, and strength? Do you believe down in your soul that "the LORD is good, a refuge in times of trouble. He cares for those who trust in him" (Nah. 1:7 NIV)? Is it your firm, inner conviction that the God who created the universe, moves the worlds like marbles suspended in space, and keeps us from killing ourselves cares and moves on your behalf? Do you really believe that in practice, or is it just something you've heard? You can say all the right words, believe in all the right things, join all the right groups, and read all the right books, but the only way to trust God is to trust Him. Herein is the dilemma of trust.

Trusting God requires you to be in a situation in which you are powerless and very often clueless. For example, when a father picks up his little daughter and tosses her around in the air, she laughs and enjoys it because she trusts in her daddy. Even though she finds herself upside down eight feet off the ground with nothing supporting her, she doesn't fear because she trusts her father's heart and hand. This is how you develop firsthand faith. Like the little girl, you learn how to trust God by allowing Him to place you in a posture where all you can do is trust Him.

You learn how to be a parent by being a parent, not by reading a book on parenting. How'd you learn to drive a car? By reading a book? No, you learned by getting behind the wheel of a car and daring to put it in gear and give it gas. Therefore, trusting God is not a passive academic endeavor or an abstract religious theory. You can't learn how to trust God while sitting in a pew, reading about other people's experiences, or nodding to the faith of your parents.

Once you understand that faith requires action, you run into the second brick wall of trust. Simply put, given the chance, you will do almost anything to avoid having to trust God. You will do almost anything to keep from being put into a place where you have to trust God. The cure for this dilemma is to understand God's great delight in regularly placing you in positions where all you can do is trust Him. You are probably in one of these positions as you read this book. You may be questioning, "What did I do to deserve this?" or "How can anything good come from this?" But take heart. God shows up strongest in your weakness. Everyone you meet is in one of three places—in trouble, coming out of trouble, or getting ready to get into trouble. This is how life works.

God forces you to trust Him because trusting Him is what you were made for. So, if "the LORD is my light and my salvation; whom shall I fear?" (Ps. 27:1 KJV). War? The economy? In the midst of a place and a time when so many people are fearful and fretful, I choose faith. Trusting God is both the hardest and the easiest thing to do. It's the hardest when you have other options open. It's the easiest when you don't, unless, of course, you feel obliged to opt for despair.

As for me, my entrance into the life of faith was much like a drowning man groping around for something solid to take hold of in the dark of a moonless, motionless ocean. How much faith does it take for a drowning man to decide which life preserver to grasp when only one is being offered? If he wants to live, he takes hold of anything offered him that will bear his weight. He can worry about who made it later. There will be plenty of time to ask about the means and manufacture of his rescue once he is back on solid ground. Firsthand faith grows by the trust-and-see method.

Firsthand Faith

We've all met people who boast of their great faith but live as slaves to fear. Their words speak of experiences they never had, and they glibly traffic in truths they know nothing of. Too few are able to speak of faith in the first person. Even more settle for living like beggars who never dare dream of a meal at the King's table. It is not enough to say, "Have faith, brother, and all will be well." Faith says, "Let's join hands and lock arms and storm the gates together." It doesn't sit around reminiscing about yesterday. Yesterday's wins will not sustain you for today's woes.

Faith comes in two basic versions: secondhand faith and firsthand faith. Secondhand faith, which I guess is better than no faith at all, is too far removed from real life to do much good. By definition, secondhand faith is someone else's faith. It is good and inspiring to hear other people's stories of God's faithfulness. But that is exactly the problem, isn't it? Their stories are their experiences, and their certainties not yours. Hearing other people speak of victory is too far removed from the actual experience to affect me. It's like listening to a group of guys spin yarns about the glory days when they played football or baseball.

To develop firsthand faith, let's go to the book of Hebrews and learn from the heroes of faith:

> What is faith? It is the confident assurance that something
> we want is going to happen. It is the certainty that what
> we hope for is waiting for us, even though we cannot see it
> up ahead. Men of God in days of old were famous for their
> faith. By faith—by believing God—we know that the
> world and the stars—in fact, all things—were made at
> God's command; and that they were all made from things
> that can't be seen. (Heb. 11:1–3 TLB)

The first trait of firsthand faith is confidence. Men of God were famous for trusting God. Somehow we get the idea that really trusting God means God is going to do weird things with our lives. If we trust God, He'll make us missionaries to some country whose name we can't pronounce. He says, "Faith is the confident assurance that something you want is going to happen. It is the confidence to see and believe your heart before you actually hold it in your hand."

Years ago a military officer and his wife were aboard a ship that was caught in a raging ocean storm. Seeing the frantic look in her eyes, the man tried unsuccessfully to allay her fears. Suddenly, she grasped his sleeve and cried, "How can you be so calm?" He stepped back a few feet and drew his sword. Pointing it at her heart, he said, "Are you afraid of this?" Without hesitation she answered, "Of course not!" "Why not?" he inquired. "Because it's in your hand, and you love me too much to hurt me." He replied, "I know the One who holds the winds and the waters in the hollow of His hand, and He cares for us!" The officer was not disturbed because he had put his trust in the Lord of the storm.

As human beings, we often say, "I'll believe it when I see it." God says, "No, you've got it backward. Some things you have to believe in order to see." Whether you're an architect planning a building, whether you're an artist creating a sculpture, whether you're an Olympic athlete trying to break a world record, or whether you're a scientist trying to send a man to the moon, you have to believe it before you can see it. All of these things require faith. You have to believe it's possible in advance, long before it will ever be possible. That's what the Bible says faith is—believing when you don't see it.

Wernher von Braun, the father of the space age, said, "There has never been any significant achievement in human history that was not accompanied by faith." Someone who dared to believe it was possible started every great achievement and advancement of humankind. If you can conceive it in your heart and believe it in your head, you can achieve it with your hand. Faith can turn dreams into reality, ideas into inventions, and scarcity into abundance, but faith can do even more.

The second trait of firsthand faith is certainty. This means that I have learned to trust God even when I can't wrap my brain around a situation or it just doesn't make any sense. The truth is, "you can never please God without faith, without depending on him. Anyone who wants to come to God must believe that there is a God and that he rewards those who sincerely look for him" (Heb 11:6 TLB).

For me, believing there is a God is a no-brainer. But I've dealt with people on their journey who say, "I just don't believe in God." Most people who have said that to me were wounded by a religious phony. I've never had a hard time believing there's a God, but I do have a hard time understanding why He cares two cents about me. I am suspicious of His motives. I believe He exists, but believing He is favorable toward me is a much greater stretch for my guilt-ridden, shame-bound heart.

If you're going to follow God, He's going to ask you to do some things that may not make sense today, but will make perfect sense tomorrow. The example we're given here is Noah:

> Noah was another who trusted God. When he heard God's warning about the future, Noah believed him even though there was then no sign of a flood, and wasting no time, he built the ark and saved his family. Noah's belief in God was in direct contrast to the sin and disbelief of the rest of the world—which refused to obey—and because of his faith he became one of those whom God has accepted. (Heb. 11:7 TLB)

It had to be a red-letter day in the neighborhood when Noah and his clan moved in and immediately set up shop for a major building project in his backyard. The neighborhood association must have sent him a ton of letters reminding him that constructing such a gargantuan structure, which no doubt loomed over his and all the other neighbors' houses, was in violation of all codes and restrictions. How would anyone on his street ever sell his house with an ark parked in Noah's backyard for 120 years? People whispered while property values went down. I'm sure Noah too had more questions than answers. After all, in Noah's pre-flood world it had never rained. Each morning a mist, which came up from the ground like dew, provided all the moisture plants required, and deep earth springs provided all the water people needed. How was God going to find enough water to cover the entire face of the earth so that even the tallest mountains would be submerged?

Noah had big questions, but a bigger faith. His faith overshadowed and overpowered his fear of looking foolish. If God wanted a boat built on dry land, Noah was going to be the man to build it. Aren't we all thankful Noah obeyed when all the facts didn't add up? I'm glad he undertook the undertaking even when he couldn't understand it. He accepted the ridicule and snickers of those who were convinced that Noah's "cheese had slipped off his cracker." The Scriptures give us this insight into what he encountered: "Noah's belief in God was in direct contrast to the sin and disbelief of the rest of the world—which refused to obey—and because of his faith he became one of those whom God has accepted" (Heb. 11:7 TLB).

Firsthand faith obeys when it isn't the reasonable or fashionable thing to do. Religion demands that God's commands be reasonable. But mere religious interest cannot drive out fear or feed faith. For faith to display virtue and valor in the face of what appears at the moment an irrational assignment, God and the supremacy of His wisdom must reign without rival on the throne of your heart. When you say, "I trust God," it's your obedience that unleashes faith's power. And until you act, it's just theory or a nice story to teach the children when they want to know what's worth trusting. Another giant of firsthand faith is the father of the nation of Israel—Abraham. The Bible says, "By faith Abraham, when called to go to a place he would later receive as his inheritance, obeyed and went, even though he did not know where he was going" (Heb. 11:8 NIV). At the ripe old age of 75, God asks Abraham to abandon all that he has known and go to a strange country simply called Ur (which today is the country we call Iraq). He was probably looking forward to retirement, but God had other plans. God choose Abraham to head up his new project in nation building. And Abraham must have had a lot of questions like, "Where is Ur?" God said, "I'll tell you when we get there." Surely he asked, "How long is the journey?" God said, "You don't need to know, just follow me." Although he was challenged to start all over again in a new place with no guarantees other than the inner conviction to which God was calling him, Abraham obeyed. And the fruit of his faith can still be seen today in the nation of Israel, which occupies a central role in the region's geopolitical affairs to this very day. For Abraham's willingness to relocate he is remembered as the father of faith.

In the Old Testament alone, there are over a thousand promises where God commits His blessings to those who love Him enough to trust Him and trust Him enough to obey Him. And every promise is an invitation to conquer your fears and feed your faith as you experience His faithfulness firsthand. It is the power to act on your faith that conquers fear. It's not talking about it or theorizing about it or even planning to do it someday, but it is doing in this moment what doesn't make sense, confident that God will come through in the end.

God is not only wise, but He loves you with a perfect love. He alone has your best interests at heart, but when you turn a deaf ear to His call or a defiant attitude toward His commands, you remain twice the prisoner of fear and ignorance. For example, when God says to forgive and you opt for unforgiveness, you feed fear and starve faith. When God says that you are to bless those who curse you, does that sound like the kind of thing you want to do with the sting of their slander still a fresh memory? No, because I am good at getting even (or so I think). God says don't be resentful because it always hurts you more than them. When you do what God tells you to do, even when it seems absurd, you free God to bless you. On the other hand, if you disobey and go your own way, you tie His hands because He cannot bless unloving, unforgiving, or disobedient people.

The third trait of firsthand faith is clarity. This is faith's ability to see what matters over time, when the circumstances tempt you to take a shortcut. Too many good men and women sacrifice their futures for the promise of a shortcut to the good life. One of the best examples of clarity in the faith hall of fame was a son of Adam and Eve—Abel. The Bible tells of his faith this way: "It was by faith that Abel obeyed God and brought an offering that pleased God more than Cain's offering. God accepted Abel and proved it by accepting his gift; and though Abel is long dead, we can still learn lessons from him about trusting God" (Heb. 11:4 TLB). The Cain and Abel story has been told and retold in thousands of novels, plays, and movies. Why is the story so engaging? Maybe it's because it's so enduring.

Abel's actions are significant because his offering was a reflection of his attitude. It was true then and it is true now that God is far more interested in the condition of our hearts than the content of our offerings. Abel built no boats, discovered no lands, and fathered no new nations, but we still remember him to this day for the faith in his heart. Abel pleased God, because he had a sense of clarity about what matters to God. Cain is remembered as an example of what happens when you live a shortsighted, faith-starved life. Remember, where faith grows weak, fear grows strong.

Firsthand faith not only gives you clarity about what to do, but the courage to do it. Moses, the great liberator of Israel, is a perfect picture of this. He led an entire nation out of four hundred years of slavery across the wilderness, through the Red Sea, out on to the Sinai Peninsula, and they traveled around in circles for forty years, waiting for God to get the people ready to go into the Promised Land. Forty years is a long time to wait in a desert.

> It was by faith that Moses, when he grew up, refused to be treated as the grandson of the king, but chose to share ill-treatment with God's people instead of enjoying the fleeting pleasures of sin. He thought that it was better to suffer for the promised Christ than to own all the treasures of Egypt, for he was looking forward to the great reward that God would give him. And it was because he trusted God that he left the land of Egypt and wasn't afraid of the king's anger. Moses kept right on going; it seemed as

though he could see God right there with him (Heb. 11:24–27 TLB).

Moses trusted God when everything around him was going well. He had been adopted by Pharaoh and raised as his own in the lap of luxury. He was sent to the best schools and was used to getting what he wanted when he wanted it. His clothing displayed the chevrons of power; his presence commanded respect. He had it made in the shade with nothing but smooth sailing ahead. He had one problem; he was Hebrew. Not even the prestige or privilege of Pharaoh could quiet the inner stirring and compassion he felt for his people.

Add to that the fact that the faith of his fathers was in direct conflict with the faith of his foster father, and you have brewing in the heart of a great man all the makings of greatness. Moses knew he had to show his true identity. Would it be with the ones who had shown him kindness, or would it be with the slaves with whom he shared kinship? Moses conquered whatever fear he might have had of Pharaoh's anger with the courage of his conviction that it was better to suffer for the promised Christ than to compromise for comfort. He had the ability to take the long, long look to an ultimate inheritance that was more compelling than the temporal inheritance for which he had been groomed.

Don't forget that all of these people—Abel, Noah, Abraham, and Moses—developed their firsthand faith from a position where they had much less evidence to go on than we do today. The Bible is divided into two major parts, the Old Testament and the New Testament. The word *testament* is an archaic way of saying "covenant." All of the men and women listed in Hebrews 11 lived under the old covenant, which means they didn't have a leather-bound Bible to tote around. They didn't have the indwelling of God through the Holy Spirit. In Old Testament times, the Holy Spirit came and rested on people for a time and a task and then left. They didn't have the historical events of the Crucifixion and the Resurrection. They accomplished all of these amazing feats by firsthand faith.

We live on this side of the covenant. The old covenant was written on stone tablets; the new covenant is written on our hearts. The old is a covenant of guilt; the new is a covenant of grace. The old is a covenant of law; the new is a covenant of liberation. The old covenant looked forward to the coming of the Messiah; the new covenant looks back to the crucified, resurrected, and soon-coming King—the Lord Jesus Christ.

On this side of the Cross, we have it better. If those people could trust God with as little light as they had, how much more should we be able to trust God with all of the light we have? We possess not only all of their history, but all of the history of the church of Jesus Christ, all the witness of the martyrs of the faith. Scripture tells us, "we are surrounded by so great a cloud of witnesses" (Heb. 12:1–2 NRSV) who bear true faith with us. That faith conquers fear, moves mountains, and sets the captives free.

In his book *The Ragamuffin Gospel*, Brennan Manning tells about an incident that took place one day when a two-story house caught on fire. The family was making its way out of the house when the smallest boy became terrified, tore away from his mother, and ran back upstairs. Crying hysterically, he appeared at a smoke-filled window. Standing outside, his father shouted, "Jump, son, jump! I will catch you." The boy cried, "But, Daddy, I can't see you." "I know," his father called. "But I can see you."[1] That's all that really matters in threatening situations, isn't it? Knowing our heavenly Father sees us, knows what we're going through, and can and will rescue us in His time.

How do you become an Olympic or professional athlete? Hours and hours of discipline and training. Ask an Olympic athlete, "Do you always feel like working out six or eight hours a day?" Of course not. Ask a master musician, "Do you always feel like practicing several hours a day to excel at your instrument?" Of course not. How does a supersalesman become a supersalesman? He or she continues to make the calls after others have gone home because they don't feel like making any more calls. That's how he or she becomes so successful. A godly man or woman who displays excellence in every area of life didn't get to that level by accident. Each chose to do the right things and to develop habits that strengthen the inner life, whether he or she felt like it or not. Mark Twain said it this way: "Twenty years from now you'll be more disappointed by the things you didn't do than by the things you did. So throw off fear and loneliness. Sail away from safe harbor. Catch the trade winds in your sails. Explore, dream and discover." The trick is not to rid your stomach of butterflies, but to make them fly in formation.

Firsthand faith gives me the ability to trust God when I can't control the outcome. Have you ever heard the story of the falling down of the walls of Jericho? "By faith the walls of Jericho fell, after the people had marched around them for seven days" (Heb. 11:30 NIV). Joshua said, "We're going to conquer the most forti- fied city in the world. We have no Bradley fighting vehicles, no smart bombs, not even a sword. We're going to march around the walls, unarmed, once a day for six days. On the seventh day, we're going to march around it six times, then on the seventh time around, we're going to turn around and shout. What do y'all think?" Joshua added, "Oh, by the way, I don't want to hear any of you talking to each other. Don't say one word to each other the whole time."

It takes only one sad dog spreading gloom to ruin an entire group of excited, positive, happy people. Can't you just hear those people, if they had been allowed to talk, walking around those walls? "I can't believe we're just walking around the wall. Boy, are we going to look stupid! We've got to walk around this thing six more days!" Then Negative Nellie said, "That ain't the half of it. The last day we've got to walk around this thing seven times." And Complaining Clarice groaned, "That ain't nothing. After we walk around seven times, we've got to shout."

I mean, come on. Let's be honest. The whole thing sounds silly, doesn't it? Do you think for one second the shout knocked it down? No! Their obedience to God's command, motivated by confidence in His power, did the trick and won the day. And even today, historians who excavated Jericho have found that the walls did not fall in, as they usually do when a city has been invaded from the outside in. The walls fell out like a mighty wind had blown them over from inside the city outward.

Faith does not just believe that God can do something; it's the conviction that God *is* doing something right now. He's working behind the scenes, and the answer is already on its way. Firsthand faith believes God is moving the pieces into place for a miracle even as we speak. It is the conviction, though God may be silent. He is never still, never early, never late, never in a hurry, and never taken by surprise.

Notice the extension of firsthand faith into the next life: "These were all commended for their faith, yet none of them received what had been promised. God had planned something better for us so that only together with us would they be made perfect" (Heb. 11:39–40 NIV).

Hope is faith's promise of something good just ahead, even though you can't see it yet. When my girls were young and we set out on a road trip of any length, I knew it wouldn't be long before I would hear a faint little voice from the backseat ask, "Daddy, are we there yet?" I would say, "No, we're not there yet. We just left the house a few minutes ago." Then another would ask, "How long will it be?" I'd say, "It's a hundred miles to Grandma's house, and we've just gone five, so we've got ninety-five miles to go." Then another angelic voice would ask, "Is ninety-five miles a long time away?" I'd say, "Well, it's about an hour and a half away, provided we don't have to stop for a bathroom break." Then one would ask, "Is an hour and a half a long time?" I'd say, "Not too long." There would be silence for a while. But after they became bored playing with a doll or working a puzzle, another voice would ask, "Are we there yet?" And then we'd go over the whole previous conversation again. It dawned on me that they had no perception of distance or time. How could they? They were kids. I'd be frustrated with their inability to grasp these very grown-up concepts of time and distance. I was frustrated because I couldn't help them understand that they didn't have to worry about getting there safely and on time. It was my job to provide a good car, take the right roads, obey the speed limits, and deliver them to Grandma's on time. It was their job to sit back and enjoy the trip, have fun, count cows, read billboards, and trust me to get them there.

How could I get my kids to trust me when we took a trip? Then it dawned on me when Lindsey asked, "Daddy, will you take the shortcut?" At first I tried to explain that there are some places you can't take a shortcut to, but that only confused her. Then I finally said, "Yes, we'll take the shortcut everywhere we go from now on." That simple assurance did the trick. Isn't that what firsthand faith is? Trusting God to get us where we ultimately want to go in the shortest time possible. Firsthand faith conquers fear because it knows how to wait. It can wait for what's coming because it allows us to trust our heavenly Father. It is His job to get us home safely. It is our job to trust that the trip He is taking us on is the shortest, best route possible. When we say, "Father, are we there yet?" He says, "Trust Me." One of the hallmarks of maturity is the ability to wait, to push forward, and to realize there is no shortcut to any place worth going.

Martin Luther King Jr. advised, "We must accept finite disappointment, but never lose infinite hope." Firsthand faith is not the way around pain; it is the way through pain. Faith doesn't give you the winning point at the last second, though it may tie the game and send you into overtime. Faith doesn't hand you the solution; it forces you to find it. Faith doesn't teach you at the moment; it teaches in retrospect. Faith doesn't provide a net to fall into when your fingers are about to give way as you hang suspended over the cliff; faith gives your fingers the strength to hang on just a little longer.

I read the story of a young father who had been away on a weeklong business trip. His two young sons couldn't wait for their dad's return. The night before his return, he told them that he would take them both to the local toy store as soon as he got home. He promised to buy them any "one" gift they wanted. The next day came, and the dad arrived. Waiting for him at the front door, the boys ran to the car and begged him to fulfill his promise to them right then and there. True to his word, he piled them into the car and off to the toy store they went.

Arriving at the store, the boys burst through the front door and ran for the first thing they could find, two brand-new water bazookas. They immediately begged their dad for the water guns. The dad said, "We just got here. Let's keep looking." They threw down the water cannons and ran to the middle of the store where they found two brand-new big-league, genuine leather baseball gloves. They said, "Dad, can we have these? It's almost summer-time, and we're playing on the Little League team this year with all the big kids. Can we have these, Dad, please?" Dad looked at the boys and said, "Boys, these are great, but let's look a little longer." This happened two or three more times, and each time the boys swore up and down they had found the perfect toy for the upcoming summer, and each time their dad responded, "Boys, let's look for something better."

The boys started sulking as they shuffled their feet to the back of the store. One whispered to the other, "Daddy broke his prom-ise. He said he would give us anything we wanted, but he just keeps saying, 'Let's look for something better.'" The other brother said, "Yeah, you're right, and since he has been gone for so long, I bet he doesn't even love us. He just says he does and then leaves and makes us wait!"

As the boys were talking of their growing resentment for their father, they looked up and found themselves staring, just a nose length away, at two brand-new cherry red dirt bikes, the kind the professionals use during the extreme games. They turned to see their dad with a huge grin on his face. Their faces lit up, too, as they realized the bikes were what their dad had in mind even before they entered the store. As a matter of fact, he ordered the dirt bikes before he left on his business trip. He called the night before to make sure they had come in, and he asked the store manager to hang the bikes on the back wall for a reason. He wanted to give the boys something special, and he wanted to use the occasion as a teachable moment.

He placed his arm around his sons to draw them into a close

huddle. The young dad looked into their eyes and said, "Boys, I love you both more than I can say or you can understand. I want only the best for you. I knew when we came in here today there would be a lot of bright, flashy toys that would catch your attention. I knew you would think you wanted some of them so badly you couldn't imagine anything better. And I could see your disappointment each time I said no. I know you guys began to think I was playing a trick on you. But I want you to remember what you've learned today. All of life's best things are at the back of the store. There will be lots of distractions, and you will be tempted to settle for second best. Remember your daddy loves you and he knows what's best for you. When you have to wait, you can trust the trip to the back of the store will be worth it." With that, he took the bikes off the wall, and the boys never forgot the gift and the lesson of the day.

To excel where you are is to trust God knows where you are and what you need. Because you are His child, He has taken on the responsibilities of a father. He can get you to the back of the store where all of His best gifts are, and more important, He will get you there safely. Your job is to trust Him. Even when you're faced with the fear of looking dumb or appearing foolish, He says, "Trust Me." It is all He needs and everything He demands.

6

I Will Live Courageously

◦

Without courage, all other virtues lose their meaning.
—Winston Churchill

You are a living example of God's commitment to excellence. In His superlative and exquisite design, He gave you a multibillion-dollar body governed by several hundred systems of control, each interacting with and affecting the other. For example, your brain has 10 billion nerve cells recording and cataloging all you hear, see, smell, taste, and touch. Your skin has more than 2 million tiny sweat glands—about 3,000 per square inch—all a part of the intricate system that keeps your body at an even 98.6 degrees in winter or summer. You have a living pump in your chest about the size of your fist, through which your blood is pumped while traveling approximately 168 million miles a day or the equivalent of 6,720 times around the earth! The lining of your stomach contains more than 35 million glands, which aid the process of digesting that Mexican food you insist on eating. In one 24-hour period you breathe in more than 23,040 times as you fill your lungs with 438 cubic feet of air.

On an average day you will consume 3.5 pounds of food, drink 2.9 quarts of liquid, and lose 0.88 pound of waste. In one day's activity you will speak more than 4,800 words, move 750 muscles, and exercise 7 million brain cells. Your body has the power to repair and rejuvenate itself as it fights off disease and in-fection. And these are but a few wonders operating every day, every hour, and every second of your life. I read in *USA Today* re-cently that the average life span in America is 77.4 years, the longest in history. Although all of this is amazing, you are still only one heartbeat or one wrong turn away from ending this most precious thing you take for granted—your life.

What if today you discovered you had only a few more months to live; how would you live those last days? Would you make the same choices you've been making? Would you con-tinue to avoid or delay some of the things you know you should do? How would you live differently? Would you lie down and give up, or would you refuse to go silently, investing the rest of your days making waves? Not just noise, trouble, or screams, but waves that move things, stir things up, and make a difference.

The 1995 Academy Award–winning movie *Braveheart* tells the story of a common man named William Wallace (played by accomplished actor Mel Gibson), who leads Scotland to freedom from English rule. At the end of the movie, Wallace is betrayed to the English, and he sits in prison awaiting execution. The Princess of Wales asks him to recant his rebellion to save his life. Submitting to the English king would spare him torture and death. Wallace sees clearly what is at stake, and he stands his ground without wavering. The princess says, "I come to beg you to confess all and swear allegiance to the king so that he may show you mercy."

Wallace says, "If I swear to him, all that I am is dead already." Weeping, the princess says, "You will die. It will be awful." "Every man dies. Not every man really lives," Wallace replies. Anything that keeps you from living courageously in this moment is rob-bing you of your birthright and legacy.

The terrible tragedy of life is not that it ends, but for far too many timid souls, it never really starts. How about you? Are you stuck at the starting gate waiting for life to even out before you begin?

The Unevenness of Life

While riding my motorcycle down an interstate highway at seventy miles an hour, I came upon a long stretch of road that was being resurfaced. As a result, the lanes were uneven by more than an inch and a half. My exit was coming up and I needed to change lanes, but I wasn't sure how. I scanned my mind to recall whether this specific road condition had been covered in my weeklong training course that my wife had made me take before allowing me to own a motorcycle. If the teacher covered it, I couldn't remember it in the middle of merging traffic. I surmised that if I tried to edge up to the higher level, my bike would become unstable. To go from one lane to the other meant I had to attack the unevenness of the road. I tried it and it worked. I've learned the same thing is true in life as in motorcycles. Sometimes you throw timidity to the wind and attack the unevenness of life.

The vicissitudes of life have a way of making cowards of us all. If they rattle you enough, they will persuade you to take your eyes off the peaks and settle for a dull existence in the flatlands. If fear is allowed to blind the heart to courage, cowardice will attack resolve and repress your spirit. Solomon, the wise man, noted, "All his days he eats in darkness, with great frustration, affliction and anger" (Eccles. 5:17 NIV). It is still true in our day. When I look into the eyes of the people I meet, I see fear and frustration in most.

It can be downright tough being courageous with the avalanche of daily bad news we have to dig our way out from under. If it's not the TV, it's the radio or the billboard on the way home that shocks our sensibilities to the day's latest scandal or outlandish stunt. There's even a Web site aptly called despair.com. On this Web site you are invited to join the "chain of pain." This will bring to your inbox a daily dose of discouraging news and demotivating sayings. I don't know about you, but I don't need that much help.

These obstacles are not new, but we face them in a new way that no other generation before us has experienced. We are the first generation to experience the "death of distance." Because of CNN, the Internet, and the freedom and affordability of travel, our planet is shrinking. We now know instantly all the bad news everywhere on earth. I remember watching the Vietnam War every night on the evening news when I was a kid. I felt as though it were being fought right there in my living room on my parents' black-and-white Zenith.

In his book *Bias*, Bernard Goldberg recounts a pivotal moment in television news. In the early 1970s, CBS president Dick Salant told staffers, "I have some good news and some bad news. The good news is, for the first time in history, CBS News made money last quarter. The bad news is, for the first time in history, CBS News made money last quarter." Goldberg writes, "Salant knew, everyone knew. If news could actually make money, the suits who ran the networks would expect just that. Sure, they would want quality in theory. But they wanted ratings and money in fact." In the words of Don Hewitt, creator of *60 Minutes*, "Before they would say, 'Make us proud.' Now they tell us, 'Make us money.'"[1] Maybe this is why the TV schedule is packed from one end of the listings to the other with bad news. Bad news sells.

All of a sudden I am not only aware of my fears and frustrations, but I am also saturated in the futility of life throughout the world. Who can stand with any degree of courage and hope when he is dipped in the despair and misery of the entire world during the nightly news? On the Google News Web site, they tell you the date of the story and how many minutes ago the event actually happened. Do we really need that much information?

The only benefit from this oversaturation of sad news is, we won't soon forget there are three forces at work in the world—evil, good, and futility. Evil is easiest to identify and sell. Good is also alive and well, but stories of husbands who love their wives, CEOs who lead their companies with integrity, and children who respect their parents are not sensational enough to sell. There is a third force afoot called futility. Like good and evil, futility is nothing new. Solomon described it so well: "What does a man get for all the toil and anxious striving with which he labors under the sun? All his days his work is pain and grief; even at night his mind does not rest. This too is meaningless" (Eccles. 2:22–23 NIV).

Futility has a divine purpose. God uses it as a tool to draw you to Him of your own free will. Although that may sound odd, I can assure you it is an act of courageous love on His part. God will not force you to love and honor Him, but He will make it impossible to be happy until you do!

God's antidote to fear and futility is confident courage, but such courage is not easily won. The overpowering presence of fear seeks to dominate our lives. We long for the promise of Scripture, "He will make your righteousness shine like the dawn, the justice of your cause like the noonday sun" (Ps. 37:6 NIV), to be the experience of everyone. Alas, it isn't, and in light of this, we face another choice. Will our lives be ruled by fear or fueled by faith? Will you be steadfast, unmovable, and courageously resolute, especially in the face of danger or difficulty, or will you fall back into your comfort zone?

What Kind of Life?

Today we need bolder men and women who see things not as nightly news anchor Walter Cronkite used to say, "And that's the way it is," but the way things "could be." We are in urgent need of people with renewed minds and resolute hearts, who dare to live out their faith in the everyday world with class and compassion. Oh, that God would give us men and women of honor who possess the courage of their convictions and who will not be swayed by popular opinion and the latest poll. We need a courageous vision to see past our own noses and think beyond our next need. We long for men and women who are humble at heart, strong of will, and courageous as a lion on the hunt.

The world waits in anticipation for the person who can hold to his or her principles without being a tyrant and who is tough enough to bend without breaking. We scan the horizon for the person who chooses a life of courage over convenience and who has the strength to live out of love rather than lust, out of the desire to serve and bless rather than the need to get and control. Yet in spite of this need, too many have decided to take the road of least resistance, which leads to a life of complaints, cosmetics, and compromise.

Courage is a cure for the self-absorbed life. If you think, *It's all about me,* you need a bigger perspective. Don't allow yourself to become so fixated on today's distraction, you lose focus on what's going on around you. "To live in the moment" is good as long as it doesn't morph into "live only for the moment." Keeping perspective means living in the moment, in the light of eternity. What you do today counts for eternity.

Psychoanalyst Carl Jung said, "The vast neurotic misery of the world could be termed a neuroses of emptiness." When human beings cut themselves off from the root of their reality (their Creator), life turns empty, inane, and meaningless. When God goes, goals go. When goals go, meaning goes. When meaning goes, love goes, and our hearts can only turn to stone. The Bible warns, "See to it, brothers, that none of you has a sinful, unbelieving heart that turns away from the living God" (Heb. 3:12 NIV). If a man is centered on himself, the smallest risk is too great because both success and failure can destroy him. If he is centered on God, no risk is too great because success is already guaranteed—the successful union of Creator and creature, beside which everything else is meaningless.

A freelance reporter from the *New York Times* once interviewed Marilyn Monroe. She was aware of Marilyn's past and the fact that during her early years Marilyn had been shuffled from one foster home to another. The reporter asked, "Did you ever feel loved by any of the foster families with whom you lived?" "Once," Marilyn replied, "when I was about seven or eight. The woman I was living with was putting on makeup, and I was watching her. She was in a happy mood, so she reached over and patted my cheeks with her rouge puff. For that moment, I felt loved by her." Was it the rouge that made Marilyn feel loved, or was it the pat of a loving hand on her small cheek? Cosmetic cover-ups may fool those who look from a distance, but there is no cosmetic that can make up for a heart that feels abandoned, no prosthetic that can replace an amputated spirit.

Psychologist Ruth Brenda performed an interesting experiment with teenagers. To show how people handle group pressure, she tested teenagers in groups of ten. Members of each group were instructed to raise a hand when the teacher pointed to the longest line on three separate charts. What one person didn't know was that nine of the others in the room had been instructed ahead of time to vote for the second longest line. The lines were not even close. But the desire of the psychologist was to determine how one person reacted when completely surrounded by a large number of people who obviously stood against what was true.

The experiment began with nine teenagers voting for the wrong line. The stooge typically glanced around, frowned in confusion, and slipped his hand up with the group. The instruction was repeated, and the next card was raised. Time after time, the self-conscious and unwitting participant would say a short line was longer than a long line simply because he lacked the courage to challenge the group. This remarkable conformity occurred about 75 percent of the time, and was true of small children and high school students.

When you lack a strong, inner sense of conviction, which rises from your core faith in God, just about anything can turn your head and steal your heart away. Whether it's the lust for money or your need to be accepted by a certain group, you need an inner compass to guide you and give you courage. Cowardice asks, Is it safe? Consensus asks, Is it popular? Courage asks, Is it right?

Benjamin Franklin affirmed, "A man without courage is a knife without an edge." If you doubt whether Jesus Christ is still edgy today, just mention His name in mixed company. Some revile Him; others revere Him. Those who revere Him have many reasons, not the least of which was His courage. He had the courage to stay on mission when the time for talk was over. His mind was always fixed on the mission for which He was born. He moved forward without wavering to the place and time that His life would be offered in one climactic act of courage where He would die as the innocent for the guilty.

In part, that's why we still esteem Him to this day. He was a man of courage who did the right thing at the right time for the right reason. Thucydides, an ancient Greek historian, said, "The bravest are surely those who have the dearest vision of what is before them, glory and danger alike, and yet notwithstanding go out to meet it." This is the legacy of Jesus who, we are told, "when it came close to the time for his Ascension . . . gathered up his courage and steeled himself for the journey to Jerusalem" (Luke 9:51 THE MESSAGE). What a statement of the kind of man He was and the kind of life He lived!

The Intelligence of Courage

Courage endows you with unique intelligence. It's hard to dissect and quantify, but as best I can tell, it is the fusion of wisdom with will. Legendary actor John Wayne declared, "Courage is being scared to death but saddling up anyway." Courage is the wisdom to do the right thing for the right reason, and the will to do it in the right way at the right time. It is saying the right word in season as well as withholding it in the wrong season. Jesus said, "You are the salt of the earth" (Matt. 5:13 NIV). Like salt, courage adds flavor and seasoning to an otherwise bland and tasteless life. Courage knows what to do and does it.

Courage is the willingness to step up and be counted, but it is equally the strength to shut up and be silent when everything in you wants to scream out. Abraham Lincoln stated, "To sin by silence when they should protest makes cowards out of men." To say what needs saying when it needs saying—and in the way it should be said—is the genius of courage. Submit to pressure from peers, and you move down to their level. If you move with the crowd, you'll get no farther than the crowd. Even if the majority

believes in a dumb idea, it's still a dumb idea. Swimming with the
tide of popular opinion can leave you stranded on the beach of
bad judgment where you'll flounder. So if you believe in something honorable, honest, and helpful, stand up for it. Maybe your
peers will get smart and drift your way.

Courage knows when to stand up against injustice and the
wrong treatment of others. It knows when to stay up with a
friend in crisis. It knows when to show up and defend the right
or oppose the wrong. The courage to discover who you really are
and what you really believe is strength and freedom.

Courage is the intelligence to know when to suit up and get
out on the playing field as well as when to nurse injuries suffered
on the playing field. Courage speaks when fear and self-doubt
whisper, "Don't say anything. You might be misunderstood and
make someone mad." It also knows when to shut up when hurt
and humiliation compel you to use words that cut and cripple.

Courage knows that sometimes staying put is the best option,
even though your emotions say, "Run away and hide." At other
times courage says to get up and get out when the fear of abandonment keeps you in bondage to a bad marriage, a toxic relationship, or a dead-end job.

Courage is the wisdom and will to take the right risk. It is the
resolve required to face forward, take the first step, and stay on
course until the war is won, the sea is crossed, or the job is finished. It is the guts to get up and get in the fight when your name
is called. And trust me, if you dare to do more than exist, it will
be called.

What to Do When It's You

An enduring example of courage in the Scriptures is the story of
Joshua. He was one of only three people who lived through the
forty years of wilderness wandering. All that time he was being
groomed for greatness. He was the one slated to stand in the big
shoes that Moses left behind when he died. God told Moses,

"Your assistant, Joshua son of Nun, will enter it. Encourage him, because he will lead Israel to inherit it" (Deut. 1:38 NIV). Moses left plenty for Joshua to do. The wilderness wandering and the days of waiting were behind them, and the promised land was ready to be taken. But it wouldn't be easy and would require a new level of courage.

Joshua was one of the best-prepared leaders in history. He had spent his life preparing to assume the heavy mantle of leadership. He had lived for more than forty years in the shadow of a giant—Moses. Upon Moses' death, Joshua heard the words he'd dreaded, but knew he would hear someday, "Moses my servant is dead. Now then, you . . ." (Josh. 1:2 NIV). I can't read the words "Now then, you" without feeling the glaring heat of the spotlight. And yet those three simple words were the call to action he'd been training for and knew one day would come. It was Joshua's time to line up in front of the people and lead the way ahead. What angst and emotion those words surely evoked in Joshua, but the time had come to step out of the shadow of Moses and into the limelight of leadership.

I remember hearing that call from my high school football coach just before my first big high school game. He said, "Men, the time for practice is over, and the moment we have been training for is at hand. Here is the lineup for tonight's home opener." I listened as the names of the starting lineup were read, and when my name was spoken, I felt a sinking sick feeling in the pit of my stomach and at the same time the exhilaration of the call to action. The time had come to line up and go out on to the field of play, and this time it was for real. The two-a-day practices of summer were over, and the time for serious football was upon us. I don't know if God does football, but I did my share of praying that night and I'm sure Joshua was doing his fair share as he stepped forward to lead.

I have discovered that if you want to be distressed—look within; if you want to be defeated—look back; if you want to be distracted—look around; and if you want to be dismayed—look ahead. But if you want the courage to drive ahead—look up. At the same time Joshua was called to line up and take the lead, he was told to look up and take heart. God promised, "I will give you every place where you set your foot. . . . No one will be able to stand up against you all the days of your life. As I was with Moses, so I will be with you; I will never leave you nor forsake you" (Josh. 1:3–5 NIV).

With the words "Now then, you" ringing in his head, I'm sure the promise, "I will be with you," was like music to his heart. The leaders may change, but the Lord remains the same, which places the emphasis where it should be—on God. Sometimes I'm tempted to think, *It's all about me,* but it's not. God reminded Joshua that his predecessor (Moses) didn't produce water from the rock, manna in the morning, or quail for those on a high-protein diet. Moses was a willing vessel to be filled with God's favor. Now it was Joshua's turn to trust that the same God who parted the sea for Moses would stop the flow of the Jordan for him.

Anytime there is a change in leadership, there is speculation. What will the new leader be like? Will he be as forceful as Moses, or will he try to kowtow to certain people jockeying for position in the new administration? That's why God told Joshua, "Be strong and very courageous. Be careful to obey all the law my servant Moses gave you; do not turn from it to the right or to the left, that you may be successful wherever you go. Do not let this Book of the Law depart from your mouth; meditate on it day and night, so that you may be careful to do everything written in it. Then you will be prosperous and successful" (Josh. 1:7–8 NIV). God was telling Joshua to listen to Him, not the people around him. It takes courage to say no to the "experts" and yes to God. You will ruffle the feathers and break the traditions if you have the courage to let God lead you. God told Joshua to think, ponder, meditate, and act on the words of God, not the ever-changing opinions of men.

God encouraged Joshua to "be strong and courageous. Do not be terrified; do not be discouraged, for the Lord your God will be with you wherever you go." God gave Joshua the courage to lighten up. He was probably feeling fairly overwhelmed by that time. He was discovering that there is a big difference between the weight of leadership and the wait for leadership. The load that Joshua had to carry was enough without adding to it the unnecessary burden of trying to figure out how he was going to get the Jews into the Promised Land. God promised to be with him every step of the way.

The same is true for you. If you commit to a life of excellence, you'll be tempted plenty of times to lose courage and compromise. That usually happens when we take on more than we need to carry. Maybe God is saying to you right now, "Don't be discouraged. I will be with you wherever you go." Take courage when you hear God say, "Look up; listen up; lighten up."

After Joshua was assured of God's protection and provision, God told him to call the people to load up for the battle ahead. Joshua sent his officers through the camp to tell the purpose for battle. Even the half tribes of Manasseh were instructed, "Your wives, your children and your livestock may stay in the land that Moses gave you east of the Jordan, but all your fighting men, fully armed, must cross over ahead of your brothers. You are to help your brothers until the LORD gives them rest" (Josh. 1:14–15 NIV).

Buzz Aldrin, the second man to walk on the moon, said, "Bravery comes along as a gradual accumulation of discipline." All the years of training and all the long hours of drilling were going to pay off. Together, they were going to achieve in real time what God had promised to Abraham long ago. Joshua couldn't do it alone; the tribes of Gad and Manasseh couldn't do it alone. But together, behind the power of God's promise, victory was sure. They needed only to guard their courage because courage leaks and vision tends to drift.

There is an old Arab proverb that says, "An army of sheep led by a lion will defeat an army of lions led by a sheep." Joshua was the new lion on the block leading the same old sheep, and Israel was, once again, at a defining moment. The people had a new leader with whom to face an old enemy. Joshua needed to demonstrate strength and courage because he had watched Moses in action enough to know that the leader makes the difference when the battle is about to begin.

The movie *Braveheart* tells the story of how William Wallace led Scotland to freedom from English rule. After winning several battles, Wallace was asked to confer with the Scottish nobles, but the meeting fell apart as the nobles argued over which of them had the right to be Scotland's new king. Disgusted by their self-ishness, Wallace stomped out of the meeting hall to fight the English without them. Robert the Bruce, one of the few nobles who hoped for a free Scotland, followed after Wallace. Robert argued that Scotland "has no sense of itself," which meant they needed the nobles to win.

Wallace turned on him and reframed the situation: "You think the people of this country exist to provide you with position. I think your position exists to provide those people with freedom. Noble—what does it mean to be noble? Your title gives you right to the throne of our country. But men don't follow titles. They follow courage." In Israel's case, their trusted leader was dead. The responsibility fell to Joshua. The question was, Would people follow him? Would Joshua be a man of courage and thereby be lifted up to the place of leadership? It wasn't a matter of nostalgia; it was a matter of character. And when character and courage are called for, the strength of a man's faith and the condition of his heart carry the day.

Take Heart

Robert Louis Stevenson wrote, "Every heart that has beat strongly and cheerfully has left a hopeful impulse behind it in the world, and bettered the tradition of mankind." The call to courage is answered first by the heart. While fear lurks in the background ready to steal our confidence, it's the heart that knows it's not alone, that knows the boldness of courage.

The God who has placed you where you are in this moment and calls for the best you have has not left you powerless.

You have everything you need to respond to each of life's obstacles with courage and bold resolution. I take heart each time I hear the call "Now then, you," when I remember God has promised me access to His throne, the assurance of His promises, and the audacity to act in faith knowing the battle I face is not mine, but His.

I take heart when I consider my access to God. I heard about some newlyweds who in the wee hours of their wedding night were escorted to the bridal suite of their high-priced hotel. Once in the suite, they saw a sofa, chairs, and table, but they couldn't find the bed. They spent the first night of their honeymoon on the sofa, which was turned into a hide-a-bed with a lumpy mattress and sagging springs. After a fitful night with sore backs, the next morning, they went to the hotel desk to give the management a tongue-lashing. "Did you open the door in the room?" asked the clerk. "What door?" they replied. Accompanied by the manager, they went back to the room. He opened the door they had thought was a closet. There, complete with fruit baskets and chocolates, was a beautiful bedroom! They had wasted the first night of their honeymoon because they didn't open the door.

Are you right now living a cramped-up life only because you think your current situation is all there is? Open the door and discover there is a big, beautiful world out there. You have access to the very throne room of the One who owns it and runs it. There is nothing stopping you from approaching His throne to ask for a courageous heart and a brave hand. If Jesus is your Lord and God's will is your passion, then you have the right to go into the Holy of Holies.

As Christ hung on the cross, He cried out, "My God, My God. Why have You forsaken Me?" When I was a kid, that bothered me. I was thinking, *If You don't know, I don't know, and we are in deep trouble.* But as I studied the meaning of His question, I came to believe that Christ wasn't asking, "My God, how did I end up on this cross?" He was saying, "Show them why." He wasn't asking, "My God, My God. Why have You forsaken

Me?" He was saying, "Show them *why* You have forsaken Me." In response to that request the veil around the Holy of Holies was torn in two from top to bottom. From that day forward no barrier would exist between God and His worshipers. Christ took it away, so you and I now have direct access to the holy place.

The high priest went there once a year on the Day of Atonement. If he went into the Holy of Holies on the Day of Atonement without having gone through all of the purification rituals perfectly, he would die. If he died there, he would be pulled out using a rope around his ankle. You didn't mess around with holy things in the Old Testament, and you still don't. But in Christ, we now have direct access. Why should we ever lose courage since we have direct access to God through our Savior without having to go through the priest?

Here's another definition of the same thing illustrated in the book of Hebrews:

> Seeing then that we have a great high priest, that is passed into the heavens, Jesus the Son of God, let us hold fast our profession. For we have not an high priest which cannot be touched with the feeling of our infirmities; but was in all points tempted like as we are, yet without sin. Let us therefore come boldly unto the throne of grace, that we may obtain mercy, and find grace to help in time of need. (4:14–16 KJV)

We live courageously because we have assurance, "and since we have a great priest over the house of God, let us draw near to God with a sincere heart in full assurance of faith. . . . Let us hold unswervingly to the hope we profess, for he who promised is faithful" (Heb. 10:21–23 NIV). The one thing of which I am absolutely, positively sure after a lifetime of walking with God is that He is faithful. He is relentlessly, graciously, faithful.

Someone sent me this version of the "Twenty-third Psalm for the Workplace":

The Lord is my real boss, I shall not want.
He gives me peace when chaos is all around me.
He reminds me to pray before I speak.
And to do all things without murmuring and complaining.
He reminds me that He is my source and not my job.
He restores my sanity every day and guides my decisions.
That I might honor Him in everything I do,
Even though I face absurd amounts of e-mails,
System crashes, unrealistic deadlines, budget cuts,
Gossipy co-workers, discriminating advisors and
An aging body that doesn't cooperate every morning.
I will not stop for He is with me.
His presence is peace and His power will see me through.
I will stop for He is with me.
His joy is mine and it is new every morning.
He raises me up even when they fail to promote me at work,
He claims me as His own even when the company
    threatens to let me go.
His faithfulness and love are better than my bonus check.
His retirement plan beats every 401K there is.
When all is said and done,
I'll be working for Him a whole lot longer than the
    people I'm working for now.
So bless His name.

In George Lucas's film *The Empire Strikes Back*, nine-hundred-year-old Master Jedi Knight Yoda is attempting to train Jedi-hopeful Luke Skywalker to use the Force. On the isolated planet Degobah, Yoda challenges him to balance himself upside down on one hand with Yoda perched on his feet. Luke then raises a basketball-sized rock in the air using the Force. Yoda tells him, "Use the Force . . . feel it." Suddenly, Luke is distracted by the sound of his starship sinking to the muddy lake's bottom. He falls forward, and Yoda tumbles down. Seeing only the tip of his ship's wing sticking out from the swamp, Luke says in despair, "We'll never get it out now!" Yoda sighs and answers, "So certain are you? Always with you it cannot be done. Do you nothing that I say?"

"Master, moving stones around is one thing. This is totally different." Yoda insists, "No! No different! Only different in your mind. You have to unlearn what you have learned." Luke nods and says, "All right, I'll give it a try." Yoda, somewhat exasperated, says, "No. Try not. Do. Or do not. There is no try." Luke tries to mentally raise the ship out of the water using the Force, but fails miserably. Exhausted by the effort, he sits down beside Yoda and tells him, "I can't. It's too big." Yoda concentrates and mentally raises the ship out of the water and onto the shore. Luke walks around the ship in amazement and tells Yoda, "I don't . . . I don't believe it!" Yoda responds, "That is why you fail."

Yoda did for Luke what we are to do for one another. The writer of Hebrews said, "Let us consider how we may spur one another on toward love and good deeds" (10:24 NIV). Our job is to master the art of advocacy. For grace and goodness and God, we encourage and lift each other up. It's a great way to live! Why should we have any fear? We have the greatest truth in the entire world. It has prevailed, without interruption, for thousands and thousands and thousands of years. We are advocates for the people we work with. Paul said it this way: "We are . . . Christ's ambassadors" (2 Cor. 5:20 NIV).

As courageous advocates of grace, we turn on the light in a dark place. We build bridges and tear down barriers. God, in this chaotic world, uses us and makes us fearless because we're supposed to be steadfast, unmovable, always abounding in the work of the Lord. He is constantly at work in this world, and while at times we may feel helpless, we are never, never, never, in Christ, hopeless. We have God's promises, His power, His providence, and His presence.

Commitment #3

EXCELLING WITH WHAT I HAVE

*When we do the best we can, we
never know what miracle
is wrought in our life, or
in the life of another.*
—HELEN KELLER

7

I Will Serve a Noble Cause

*When great causes are on the move in the world,
we learn that we are spirits, not animals.*
—WINSTON CHURCHILL

Two warring tribes in the Andes Mountains had a long history of harassing each other. One tribe lived in the mountains while the other tribe occupied and cultivated the valley below. One night the mountain people, under the cover of darkness, swept into the camp of the valley people, stealing food and terrorizing them. Imagine the outrage they felt when it was discovered a baby was stolen from his mother's arms.

For several days the valley people gathered a raiding party of their strongest and fiercest warriors for a rescue mission. As they attempted to climb the mountain, they found the going much harder than they had imagined. They were valley people, after all, and had no experience climbing treacherous mountain passes. After three and a half days of frustrated efforts, they had moved only a couple of hundred yards up the mountainside. Maneuvering the cliffs and gaps in the trail was a daunting task.

Utterly discouraged and despondent, confident the baby was by then dead, they voted to abandon their mission and return to the valley. They were gathering their gear for their descent when they saw a small figure moving down the mountain toward them. As the person got closer, they were stunned to see one of their own women cradling the rescued infant in her arms. How had she done alone what all of them together had not come close to doing? One of the leaders asked, "How on earth were you able to climb that mountain so quickly and retrieve the child, a feat all of us combined were unable to do?" The young woman looked at them and simply said, "It wasn't your baby."

This story illustrates the power of a mission fueled by love and aimed at freedom. These two ingredients provide the motivation and mission at the heart of a noble cause. Motivated people on a mission can accomplish extraordinary things. If you have a noble cause, your life will never be boring, boxy, or benign. But nothing—not money, not talent, not education, not power—can make up for the lack of a noble cause.

To excel at being who you are is a matter of acceptance, authenticity, and audacity. To excel at being where you are requires facing problems and fears with courage and resolve. It was true then and it is still true today. But to excel with what you have is to find a mission for which you have a substantial passion and motivation. This is the pathway to nobility and the supreme resource in a life committed to excellence

Think back. We start out in life full of energy and excitement. If you doubt that, watch a group of children at play. A group of girls will be giggling and laughing. A group of boys will be running and shouting. They have an innocent, unbridled passion for life. But as they get older, they'll be told to shut up, straighten up, and stand still. We've all been told to behave, be good, and calm down. And that's what we end up doing. In the maturation process, too often we lose the sheer wonder and delight of just being alive. We can't afford the death and demise of our passion because it is the unique spark that sets us apart.

Saint Irenaeus said, "The glory of God is man fully alive." That's the whole thing said in a nutshell, isn't it? That's how we were, if only for a few fleeting moments, and isn't that what we all yearn to recover? If you possess a heart fueled by the passion to be fully loved, fully alive, and fully engaged in a noble cause, that's the power to excel.

Passion is a great equalizer in life. The passion of the young mother who loved her child made up for a lot of other things she didn't have. The Scriptures admonish, "Never be lacking in zeal, but keep your spiritual fervor, serving the Lord" (Rom. 12:11 NIV). Paul advised, "It is fine to be zealous, provided the purpose is good" (Gal. 4:18 NIV). And Henry Ward Beecher maintained that, "in things pertaining to enthusiasm, no man is sane who does not know how to be insane on proper occasions."

You can stop searching for the magic possession that will fill your life with purpose and meaning, for you already have it. It's not your good looks or your youth. It's not your money, position, or power, but your God-given ability to give and receive love. The Scriptures rate this divine ability above all others when they warn, "If I speak in the tongues of men and of angels, but have not love, I am only a resounding gong or a clanging cymbal. If I have the gift of prophecy and can fathom all mysteries and all knowledge, and if I have a faith that can move mountains, but have not love, I am nothing" (1 Cor. 13:1–2 NIV).

Love makes up for a multitude of missing abilities. Its lack causes all kinds of terrible trouble. Love for her child moved that young mother up the side of an "unscalable" mountain and gave her the audacity to get her child back. Love moved God to become a man and suffer humiliation, even death on a cross. Love is what you have the capacity to give and receive, and when it is directed at a mission of seismic proportions, the impossible becomes possible, the undoable becomes doable, and miracles happen.

Deadly Distractions

There is a war going on right now for possession of your heart. It is not a visible onslaught from an enemy who dares show his face. It is a subtle, tactical war fought in the shadows and back thoughts of a mind distracted and a heart divided. You feel it every day in the ways you're pulled downward. It's the daily drain that sucks the joy out of living, much like headlights left on all night kill a car's battery. It's the dizzying, downward effect of being spun round and round on a merry-go-round of mundane and meaningless materialism.

We are caught up in a tipping point in our cultural ethos where we are materialistic, and worse than that, we are becoming emotionally depleted and desensitized. I heard a friend say recently, "We don't sing; we don't dance; we don't even commit sin with very much enthusiasm." If you take the warnings of Scripture seriously, then you know this is the result of a frontal attack from Satan: "Be careful—watch out for attacks from Satan, your great enemy. He prowls around like a hungry, roaring lion, looking for some victim to tear apart" (1 Pet. 5:8 TLB).

Gregg Easterbrook in his widely acclaimed book *The Progress Paradox* documents the enormous improvement in American lives over recent generations. He notes things like the average life expectancy doubling since 1900, the development of central heating and air-conditioning, and the availability of advanced medical care. Easterbrook's conclusion is that if America has ever had a Golden Age, it is "right here, right now." But my question is, Are we any happier? On a recent trip to south Florida, the retirement mecca of America, I saw more angry, frustrated people than I'd ever expect to find among the rich and retired. The truth is, we have added more years to our lives, yet we have not added more life to those years. What good is it to have twice as much of what we are already not using or enjoying?

Johnny Cash, just months before his death, gave a courageous, artful testament to the fleeting, fickle nature of fame in his award-winning song "Hurt." He talked about all he had amassed over a lifetime as his "kingdom of dirt." The worst judgment I can imagine is a man or woman with everything to enjoy except the power to enjoy it. More than a few of us are blinded by greed. Even though Jesus warned, "Take care! Protect yourself against the least bit of greed. Life is not defined by what you have, even when you have a lot" (Luke 12:15 THE MESSAGE), we keep trying to prove that the one with the most toys at the end wins.

Greed is a disease of the heart. Its symptoms are insatiable hunger, unquenchable thirst, and feelings of emptiness and restlessness in spite of apparent wealth. The more we get, the more we want to get. And once we are tired of legal getting, we quickly turn to what the Scriptures call lust. A lot of people have confused lust with love. The big difference between love and lust is that love commits! How many young girls have been seduced by the words, "Oh, honey, I just love you so much; let's live together and see if we're compatible," only to find themselves used and discarded when the "man of their dreams" moves on to greener pastures and a younger, less demanding model?

Added together, greed and lust lead to aggression and arrogance. They feed the brutish, lower angels of our nature. These unholy pursuits destroy an otherwise beautiful, intelligent, gifted, capable person. It doesn't happen all at once, but by the time their work is uncovered, the damage is done—just like discovering termites have been in the foundation of your house. These are the tools of Satan. These are the ways in which, by stealth and deception, he zaps our energy, our drive, our passion, and our love, leaving us feeling dirty and demoralized.

All of us want to be moved in ways that are good, clean, and honorable. But these are the first virtues Satan sets out to destroy. He whispers in our ears as he did to our parents in the Garden of Eden, "Did God really say, 'You must not eat. . . .'?" (Gen. 3:1 NIV). He knew then what he knows now: a frontal attack wouldn't work. But creating the slightest breach in our spiritual boat would cause a hairline fracture that, with time, grows into a full-fledged flood of doubt about our worth and God's true motives toward us. His "God is trying to keep you down" suggestion takes on a life of its own. Yet God is still clear about His intentions: "If you will humble yourselves under the mighty hand of God, in his good time he will lift you up" (1 Pet. 5:6 TLB). If I humble myself before God, He will promote me? Then the Bible urges, "Let him have all your worries and cares, for he is always thinking about you and watching everything that concerns you" (1 Pet. 5:7 TLB). These and other promises from God are the very treasures that Satan hopes to bury in the seas of our forgetfulness. Forgetting what we should remember is the one thing we've gotten good at.

Excitement and energy are the first to go when love grows old and cold. We're not excited about being married anymore. We're not excited about going to work anymore. We're not excited about reading the Bible anymore. We're not excited about our friends. We're not excited about anything! When love drains away, we are left sad, sullen, and apathetic. God save us from the apathetic "whatever" attitude seeping in and sapping our passion for life and love for one another.

No one has so much he or she can afford the high price of apathy. Its price is ignorance, self-centeredness, and unconcern. Apathy makes smart people stupid, good people bad, and things God meant to be beautiful, ugly. Its fruits are needs going unmet, discoveries going unmade, hurts going unhealed, and resources going unused. I choose to employ my passions in the service of life rather than dishonor my life in the service of my petty passions.

The Anatomy of a Noble Cause

How can you distinguish a noble cause from other ambitions? I mean everyone is working a scheme or angle. What guarantees do you have that if you give your love and life away in full devotion to a cause, you won't wind up regretting wasting your time and life on something that is doomed for failure?

In the movie *First Knight*, Lancelot (played by Richard Gere) is a highly skilled swordsman for hire. Seeing a princess under attack in the woods, he fights to rescue her. Attracted to the princess, Guinevere, he later visits her in Camelot, where an annual festival is taking place. Unfortunately for him, she is to be wed to King Arthur (played by Sean Connery) at a later date.

Following Lancelot's success at running the gauntlet, an impossible obstacle course of swinging boulders and axes, King Arthur privately meets Lancelot. Arthur is impressed with Lancelot's ability to run the gauntlet and wants to know how he did it. Lancelot responds, "I have nothing to lose, so what have I to fear?" He has no home and no family and no cause.

As they walk toward the room that houses the Round Table, King Arthur tells Lancelot about Camelot's values: "Here we believe that every life is precious, even the lives of strangers. If you must die, die serving something greater than yourself. Better still, live and serve." He explains, "The table has no head or foot; they are all equal, even the king." Lancelot reads the inscription on the table: "In serving each other we become free." King Arthur remarks, "That is the very heart of Camelot. Not these stones, timbers, towers, palaces. Burn them all, and Camelot lives on. Because it lives in us, it's a belief we hold in our hearts." As he's leaving, King Arthur whispers, "Lancelot, just a thought. A man who fears nothing is a man who loves nothing. And if you love nothing, what joy is there in your life?" Not a bad question to ponder in our postmodern world.

French poet Jean de la Fontaine said, "Man is so made that whenever anything fires his soul impossibilities vanish." The fuel of the soul is love. That's why the Scriptures declare, "Let love and faithfulness never leave you; bind them around your neck, write them on the tablet of your heart" (Prov. 3:3 NIV). These are the true motivations of an individual in pursuit of personal excellence.

When asked, more as a trap than as the pursuit of truth, "What is the greatest commandment?" Jesus quoted the Old Testament command, "Love the Lord your God with all your heart and with all your soul and with all your mind and with all your strength" (Mark 12:30 NIV).

On October 28, 1886, France unveiled its magnanimous gift to America, the Statue of Liberty. Including the pedestal, the statue stands more than 305 feet tall and weighs 225 tons. At the base is a portion of the poem by Emma Lazarus articulating the basic philosophy of American democracy. The two most famous lines are, "Give me your tired, your poor, / Your huddled masses yearning to breathe free." Freedom has been our national battle cry and our social bonding agent since our inception. We are a country of mavericks, pioneers, individuals, and free thinkers who can't agree on much of anything except freedom. For the love of freedom, we have fought wars, shed blood, and sent our sons and daughters into harm's way. Freedom is our battle cry because it is the heart's longing.

Freedom is what we want more than anything else for the world because it is what we want so badly for ourselves. The good news is, Jesus Christ came to earth with that very mission in mind. To start the public phase of His ministry, He went to a synagogue on the Sabbath and stood up to read,

> God's Spirit is on me;
>   he's chosen me to preach the Message of good news to
> the poor;
> Sent me to announce pardon to prisoners and recovery of
>   sight to the blind,
>   To set the burdened and battered free. (Luke 4:18 THE
> MESSAGE)

Freedom is the reason why Jesus came and why He was considered so dangerous. With His message of freedom from the tyranny of sin and slavery, both personal and national, He stirred up trouble and set people talking. He spoke with authority about sorrow, anxiety, sickness, death, and separation; He penetrated the dark corners of human suffering. Like no man before or since, He shattered illusions and myths about God and spoke of the power of love and the cause of freedom. And make no mistake, this very message and mission make some love Him and others loathe Him. He dared make love the highest motivation, and freedom the noblest mission. But others have spoken of love, and certainly others have led rebellions in the name of freedom. What makes His cause the most enduring and ennobling of them all? Jesus dared frame the concept of love and freedom in the context of a personal relationship with God.

The Four Levels of Love

Love is the most powerful and mysterious force on the planet. It can break hearts and mend them again. It can be healthy and freeing or dangerous and toxic. It helps to understand love in its levels of maturity. *The first level of love, in its most immature expression, is the love of self for self's sake.* This is the kind of love a baby demonstrates. When Paula and I brought our first daughter home from the hospital, we learned quickly that a baby wants what a baby wants when a baby wants it. This is the nature of a baby, and it's okay, for a baby's world is only as big as her present need. When she is hungry, the world is hungry; when she needs changing, the world needs changing. If this type of infantile behavior is allowed to spill over into adulthood, you have a mess. The Scriptures describe it as "the ambition to buy everything that appeals to you, and the pride that comes from wealth and importance— these are not from God" (1 John 2:16 TLB).

The second level of love's maturity is the love of God for self's sake. This is expressed in the belief that God exists for my pleasure. He's "up there" to provide me with things. God is like a cosmic Santa Claus or the equivalent of a rich uncle. This type of love uses God, and everyone else in sight, to get what we want. God is like a dispenser of all things good. He is like the person who takes the order at the fast-food drive-through. We talk into a speaker, place the order, and expect it to be filled perfectly in the time it takes to drive to the next window. It seldom works that way in real life, and it never works that way with God.

Paula and I were staying in a nice hotel as a part of celebrating a recent wedding anniversary. We were getting ready to call it a night when she asked if I would go down the hall and get her a soda from the vending machine. She said it would cost a dollar and handed me one with that "you're so sweet" look that wives give their husbands on such occasions. I sauntered slowly down the long corridor until I found the dingy room with the noisy icemaker and the brightly lit sign on the drink machine: "$1.00."

I inserted the dollar bill, pushed the button, and waited for the can to drop, but nothing happened. I was tired, poorly dressed, and frustrated that the stupid machine stole my dollar. So I responded like any guy from out of town and kicked the stupid thing. Why do we feel that we have to talk to machines at a time like this? But I shook my finger at it and said, "I'm going to go back and get another dollar, and give you one more chance." I shuffled back to the room, got another dollar, and hurried back to try again. I hand-fed the dollar to the machine, pushed the button with a little extra gusto this time, as though pushing harder would let it know I meant business, and sure enough out came my wife's diet soda. The machine had done its job, and I had won the war. That's the way I like life; output equals input.

I'm embarrassed to admit I often love God like a cold drink machine. I send up my prayers, give my dollar, or attend a church service once in a blue moon, and I expect the blessings to come down. When they don't, I'm insulted. I threaten to withhold my affection, as though that would diminish His deity. I sulk, He's saddened, and I lose. How silly and infantile this must seem to God, yet He remains faithful and does not treat me as my childish behavior warrants.

The danger in this level of love is that it appears to be genuine from a distance. Jesus warned of the damage this deception can cause when He said, "Many will say to me on that day, 'Lord, Lord, did we not prophesy in your name, and in your name drive out demons and perform many miracles?' Then I will tell them plainly, 'I never knew you. Away from me, you evildoers!' " (Matt. 7:22–23 NIV). It sounds a little harsh from a distance, but a closer look confirms the corrupt heart that dares to commercialize God's love.

The third level of love is the love of God for God's sake. This type of love sees God as a far-off deity to be feared and appeased. If the second level treats God as a waiter, this level sees God as a tyrant. In this equation, I exist only as a thing to bring God some type of sick satisfaction. On this level I am connected to God only by a set of religious rules. I must obey or suffer the consequences. In religious terms, this is legalism. Its adherents live by lists, and the longer the better.

Goethe said, "We are shaped and fashioned by what we love." If this is true, and I think it is, then we look for love outside ourselves. We start with God as He is, not the idea of the God we wish or imagine. He is the One who has the power of being contained in His own person. As a person (one in essence with three personalities living together with unity and diversity in community) without obligation or constraint, He chose to create us in love, giving us the very gift He enjoys so much—life. To love God with "all your heart and with all your soul and with all your strength and with all your mind" (Luke 10:27 NIV) is to express and experience life at its highest level because it is freely given. It is a love that sacrifices without counting the cost and serves without asking why. *The fourth level of love's maturity is the love of self for God's sake.* The highest, most mature level of life is to love God and then in turn look back at myself using His eyes as my mirrors.

In the movie *The Passion of the Christ*, Mel Gibson used the word *passion* in its root Latin meaning, "to suffer." The film documents the last twelve hours of Christ's life as He suffers one indignity after another. Critics of the movie feared the violence and graphic nature of the suffering of Christ would result in a backlash of anti-Semitism. People would blame the Jews for killing Christ. But while the Romans were the means of His death and the Sanhedrin the agent of His death, I was the cause of it.

What was Christ thinking on the cross? He was thinking of you and me: "He was willing to die a shameful death on the cross because of the joy he knew would be his afterwards" (Heb. 12:2 TLB). It seems almost heretical to think it and blasphemous to write it, but for the joy of loving me He willingly satisfied the demands of God's justice on the cross. He took back death's victory and sin's sting when love raised Him from the dead. What a God! What a love! What a faith! What a life! How could I respond with anything less than love for the One who loved me enough to purchase my freedom? I want to live the rest of my life as an act of worship and adoration to the honor of the One who honored me with His love.

The Three Freedoms

While I was driving along an interstate one day, a car with New Hampshire tags passed me. Across the top of the plate it read, "Live free, or die." That's not a bad take on the truth of how the human soul thrives or dies. We were created to be free, and when we are not, something dies inside. For freedom to have its enlivening and enriching effect, we should understand it in its three dimensions: the freedom from, the freedom to, and the freedom under. Like a three-legged stool, all three are required for freedom to exist as a sacred and sought-after virtue.

I need to be rescued from myself. I've tried to free myself, but just like a quickie diet, the weight of my sin comes right back when I stop denying myself. The great missionary Paul expressed everyman's exasperation with self-bondage when he cried out, "Oh, what a miserable person I am! Who will free me from this life that is dominated by sin? Thank God! The answer is in Jesus Christ our Lord. So you see how it is: In my mind I really want to obey God's law, but because of my sinful nature I am a slave to sin" (Rom. 7:24–25 NLT). We are in bondage from which another must set us free. Our liberator is Christ, the One who has crushed the head of Satan and set the captives free.

Freedom From

In Christ I find freedom from the constant fear of abandonment. He has promised to never leave me or forsake me; I will never be destitute or deserted—ever. In Christ I am freed from the fear of being an insignificant nobody. I need never wonder whether my life matters to anyone of any importance. I matter to God. You matter to God. Every person you meet on the street, pass in the hallway, or sit beside at a ball game matters to God. Therefore, we matter—period. We had essential dignity the day we were born.

Christ the excellent One, the One better than the angels,

thinks you're worth loving. That love frees you from feeling inferior, incompetent, or insignificant. All of us tend to think we are messed up in a way unique only to us, but His love frees us from all guilt and shame. You are loved and wanted by the One of highest value; therefore, you can never be worthless or unwanted.

You are free from the bondage of rules and dead religious obligation. You are free from obligation (as a matter of law) for the sake of obedience (as a fruit of love). God doesn't need your passive compliance or surface conformity. He waits for your willing and eager thirst for righteousness, a hunger for which He has promised satisfaction not by ritual but by relationship.

You are free from blind, superstitious allegiance to authority figures. You are free from being talked down to or belittled. You need never submit to verbal beating in the name of God. You are free from the need to believe outrageous claims of self-anointed prophets of posterity. You need no priest to plead your case, no guru to pledge allegiance to, and no preacher to be threatened or intimidated by. In the place of these you have a loving Advocate who is "sitting at the place of highest honor next to God, pleading for us there in heaven" (Rom. 8:34 TLB). He loves you. He knows everything about you, and He loves you still. He knows how fickle and faint your love can be, and He loves you fully, faithfully, and forever.

You're free from self-destructive behavioral patterns. You're free from overworking, overspending, overeating, overdrinking, or overachieving. You're free from worrying too much, vegetating too often, pleasing too many people, and winding up filled with pent-up anger, rage, or resentment. Yea, God, for the freedom from.

In the film *Lord of the Rings: The Two Towers,* Sauron's dark forces begin to overcome the people of peaceful Middle Earth. Their only hope lies in the hands of two hobbits and a man named Aragorn. Knowing a militia of ruthless soldiers is heading for the country of Rohan, Aragorn comes to help. As he walks about the palace, he finds the king of Rohan's daughter practicing her swordsmanship. In a Gothic parlor, lit only by a few flames, she wields a long, large silver sword with grace. Although petite, she is formidable. Impressed and intrigued, Aragorn steps out of the shadows. She reacts with agility, and their swords clash.

Aragorn comments on her skill. She replies, "The women of Rohan have had to learn that just because you do not carry a sword does not mean you cannot die upon one. I fear neither death nor pain." Aragorn asks, "What do you fear?" "A cage," she says. "To stay behind bars until use and old age accept them and all chance of valor has gone beyond recall or desire."

Freedom To

The freedom that Christ offers is *freedom from* and also *freedom to*. On the cross, Jesus cried out for God to show the people why He had to be forsaken on the cross. Three things happened. The sun refused to shine, the veil in the temple was torn from top to bottom, and an earthquake opened some graves and some dead were freed. Because of the cross and empty tomb, the cage doors are not only opened; they're knocked off their hinges.

The captivity of sin, sorrow, suffering, and self is broken. Love stepped in where no other power could go and won our pardon.

Freedom from being held in bondage means the freedom to become the person God had in mind when He created me. Because I am a spiritual being having a human experience, *being* always precedes and empowers *doing*. Being comes before behavior. In Christ I am free to be real, right, and redemptive. I am free to let other people know me. I am free to love and be loved, to celebrate and be celebrated. I am free to grow and change, dream and dare. I am free to speak up when I have something to say and shut up when I don't.

One of the hardest things to overcome as a writer was the nagging, gnawing feeling that what, if anything, did I have to say that anyone wanted or needed to read? Feeling I had something to say gave me the freedom to test my voice. I've spent my life listening to other people's voices. I've held my own thoughts hostage to the old tapes in my mind too long. It was a great day when I felt the freedom to trust my voice. I am free to write, to express, to extend my deepest thoughts and feelings in hopes they might free someone else held captive by old labels and lies.

Freedom Under

For freedom to be more than another form of bondage, as *freedom from* and *freedom to* can become if left to stand alone, real freedom is also *freedom under*. Jesus prayed in the last hours alone in the Garden, "If it is not possible for this cup to be taken away unless I drink it, may your will be done" (Matt. 26:42 NIV). And as a result of His submission to God's will, Paul said, "God exalted him to the highest place and gave him the name that is above every name, that at the name of Jesus every knee should bow" (Phil. 2:9–10 NIV). When I submit my will to God's will, when I surrender my shame to His love, I place myself under His care. The question then is, What does He care about? Paul gave this answer: "God rescued us from dead-end alleys and dark dungeons. He's set us up in the kingdom of the Son he loves so much, the Son who got us out of the pit we were in, got rid of the sins we were doomed to keep repeating" (Col. 1:13–14 THE MESSAGE).

Some people chafe at the idea of living under the authority of Christ. Authority doesn't have a great reputation among us rebels. But the way I look at it, I'm going to live under the influence of one of three things. I will live under the influence of loot, lordship, or love. Money can't buy me love, and lordship is just another burden I'm not qualified to carry. But living under the lordship of a loving Savior makes me heir to His promises, providence, presence, and power. As Jesus said, "My yoke is easy and my burden is light" (Matt. 11:30 NIV).

Feeding Your First Love

We were made to serve a noble cause. With love as our motivator and freedom as our mission, we have the power to excel. These two possessions are the key and core ingredients of a life of meaning and substance. Nothing else we possess will make up for the lack of them. Money can't. Connections can't. Privilege can't. We must guard them at all cost because as essential as they are to a life of excellence, they are the first to go when we neglect them. No one should assume that they are static qualities and, once attained, always at hand. Passion leaks, mission drifts, and the heart is easily wooed and won by lesser loves.

How, then, has God equipped us to keep our love for His agenda vital and vibrant? He made us thirsty, hungry, and driven. Passion is like being thirsty. Have you ever been so thirsty that nothing would do but water? Your body cries out for cold, clean, good water. Your soul gets thirsty: "As the deer pants for streams of water, so my soul pants for you, O God. My soul thirsts for God, for the living God" (Ps. 42:1–2 NIV).

Are you genuinely thirsty for God? If you are, He invites you to drink long and deep. To the woman at the well, He said, "If you knew the gift of God and who it is that asks you for a drink, you would have asked him and he would have given you living water" (John 4:10 NIV).

I am thirsty for God. I ache for an experience with Him, a full, long, deep, satisfying one. Yet I tend to get my thirst satisfied too early. I settle for quenching my thirst with counterfeit water. That's why I resonate with Sting (writer, actor, and singer), who confessed in his autobiography:

> I have never had a genuine religious experience. I say this with some regret. I've paid lip service to the idea, certainly. But a devastating ego destroying, ontological, epiphany, I simply have not had. More devout souls than I have visited this realm through prayer, meditation, fasting, or from undergoing a near-death experience. Religious literature is full of such visionary claims and while I have no reason to doubt their veracity, I would venture to say that such experiences are rare.[1]

Dear God, I don't want this thirst within me to be satisfied by anything but You.

Passion is like hunger. It is impossible to satisfy your appetite for cake with pictures of cakes. You want the real thing. I mean, when you're famished, you want something substantial. Jesus said, "Blessed are those who hunger and thirst for righteousness, for they will be filled" (Matt. 5:6 NIV). If thirst is the key to our spiritual passion, hunger is the key to our intellectual passion. God gave each of us a trillion-dollar brain! We're inquisitive! We want to know!

Years ago, Paula and I went to London, and we wanted to visit several churches. On the only Sunday night we were going to be in the city, we went to a historic church, famous for the scholarship of its pastors. The men had inspired me with their writing. I had imagined what it would be like to sit in the pews and listen to these intellectual giants speak. But it was a different time. The attendance was meager. For a sanctuary with two balconies, the handful of people in attendance that night would have barely filled the front three rows. I wondered why the crowds were no longer gathering at this historic bulwark of faith in England. I got a hint when I read the topic for the evening, "Can a Man Be a Christian and an Intellectual?" That struck me as odd, but I was willing to hold my judgment until later. The conclusion; it's possible to be a God-lover and an intellectual, but not probable. I didn't leave with my heart warmed or my thirst satisfied. I went hoping for a spiritual and intellectual banquet of biblical scholarship served with passion and hope. I left with the equivalent of religious beanie-weenies served on a paper plate of platitudes.

God gave you a brain to know Him, a heart to feel Him, and a will to obey Him. The more about God I discover, the more passionate I become. Listen to what the Scriptures say:

> How sweet are your words to my taste,
>   sweeter than honey to my mouth!
> I gain understanding from your precepts;
>   therefore I hate every wrong path.
> Your word is a lamp to my feet and a light for my path.
> (Ps. 119:103–5 NIV)

The Word of God thrills my soul because, from cover to cover, its history, its psychology, its spirituality, its salvation, and its hope thrill my soul and feed me where I'm hungry and fill me where I'm empty.

I remember the place and time when I committed my life completely to the nobility of love and freedom. I had moved to Memphis to begin seminary. Paula and the girls remained in Kentucky until I could secure housing and find a job. For several weeks, I slept on the floor of a friend's apartment. I missed my family. I enjoyed the academics okay, but I had a growing feeling of panic with each day. Why wasn't God showing up for me? I'd quit a good job and moved three hundred miles to train for a life of service to the gospel of Christ. I had found my noble cause and I was willing to sacrifice for love and freedom, but where was God?

Mad at God, I got in my car one day—I packed up and quit. I pointed my car north toward Kentucky with the intention of leaving this God-forsaken place, never to return. I was mad, hurt, and scared. Had I taken "the call" too seriously? It was bad enough I had placed myself in a crisis situation, but I had dragged my family into the ditch with me. All I could hear were the voices of friends who had warned me it was a bad idea: "Why would you leave a great job? Why would you place your family in jeopardy? Why? Why? Why?"

As I was listening to all those dissonant voices in my head, a feeling of dread came over me. It was as though a presence uninvited and unfamiliar was in the car with me. And to this day, I'm not sure I heard an audible voice, but at least in my mind I heard these words: *If you cross Canada Road, it's over.* Now I didn't—then or now—believe it meant, *If you cross Canada Road, I'm gonna kill you.* But what I felt—then as now—was God saying, *If you cross Canada Road, you can just sit this one out. You'll be a nice guy and float through life. I'll love you and bless you and all the rest of it. But what you want from Me, what you have cried out for, what you say you thirst and hunger for, lies on the south side of Canada Road.* It was a defining moment for me. My life with God transformed from a career path to a noble cause.

Thank God, I did not cross Canada Road that day. I turned around and headed back to seminary. God could have materialized before me that day, and the experience would have not been more real. It was a turning point, of which I've had only a few, but they helped me get committed to my commitments.

That's why that young mother could climb that mountain and negotiate the return of her child. She wasn't just committed to her noble cause. She was committed to the commitment. The warriors were committed, but theirs was more from pride and outrage. Such motivations can't rise to the level of a noble cause.

The one whom God uses greatly, He first wounds deeply. I think it's because you'll never understand that Jesus Christ is all you need until Jesus Christ is all you have left. When you emerge from that dark place, and as sure as God is in heaven you will, you will have new motivation—love—and a new mission—freedom. From these you get the power to excel at being who you are, where you are, with what you have, while you can. Who could hope for more this side of heaven?

8

I Will Act on My Ideas

∽

*Everything has been thought of before, the problem is to
think of it again.*
—JOHANN WOLFGANG VON GOETHE

In 1877 the Methodists in Illinois held their annual conference
at Westfield College. The president of the college said, "I
think we live in a very exciting age." A presiding bishop
asked, "What do you mean?" The college president responded, "I
believe we are coming into a time of great inventions. For example, I believe men will fly through the air like birds." The bishop
said, "This is heresy! The Bible says flight is reserved for the angels so we'll have no such talk here." After the conference, the
bishop, whose name was Wright, went home to his two sons,
Wilbur and Orville, with no clue about what they were up to.
Unbeknownst to him, his sons personified the audacity to act on
ideas, no matter how strange they might sound or impossible they
might seem.

Predicting what can or cannot be done in the future is point-
less. Just think of the great things we enjoy today that were considered impossible in the past. For example, the first cast-iron
plow was invented in the United States in 1797, but was initially
rejected by New Jersey farmers because it was believed that cast
iron poisoned the land and stimulated the growth of weeds.

At the introduction of the railroad, it was widely believed that
insane asylums would be needed for the people driven mad with

terror at the sight of locomotives rushing across the country. In Germany "experts" proved that if trains went at the frightful fifteen miles an hour, blood would spurt from the travelers' noses, and passengers would suffocate when going through tunnels. Commodore Vanderbilt dismissed George Westinghouse and his new air brakes for trains, stating, "I have no time to waste on fools." Those who loaned Robert Fulton money for his steamboat project required their names be withheld for fear of ridicule were it known they supported anything so "foolhardy."

In 1881, when the New York YWCA announced typing lessons for women, vigorous protests were made on the grounds that the female constitution would break down under the strain. Joshua Coppersmith was arrested in Boston for trying to sell stock in the telephone. "All well-informed people know that it is impossible to transmit the human voice over a wire," intoned the experts.

God has created humankind to move onward and upward by the boldness of people who dared to act on their ideas. Consider this admonition: "Whatever is true, whatever is noble, whatever is right, whatever is pure, whatever is lovely, whatever is admirable—if anything is excellent or praiseworthy—think about such things" (Phil. 4:8 NIV). Contrary to what some people think, God is not opposed to our dreaming big and daring greatly. For example, we start out in life as natural-born risk takers. As Job said, "Naked I came from my mother's womb, and naked I will depart" (Job 1:21 NIV). For a while we are fearless. We run into rooms, climb on couches, and dig in dirt, oblivious to the presence of germs. Then after we live for a while, we have sufficient labels hung on us by the significant people in our lives; we get an education, a job, a family, and a mortgage; and we turn into caretakers. And if we're not careful, we'll spend our lives collecting things and storing them in the basement, closet, or storage unit (if we're lucky enough to find one). Then after we consume and collect for around thirty or forty years, we retire and putter around, waiting for the undertaker. We start out as spirited mavericks, but if we're not very brave, we'll end up shuffling along with the herd of other tame souls whose mediocrity is less and less inspiring and more and more demoralizing.

Refuse to be tamed by being tagged mediocre. Reject the herd mentality—go along to get along. Stay wild at heart and adventurous in spirit. Let someone else be the couch potato. Be a player, not a spectator or a speculator. A spectator watches what happens. A speculator wonders what would've happened had he or she the guts and gumption to get in the game and make things happen. The world will always be populated with people who talk the talk, but won't walk the walk. We need more people like the apostle James who said, "Show me your faith without deeds, and I will show you my faith by what I do" (James 2:18 NIV). We scan the horizon for men and women who *have* character, not *are* characters. The Proverbs ask, "Many a man claims to have unfailing love, but a faithful man who can find?" (20:6 NIV).

The Power of an "Acted On" Idea

We owe a debt of gratitude to the countless numbers of people who had an idea and the ingenuity to do something about it. Because they acted on their ideas, we have things we never knew we needed, but now wouldn't want to live without. Brand names such as Apple, IBM, and Dell computers wouldn't even be in our vocabulary if Federico Faggin, who received a patent for the first computer microprocessor, hadn't acted on his far-fetched idea. Daniel Fahrenheit, a German physicist, invented the alcohol thermometer in 1709 and the mercury thermometer in 1714, and in 1724 he introduced the temperature scale that bears his name. How many ways does Michael Faraday, who invented the electric motor, touch our lives every day? Who of us could imagine life without TV? Well, thanks to Philo Farnsworth who, while still a young farm boy of thirteen, conceived the basic operating principles of television, you don't have to. I've been staring into James Fergason's invention of the liquid crystal display for years. I've screamed with delight on many a summer vacation thanks to George W. Ferris, a bridge builder, who invented the Ferris wheel. Reginald Fessenden transmitted the world's first over-the-air voice message in 1900. John Fitch made the first successful trial of a steamboat.

Edith Flanigen received the first patent for refining petroleum and became one of the most inventive chemists of all times. Alexander Fleming discovered penicillin, thereby saving millions of lives from death by infection. Sir Sandford Fleming established universal standard time. Jay W. Forrester, a pioneer in digital computer development, invented random access, coincident-current, magnetic storage. Sally Fox rediscovered naturally colored cotton. Helen Murray Free invented the home diabetes test. Art Fry, a 3M chemist, invented Post-it® Notes as a temporary bookmarker.

One reason these ideas have become parts of our lives is that they all meet a need in society. Large or small, they all contribute to making life better. I'm glad Leo Gerstenzang thought of Q-Tips® when he saw his wife trying to clean their baby's ears with toothpicks—ouch! I'm glad Otto Diefenbach came up with the cellophane soda straws when he twisted the wrapper from a cigarette pack. Being a man, I'm exceedingly grateful that King C. Gillette got tired of using a dull razor, so he invented the safety razor with disposable blades.

A great idea not only meets a need; it also helps solve a problem. Anyone who has ever gone boating owes a nod of thanks to Ole Evinrude for getting angry when the ice cream in his rowboat melted before he got to his island picnic spot, so he invented the outboard motor. Ralph Schneider decided to form the Diners Club one night after he lost his wallet. Charles Strite was fuming at the burned toast in the factory lunchroom where he worked—and thought up the automatic toaster.

These "acted on" ideas have created prosperity not only for the people who thought of them, but also for entire industries that have sprung from many of them. Just think of the jobs created around the automobile, the computer, cell phones, and the Internet. This proves the proverb, "A generous man will prosper; he who refreshes others will himself be refreshed" (Prov. 11:25 NIV).

Breakthrough ideas in medicine, science, politics, philosophy, and psychology have expanded our knowledge base. An idea has the power to enlighten the mind and stir the slumbering soul to action. Author Orison Swett Marden said, "Deep within man dwell those slumbering powers; powers that would astonish him, that he never dreamed of possessing; forces that would revolutionize his life if aroused and put into action."

As people have bigger, better ideas, new, never-dreamed-of possibilities come into view. The most noble of these ideas go far beyond mere commerce. They have the power to literally lift the culture by bringing people together. When people come around a great idea, creative energy is channeled into productive avenues. For the lack of ideas that fire the imagination, bickering and back-biting can set in—what a waste of God-given talent and potential.

Generating Ideas

You are created in the image of God, a one-of-a-kind original. You have essential dignity, just because you were placed on this spinning planet. Motivated by love, God placed a specific design and destiny within you. He made you a problem solver, a change agent, and a noble soul living in a frail, yet fascinating body. But all of that is God's gift to you. It's what you do with what you've been given that proves the quality of your life. You weren't made for mediocre. Why? Mediocre can't arouse your creative centers to a level of focus and full engagement. The question is, Which abilities do you need to stimulate in order to generate good ideas? Only a commitment to excel at being who you are, where you are, with what you have, while you can, has the power to draw out what God has put in.

The answer is given in the pastoral prayer of the apostle Paul for the people he loved. He assured them,

I have not stopped giving thanks for you, remembering you in my prayers. I keep asking that the God of our Lord

Jesus Christ, the glorious Father, may give you the Spirit of wisdom and revelation, so that you may know him better. I pray also that the eyes of your heart may be enlightened in order that you may know the hope to which he has called you, the riches of his glorious inheritance in the saints, and his incomparably great power for us who believe. That power is like the working of his mighty strength, which he exerted in Christ when he raised him from the dead and seated him at his right hand in the heavenly realms. (Eph. 1:16–20 NIV)

Paul prayed for the eyes of their hearts. What an interesting insight to our inner makeup! I'm not sure about everything that phrase means, but I offer three suggestions that are germane to our discussion. Could Paul be asking God to enlighten the power of our imagination, inspiration, and insight? Each one of these capacities is crucial to being thinking, feeling, and acting individuals.

Imagination

Doug Marlette is a cartoonist. His job is to draw a new cartoon every day. He doesn't consider it pressure; he enjoys it. He said, "I have learned to love a blank sheet of paper. It braces me with its endless potential." Every day you are given a blank sheet of paper: a new day with powerful possibilities. You can fill the page with whatever you want: holiness, love, praise, service—or selfish ambition and bitterness. It's your choice; use it or lose it.

Oliver Wendell Holmes observed, "Man's mind once stretched by a new idea, never regains its original dimension." God gave you the capacity to imagine a better future. You're not limited by what you put on the page yesterday. Each day is like a blank page on which you may write a nobler chapter to your story. To this end, God has promised to add His loving promise: "Because of the LORD's great love we are not consumed, for his compassions never fail. They are new every morning" (Lam. 3:22–23 NIV).

Inspiration

I briefly mentioned the inventor of Post-it® Notes, Art Fry. The inspiration behind his discovery was the search for a bookmark for his church hymnal that would neither fall out nor damage the hymnal. One of Fry's colleagues at 3M, Dr. Spencer Silver, had developed an adhesive that was strong enough to stick to surfaces, but left no residue after removal and could be repositioned. Fry took some of Dr. Silver's adhesive and applied it along the edge of a piece of paper. His church hymnal problem was solved! Today, we see Post-it® Notes peppered across files, computers, desks, and doors in offices and homes throughout the country. From a church hymnal bookmark to an office and home essential, the Post-it® Note has colored the way we work.

Author Paul J. Meyer lamented that "the human scene is crowded with the people who have gone as far as they're going simply because their goals aren't high enough." What are the sources of inspiration you open yourself up to every day? Inspiration can hit at any place and any time. How many musicians were inspired to take up their instruments at a concert of their favorite bands? How many children were inspired to go into careers by the example of their parents, grandparents, or someone they greatly admired?

I find great inspiration in movies, books, and music. The Bible, though it was a big book of rules when I was young, has become a major source of inspiration during my adult life. Inspiring people doing inspiring things are all around you. Open your mind to sources of inspiration and dissatisfaction that motivate you to fix something, finish something, or invent something.

Insight

Insight results when imagination, inspiration, and truth intersect. You'll think new thoughts and have new visions. You'll have ideas popping across the screen of your mind like fireflies on a summer evening. This might seem strange at first, but believe me, it is what you were created to do. My question is, Why don't we invest more of our time thinking in new, exciting ways? George Bernard

Shaw said, "Few people think more than two or three times a year. I've made an international reputation for myself by thinking once or twice a week." His statement only illustrates the awesome potential power of a new insight into a problem or possibility. And when you think about ways to make life better, your mind expands and new worlds appear right before your eyes. Edward R. Murrow cautioned, however, that "a great many people think they are thinking when they are really rearranging their prejudices and superstitions." The only antidote to small-mindedness is God's promise that

> I will pour out my Spirit on all people.
> Your sons and daughters will prophesy,
>> your young men will see visions,
>> your old men will dream dreams. (Acts 2:17 NIV)

I want to be one of those drenched with God-anointed, God-inspired ideas and dripping with the holy sweat of a noble cause.

How to Get a Good Idea

Louis Pasteur stated, "Chance favors the prepared mind." If that is true, then how can I prepare my mind and heart to be receptive to bold and better ideas? Let's consider a few practical ways to stimulate the creation of new ideas.

Reading is a surefire way to stimulate new ideas. I mean, except for life itself, is there anything more wonderful and enduring than a good book? Thank God, Johannes Gutenberg acted on his idea for the movable type printing press. It is still considered one of the most important breakthroughs in history. It was no accident that the first book mass-produced by virtue of this invention was the Bible. Up until that time, books were too bulky and expensive to be owned or transported.

Books contain messages from people in another place and time, through which little sheets of paper teach us, terrify us, amuse us, and amaze us. Clarence Day, writer and cofounder of

Yale University Press, said, "The world of books is the most remarkable creation of man; nothing else that he builds ever lasts. Monuments fall; nations perish; civilizations grow old and die out. After an era of darkness, new races build others; but in the world of books are volumes that live on still as young and fresh as the day they were written, still telling men's hearts of the hearts of men centuries dead."

In the best books, great men and women hand over their most precious discoveries. These distant voices of the living and the dead make us heirs of the highest thoughts and ideals. Books are true levelers. They give to all who faithfully use them, the brightest and best of our race. I have found fresh inspiration by rereading some of the classics that inspired me years ago. As I go back over ground I've covered, I'm not sure that I see in the books more than was there, but I definitely see more in me than there was before.

Prayer is an underused way to gain insight into new ways of thinking. R. A. Torrey said, "We are too busy to pray, and so we are too busy to have power." The power in prayer is not so much that I change God's mind, but He changes mine. Harry Emerson Fosdick, in his classic volume *The Meaning of Prayer*, posed an interesting question: "If God has left some things contingent on man's thinking and working why may he not have left some things contingent on man's praying?"

A form of prayer we call meditation is another discipline that can yield great results. I read an article that explained why a pigeon wobbles when it walks. A pigeon can't see where it's going because it can't adjust its focus as it moves. The pigeon actually has to bring its head to a complete stop between steps in order to refocus. In order to walk it has to stick its head forward, stop and then back and stop. Maybe we walk so crooked and wobbly sometimes because we, too, have a hard time focusing on our moves. Stopping to meditate and think from a God orientation helps us realign our lives. We need to stop between steps and refocus on where we are in relation to where God wants us to be. That's the power of taking the time to meditate and concentrate.

Sometimes in order to really pray and meditate as we seek new breakthroughs in thinking, isolating or taking ourselves out of the flow of the daily routine can be a source of idea generation. I can't list the number of times just a change in zip code has opened up the clogged arteries of inspiration and insight that the sameness and hurriedness of routine have blocked and stymied. Time to ponder allows thoughts time to percolate our insights into ideas. Meditating on promises in the Scripture such as, "Call to me and I will answer you and tell you great and unsearchable things you do not know" (Jer. 33:3 NIV), always inspires me to be bolder in my expectations of God.

At other times, I have done the very opposite of meditation and isolation; I started participating with others in acts of service and giving. These times of activity have helped me experience what's happening in the hearts and heads of real people engaged in making life work in the real world. If you're looking for a way to make a better umbrella, can there be a better way to do your research than to walk in the rain alongside someone trying to get one open in a heavy downpour? Walking a mile in someone's shoes can go a long way toward finding out what he is looking for in a new pair of shoes. What he says or how he sees things can result in new insights.

I highly recommend the discipline of journaling. I keep a notebook with me everywhere I go. Ideas not captured at the moment of inspiration are often gone forever. Don't rely on your memory; it will let you down. I have learned from bitter experience the old saying, "A dull pencil is better than a sharp mind." I have had great ideas flash across the screen of my mind in such vivid color that I thought, *There is no way I will forget this,* only to try to recall it later without a hint of its vapor trail.

Believe it or not, one of the best ways to get a breakthrough idea is to exercise. When your body is in motion, your brain is freed to work at the subconscious level. And work it will if you give it a chance. When I was developing the idea for this book, I knew what I wanted to say, but I couldn't get it organized enough to write it down. I spent hours at my desk staring at my blank computer screen, praying for imagination, inspiration, and insight, but nothing happened. I got up, put on my running clothes, and went out for a four-mile run. About the second mile, the dam burst and out poured all the things I knew I wanted to say, but couldn't access. Try it; it works. But make sure to write it down.

What to Do with an Idea

Once you get an idea worth working on, write it down in your journal. Put it in the simplest form you can. I have found that asking the questions, "What if?" and "So what?" is essential in distilling the thought into something workable. As you work through this process, bathe your idea in prayer. I ask God to give me insight into this idea. I want to be sure this is a God idea. By that I mean if it's not great for God and good for people, I don't want to waste another moment on it. It can't be about me, and it shouldn't be just about making more money. It has to meet a need, right a wrong, love a person, encourage the heart, heal a relationship, or do something that extends the loving reign of Jesus Christ in the world longing for faith, hope, and love. Remember the Scriptures warn, "Many are the plans in a man's heart, but it is the LORD's purpose that prevails" (Prov. 19:21 NIV). O God, make your purpose clear in my idea.

As I write it down and pray it up, I also want to think it through. What would this idea mean if it were wildly successful? Would it be worth my time? Can I get other people excited about it? That's when another step in the maturation process of an idea comes into play—pass it around. When like minds get together, they talk about ideas; mediocre minds talk about things; small minds talk about other people. This is so important; I will develop this idea in the next chapter, "I Will Ask for Help."

After you've clarified it through writing, crystallized it through collaboration, and offered it up in prayer, it's time to lay it aside for a while and let it breathe. A popular commercial for a California winery used the slogan, "We will sell no wine before its time." Just as wine *mellows* with time, a great idea *matures* with it. If you act on the idea, it's going to require commitment on your part, and only a handful of ideas are going to be worth throwing your full weight behind. Give your idea time to take on a life of its own. Life is full of stories of people who have gone off the deep end of an ill-conceived and ill-timed scheme. If it's an idea worth acting on, it will intensify with time. That leaves only one major roadblock in the way—the proclivity to procrastinate.

The Proclivity to Procrastinate

This can be a dangerous time for your new idea because of the proclivity to procrastinate. The word comes from the Latin, meaning "to put forward to tomorrow." Someone once asked Alexander the Great, "How did you conquer the world?" He replied, "By not delaying." There comes a time in the life of every great idea when you don't need more information, more collaboration, or more prayer. It's time to act. It's time for character and a sense of urgency to take action upon what you've already thought and prayed through.

The excuses to procrastinate are as many as there are ideas against which they work. We often justify doing nothing because we can't do everything. We listen to the lies of the old labels hung on our hearts from childhood. And even though no one erects monuments to critics, crackpots, and commentators, we allow them to erect walls in our minds. We reinforce their predictions of mediocrity by our inactivity.

Courage to act is replaced by timidity and uncertainty when we bow to the forces of FOF and FOP. These twin fears, the fear of failure and the fear of people, have wrecked more homes, way-laid more futures, and starved more dreams than any other force on earth. They are like a plague of locusts feeding off the insecurity of a soul not sure of its place in the world. No wonder the Bible warns, "Fear of man is a dangerous trap, but to trust in God means safety" (Prov. 29:25 TLB). For our fears and phobias God gives this assurance: "Though a righteous man falls seven times, he rises again" (Prov. 24:16 NIV).

Procrastination feeds on the "someday" mentality. A basic tenet of this book is that personal excellence is the commitment to start where you are with what you have. If you listen closely, you'll hear the clock ticking on your life. The old "someday" excuse is a cop-out. The Scriptures warn, "The lazy man is full of excuses. 'I can't go to work!' he says. 'If I go outside, I might meet a lion in the street and be killed!' " (Prov. 22:13 TLB). Someday I'll get serious about making my life count. Someday I'll take my life in God seriously. Someday prayer will become priority, and people will know I'm a force to be reckoned with. Someday I'll make up with those I'm mad at. Someday soon I'll tell my wife I love her and my kids how proud I am of them. Someday I'll step up. Someday I'll be strong. Someday I'll slay those demons. Someday I'll stop saying, "Someday," and start saying, "Today." When you don't want to do something, any excuse will do.

Another powerful force drawing us to mediocrity is the cultural climate in which we live. As I write this chapter, the ire of the country is raised by the recent Super Bowl halftime program during which Janet Jackson revealed one of her breasts. And even though partial nudity is all over the TV screen, this incident has stirred the sensibilities of many people. The truth is, this type of thing has been tolerated for a long time, but this one event illustrates the cooling effect of compromise. I remember one of my ethics professors asking, "How do you cook a frog?" Students looked at each other for answers. The teacher said, "To cook a frog alive, you place him in a pot of water at his favorite temperature. Start turning up the heat in small increments. The frog will sit still, adjusting to the rising temperature. Because of his ability to adapt to the hot water, he will be boiled alive before he thinks about jumping out." The application of the story was that we are just like that frog; we will adapt to the climate around us unless we resist. The mass of humanity tends to settle in the middle where mediocrity breeds best. Commitments cool. Vision leaks. Excellence tends to entropy, and energy defuses.

But after all the excuses have been offered, the truth is, many times procrastination results from everyday laziness. I have never heard this problem addressed any better than by Solomon in the book of Proverbs,

> Go to the ant, you sluggard;
>   consider its ways and be wise!
> It has no commander, no overseer or ruler,
> yet it stores its provisions in summer
>   and gathers its food at harvest.
> How long will you lie there, you sluggard?
> When will you get up from your sleep?
> A little sleep, a little slumber,
>   a little folding of the hands to rest—
> and poverty will come on you like a bandit
>   and scarcity like an armed man. (6:6–11 NIV)

We allow activities to crowd out action. Nature abhors a vacuum, so unless we fill our lives with meaningful, purposeful action, someone or something will fill them with banal, barren activity. And fill our lives we have. There is a time to do things better, and there is a time to do better things. The good overtakes the best until someone stops it. Ernest Hemingway cautioned, "Never mistake motion for action." If activity were productivity, we would be the kings and queens of getting things done.

The Power of Action

George W. Cecil, who used the pseudonym of William A. Lawrence, said, "On the Plains of Hesitation bleach the bones of countless millions who, at the Door of victory, sat down to wait, and waiting—died!" Ideas require action—deliberate, bold, daring action—because they die without it. You can have all of the great ideas in the world, but they are worthless until someone takes action. Talk is cheap because "faith by itself, if it is not accompanied by action, is dead" (James 2:17 NIV). Using the word *action* as an acronym, let's think about how to trade endless activity for meaningful action.

Accept Responsibility

Author Basil King urged, "Be bold—and mighty forces will come to your aid." When the call came for someone to step into the gap in the life of Israel, Isaiah stepped forward to accept responsibility: "Then I heard the voice of the Lord saying, 'Whom shall I send? And who will go for us?' And I said, 'Here am I. Send me!' " (Isa. 6:8 NIV).

Nothing changes until someone steps up to accept responsibility for his own choices, attitudes, and actions. I have observed that we human beings err in two ways at this point. On the one hand, some people don't act responsibly for anything in their lives. They see themselves as victims. Life acts on them, and they're content to settle for whatever cruelties and insults that fate has assigned them. They have an impressive slate of liabilities that can't be changed and, therefore, cannot be overcome. As their numbers grow, the apathy factor drags the entire culture down. We live in a no-fault society where lawsuits and litigation are more about finances than fairness.

At the other end of the spectrum are those who assume responsibility for way too much. Their basic vocabulary consists of two words, "I'm sorry." They're trying to take on the sins and sorrows of the entire world, it seems. If anyone or anything is upset around them, they feel guilty about it. As a result of labeling from their childhood, they are bound by the need to fix everyone who's broken, heal everyone who's wounded, and make everyone with a gripe happy. If that's your idea of accepting responsibility, then here is good news: it is not. Both extremes will kill your spirit and weigh down your soul.

When I advocate accepting responsibility, I am advising you to accept responsibility for your life and no more. Act on your ideas, but don't let other people scoop their agendas over onto your plate. Find your glorious idea, your "one thing," and do that full bore, all out, pedal to the metal. People won't like it. They'll call you fanatical. They'll be offended that you are focused on your mission and not available to feed them or fix them. American evangelist D. L. Moody once said of his critics, "They say of me, 'He is a radical; he is a fanatic; he only has one idea.' " Well, his was a glorious idea, with a college, a radio network, and a publishing company to show for it. I would rather have that said of me than be a man of ten thousand ideas and do nothing with them.

Clarify Contribution

Dwight Eisenhower noted, "A people who values its privileges above its principles, will soon lose both." That leads me to ask, What do you want to be remembered for? It's your life; therefore, only you can determine what your contribution should be. God did not create you to be a wandering generality. He designed you to be a meaningful specific. Paul, the great Christian missionary, said, "This one thing I do." That's always inspired me. He didn't say, "These forty things I dabble at." As you have matured, you have a solid core on which you have formed a strong character (refer to Chapters 1 and 2). Through your education and work experience, you no doubt have developed competencies that have handed you a hint about your calling. Take your character and competencies and identify your calling. Your calling will then help you clarify your contribution.

This is not a quick fix or an easy set of conclusions that can be arrived at or mastered in forty days. Remember, the genius is in the journey, not the destination. To struggle, to strive, and to pay the price of excellence are where real life longs to live. Let your legacy be that you lived "by the principles of love and justice, and always be expecting much from him, your God" (Hos. 12:6 TLB).

Take the Right Risks

I used to think of myself as a risk taker. But upon further reflection, I'm not really sure that's true. For example, I ride a motorcycle, but I wear a helmet. I'm into enough head-cracking activities without going out and not wearing a helmet. I was in Florida not long ago, cruising about seventy miles an hour on Interstate 75 in my rental car. All of a sudden two guys on Harleys blew past me like I was standing still. I was impressed until I saw that they rode helmetless. To me, that's a risk not worth taking. You might say, "Stay off the motorcycle in the first place." I understand, but I've decided that, for me, the joy of riding with the wind in my face is a risk worth taking. I wear a helmet, and I do everything I possibly can to ride safely and stay out from underneath big trucks.

I used to pride myself as a risk taker, but as I look back over my life, I see only thirteen or so really big risks I've taken. The point is not just to take risks—you do that every day just by getting out of bed in the morning—but to take the right ones. Defining moments, either good or bad, happen when you take or fail to take the risk that God is calling you to take. The Bible announces, "Many are the plans in a man's heart, but it is the LORD's purpose that prevails" (Prov. 19:21 NIV).

Taking the right risk means figuring out what God wants you to do, and doing it for as long as you can, the best that you can. Go for the goal, no matter how unlikely success may seem in the moment. The truth is, if you're not more than a little intimidated by what you're attempting to do, it's probably too tame a risk to keep your attention or draw God's support. Oscar Wilde affirmed, "An idea that isn't dangerous is hardly worth calling an idea at all." It's the shock part, the frightening part, the unknown element that makes an idea an idea in the first place. If you feel comfortable with it from the very first, take another look. It's probably not an idea.

Initiate Change

Since even good change can be a challenge, the best way to change is to initiate it gradually. If you want to lose weight, get in shape, learn a language, or acquire a skill, work these changes into the flow of your life in small, incremental movements. Calvin

Coolidge said, "We cannot do everything at once, but we can do something at once." All the good you're going to do does not have to be done today. But the principle is to do something every day. A French proverb concludes, "Young people tell what they are doing; old people tell what they have done; and fools tell what they wish to do."

Author, poet, philosopher Harriet Martineau stated, "A soul occupied with great ideas best performs small duties." You will be amazed at the progress you have made when small, consistent steps are added up. They provide momentum for greater change along the way. It takes six times as much power to start a fly-wheel from a dead start as it does to keep it going once it is in motion.

It seems to me there are only four basic kinds of change: good, bad, the kind that happens to you, and the kind that you make happen. The hardest of the four is the last one. It's hard to change when you don't have to; since you can't do everything at once, you tend to do nothing until you're forced to by some sort of crisis.

When you do get fired up for change, you tend to overestimate what you can do overnight and underestimate what you can do over time. For example, you may be ready to lose weight. Instead of taking the long view, you buy pills that promise, "Lose twenty pounds in two hours with no side effects (other than death)." This sets you up for failure. Instead of initiating change incrementally in ways that you can, you take an all-or-nothing approach, waiting for perfect conditions. Yet the Scriptures warn, "If you wait for perfect conditions, you will never get anything done" (Eccles. 11:4 NLT).

Initiating real, lasting, productive change begins with a commitment to start today! The Bible asserts, "Today, if you hear his voice, do not harden your hearts" (Heb. 3:15 NIV). Today is the day to begin. Today is the day to take your life with God seriously, if you haven't up to this point. Today is the day to say, "No more mediocre for me. I'm going to commit my life to excellence." Do today what you'll be glad you did ten, twenty, or thirty years from now. You do not want to stand at the end of your life grieving over the risks you didn't but should have taken.

Omit Distractions

The enemy of the best is not the worst, but the good. And there are so many good things to do. It's almost a given these days when I meet people and ask them how they're doing. They'll say, "I'm busy," or "I'm tired." Chronic overextension and weariness are not God's plan for us. Paul stated, "Don't copy the behavior and customs of this world, but be a new and different person with a fresh newness in all you do and think" (Rom. 12:2 TLB).

Wisdom is knowing what to do next; skill is knowing how to do it; virtue is doing it. The world is full of people who spend their lives doing good things that do not result in a lasting benefit or blessing. They are good only for the moment and end up being good for nothing. When good things get in the way of best things, good things must go. Since I have a full-time schedule of speaking, radio, and training events, I have to fit my commitment to writing into an already crowded agenda. To write, I have to forgo some leisure activities, hang time with buddies, and trips for fun. It's one or the other, and for me the trade-off is worth getting to write books that will go where I can't and live on when I'm long gone. There are a time and a place for play, but always after the work is done.

Never Quit

Thomas Edison perceived that, "many of life's failures are people who did not realize how close they were to success when they gave up." That's exactly what the Scriptures advise: "Let us not get tired of doing what is right, for after a while we will reap a harvest of blessing if we don't get discouraged and give up" (Gal. 6:9 TLB).

Longfellow could take a worthless piece of paper, write a poem on it, and instantly make it worth thousands of dollars—and it's called genius. Rockefeller could sign his name to a piece of paper and make it worth millions of dollars—and it's called riches. A mechanic can take material worth only five dollars and make it worth five hundred—and it's called skill. An artist can take a fifty-cent piece of canvas, paint a picture on it, and make it worth thousands of dollars—and it's called art.

Jesus Christ can take a broken, battered, and bruised life, and redeem it, restore it, and raise it up to think great thoughts and accomplish great things. The Lord is in the business of taking rough, raw material and using it to dream through, to love through, and to change the world through. Are you one of the people who gladly surrenders your love to God's agenda? Or are you one among the herd holding out for a better place, a better time, and a better God?

For many days a farmer had been plowing with an ox and a mule together and working them pretty hard. The ox said to the mule, "Let's play sick today and rest a little while." But the old mule said, "No, we need to get the work done, for the season is short." But the ox played sick, and the farmer brought him fresh hay and corn and made him comfortable. When the mule came in from plowing, the ox asked how he made out. "We didn't get as much done, but we made it all right," answered the mule. Then the ox asked, "What did the man say about me?" "Nothing," said the mule. The next day the ox, thinking he had a good thing going, played sick again. When the mule came in again very tired, the ox asked, "How did it go?" The mule said, "All right, I guess, but we didn't get much done." Then the ox asked, "What did the man say about me?" "Nothing to me" was the reply, "but he did stop and have a long talk with the butcher."

Thank God, you are not a mule or an ox. God made you more than a beast to bear someone else's burden. You are a person with great potential, God will take that very potential and turn it into big, audacious ideas that help, heal, and honor God and people. Refuse to accept mediocre, and aspire to be the best you can possibly be. Ask God for great ideas and the courage to act on them. Now that you have a noble cause (motivated by love whose mission is freedom) and great ideas in which you can invest your life, let's focus on the one missing ingredient. You're going to need some great people on your team.

9

I Will Ask for Help

*To be capable of steady friendship or lasting love, are the two greatest
proofs, not only of goodness of heart, but of strength of mind.*
—WILLIAM HAZLITT

It was a dream come true for thirteen-year-old Natalie Gilbert
when she was chosen to sing the national anthem at a na-
tionally televised NBA Western Conference play-off game.
Natalie stood alone at midcourt that Friday evening on April 25,
2003, in Portland's Rose Garden Arena, ready to perform before
a sellout crowd. But as she began to belt out the familiar lyrics,
she forgot the words. Closing her eyes and shaking her head, she
appeared in the grip of panic and on the verge of tears. Who
would dare help break the stalemate that Natalie faced between
singing and sobbing? She needed rescuing—and soon.

Maurice Cheeks, the head coach of the Trail Blazers, left his
team and walked out to stand with Natalie. He put his arm
around her and began singing with her. "I didn't even know if I
knew all the words, but as many times as I've heard the national
anthem, I just went over and continued to sing," Cheeks told *CBS
SportsLine.* "The words started coming back to me and I just tried
to help her out."

As Cheeks whispered the lyrics to Natalie, he moved his arm
as if leading a 20,000-voice choir in a patriotic sing-along. By the
time Natalie sang "and the home of the brave," every player, every
coach, and all the fans in the arena were singing. What started out

as a humiliation for a young teenaged singer turned into a magic moment with a little help from her newfound friends. The people in that room placed themselves in Natalie's shoes. They helped her do what she could not have done alone.

The next morning Natalie and Coach Cheeks were on the major TV networks. On ABC's *Good Morning America,* Charlie Gibson said, "Natalie, I heard you say that potentially it was the worst night of your life." Natalie replied, "It started out that way, but after everybody started singing with me and Coach was helping me out, it turned out to be one of the greatest moments of my life." Diane Sawyer asked, "I heard that you've been asked back to sing the national anthem again; are you going to do it?" Natalie said, "Oh, yes, without a doubt; I wouldn't miss it."

Natalie Gilbert's dilemma is yours and mine. We are out on life's stage, and everyone is waiting to hear how we sound. Everyone is watching to judge what we bring to the table. We open our mouths, forget the words, and we're stuck. Will anyone come to our aid? Who will come alongside us and turn what could be the worst nights of our lives into the greatest moments of our lives? If you are going to excel where you are with what you have, you're going to need more than a little help from your friends.

You were created for relationships. Solomon described it this way:

> Two are better than one,
>   because they have a good return for their work:
> If one falls down, his friend can help him up.
> But pity the man who falls
>   and has no one to help him up! (Eccles. 4:9–10 NIV)

But one of the most difficult challenges you'll ever face is establishing and maintaining friendship and intimacy with other people. People are as messy as they are necessary.

An old German proverb says, "When a dove begins to associate with crows, its feathers remain white but its heart grows

black." The Bible warns, "Do not be misled: 'Bad company cor-
rupts good character' " (1 Cor. 15:33 NIV). Show me your friends
and I will show you your future. Then show me your willingness
to ask for their help, and I can predict the impact of that future,
for "none of us lives to himself alone and none of us dies to himself alone" (Rom. 14:7 NIV).

Thoreau described modern-city life as "millions of people
being lonesome together." Even in these postmodern days of
"whateverism," the top five emotional hurts remain: emptiness,
fear, worry, aimlessness, and loneliness (number one on annual
lists). God's statement, "It is not good for the man to be alone"
(Gen. 2:18 NIV), is a timeless and timely truth. We are card-
carrying members of a nation of strangers. Author Louise
Bernikow calls loneliness "an American epidemic." AT&T urges
us to "reach out and touch someone." The television, computer,
and bank teller machine eliminate the need for personal contact;
cell phones, e-mails, and instant messaging have given us access,
but they can't cut down the distance between us.

As a cure for loneliness, we try to replace meaningful relationships with more work (a demanding distraction), more TV
(the perfect electronic sedative), faster computers (the proverbial
endless road), louder music (a way to keep the brain engaged at
all times), mystery novels (the retreat from reality into a fantasy
world), surface companionship (noncommittal relationships based
on convenience), and playing at pleasurable distractions.

Lee Strobel wrote,

> People today will admit any problem—drugs, divorce,
> alcoholism—but there's one admission that people are loath
> to make, whether they're a star on television or someone
> who fixes televisions in a repair shop. It's just too
> embarrassing. It penetrates too deeply to the core of who
> they are. People don't want to admit that they are lonely.
> Loneliness is such a humiliating malady that it ought to
> have its own politically correct euphemism: relationally
> challenged. Or its own telethon. Anything to make it safer

to confess. Because right now it's a taboo, an affliction of losers and misfits and—to be honest—of respectable people like you and me.[1]

Loneliness is a universal sickness that leaves us to carry our secrets, sufferings, and sorrows alone. In the midst of an active social life surrounded by people, it eats away from within unless we have trusted friends to whom we can unburden ourselves. The trends in our society of individualism, isolationism, segmentation, and fragmentation make meaningful relationships much harder, but far more necessary. In his book *Bowling Alone*, Robert Putman reports that over the past twenty-five years people attending local club meetings is down 58 percent, families having dinner together is down 33 percent, and people having friends over is down 45 percent.

A young man wanted to learn how to scuba dive. He asked his instructor what he should do if he were confronted with a shark. The instructor said, "You'll have a knife with you." The student asked, "Should I use it to try and stab the shark?" The instructor said, "Don't do that! You'll only make him mad." Then with a smile he went on, "If you see a shark coming after you, take out your knife, and then cut your buddy and swim like crazy." That's the "every man for himself" attitude that our disconnectedness is breeding.

Hurt people hurt people, and there are a lot of walking wounded moving across your path and into your life. Solomon cautioned, "Do not make friends with a hot-tempered man, do not associate with one easily angered" (Prov. 22:24 NIV). Demanding, draining, and difficult people are everywhere you go. They're like parasites that find someone to suck dry, then fly away looking for another host to hang onto. You will meet a lot of needy people who expect you to do for them what they should be doing for themselves. You will run into some people who will want to dominate your attention. If their sad stories can be believed, they are the victims of gross injustice. They speak in nasal tones as they bore you with their endless excuses about why they haven't been allowed to do more with their lives. Their constant whining has a draining effect.

You will be cut to the quick by some demeaning people whose sole mission in life is to make you feel as bad about yourself as they do about themselves. Remember, everyone you meet fears something, loves something, has lost something, and has been hurt by someone at some time. The point is, even though people are difficult and relationships are messy, you still need them. You can't afford the high price of doing life alone. This life is a big, scary, unfair place where the world you're sitting on top of today can roll over on you tomorrow. Philosopher Martin Buber recognized that "the world is not comprehensible, but it is embraceable: through the embracing of one of its beings." Embrace people, but choose wisely the ones you hold on to. God commands you "to love your neighbor," but you get to choose the neighborhood. Loving people does not include letting them set the standard or agenda.

Three M People

Woodrow Wilson admitted, "I use not only all the brains I have, but all I can borrow." Befriending strong, vibrant, vital people who have brains worth borrowing is not like finding ants at a picnic. It is the nature of turkeys to flock, but eagles tend to soar above the fray of pettiness. You need three eagle-type people in your life, but you're going to have to look for them. The Scriptures teach, "Be with wise men and become wise. Be with evil men and become evil" (Prov. 13:20 TLB). You need to be with three classes of people—models, mentors, and motivators.

Models
You need models to help you look up. Models are people of personal integrity who display character, class, calling, and competence under pressure. They stand head and shoulders above the ordinary and average. By the way they live, you can see evidence

of an inner strength that is attractive and attracting. It is obvious to you that they know something you need to know, but can't learn on your own. The apostle Paul wrote, "Even though you have ten thousand guardians in Christ, you do not have many fathers, for in Christ Jesus I became your father through the gospel. Therefore I urge you to imitate me" (1 Cor. 4:15–16 NIV). Now that's either audacious arrogance or authentic confession. But Paul was saying that people need models, and he was willing to serve as one. And whether you like it or not, someone is watching you too. You are an example. The question is, What kind? You need some people in your life who have their own bar set so high that they can turn around and say, "Do what I do, say what I say, and go where I go."

Before September 11, 2001, rock stars, athletes, and corporate executives were held up as models. But the currents are shifting, even if only a little. Names such as Enron, WorldCom, and Tyco, once the gold standard of capitalism, now serve as cautionary tales of corporate greed and duplicity. Professional baseball is in the middle of a steroids scandal, which threatens to taint the reputation of names like Bonds and McGwire, not to mention the ongoing embarrassment of Pete Rose's admission to lying about gambling. Basketball is more like a brawl, where players appear in courtrooms defending their behavior as often as on the court playing their game. Someone has described hockey as a fight where a game breaks out. The scandals in our land are not just corporate related or sports rooted; they reach to politicians, religious leaders, and institutions. Every time our models fall we lose. There is no time for finger-pointing because life moves on.

The new models are firefighters and first responders. We've watched a war in the Middle East where citizen soldiers leave their homes and families to go to the other side of the world to defend us and fight for freedom.

Mentors

You need many models, but only a few mentors. Models help you look up; mentors help you reach up. These people have achieved more than you have. They have skills you need. They have great character, and they have a competency you do not possess. They have successfully turned their potential into performance. They are big people with big hearts willing to pass on what they've learned over a lifetime. I've always tried to be the smallest person in my group intellectually, emotionally, and professionally. It takes courage to ask for help, but if you surround yourself with people better than you, they will pull you up to their level.

One of the best movies I've seen about mentoring is *Finding Forrester,* starring Sean Connery. It is about a reclusive writer who, after winning the Pulitzer Prize for his first novel, locks himself inside his apartment and hides from the world. Forrester lives off the royalties generated by his classic novel. He refuses to write another book, so he uses binoculars to watch the world outside. To the kids playing ball in the playground below, he is known simply as "The Window."

On a dare, a high school student, Jamal, breaks into Forrester's apartment. He is frightened by Forrester and runs off, leaving his backpack behind. Forrester opens the pack and discovers Jamal is a budding writer. He edits several of Jamal's writing journals and later throws the backpack containing the journals out the window as Jamal passes below. These events initiate an unlikely relationship. Forrester mentors Jamal, developing him into a writer of such skill that his teachers suspect him of plagiarism. Forrester helps transform Jamal from a person with potential into a person of accomplishment.

Jamal similarly transforms Forrester. As Forrester helps Jamal progress as a writer, Jamal helps Forrester end his self-imposed exile. Because of Jamal's encouragement, Forrester has the courage to go outside alone, ride his bike again, and even travel to visit his homeland, Scotland, before he dies of cancer. Largely due to Jamal's friendship, Forrester writes a second novel just before his death.

We humbly ask mentors for permission to sit at their feet and learn. Jesus taught His disciples, "When you are invited, take the lowest place, so that when your host comes, he will say to you, 'Friend, move up to a better place.' Then you will be honored in the presence of all your fellow guests. For everyone who exalts himself will be humbled, and he who humbles himself will be exalted" (Luke 14:10–11 NIV). Jesus highlighted the virtue of humility. He emphasized the importance of a teachable spirit. Mentors are lifelong learners, and lifelong learners are worthy mentors.

Motivators

I was leaving a restaurant the other day as a young girl came in wearing a T-shirt emblazoned with "Don't know, don't care." I thought, *How sad to be that young and that done.* But she serves as a warning to you and me that we need not only models and mentors, but also people in our lives who can help stave off apathy. You need motivators in your life to help you fend off the human virus of moral lethargy. Motivators personify the proverb, "As iron sharpens iron, so one man sharpens another" (Prov. 27:17 NIV).

The history books are full of stories of gifted persons whose talents were overlooked by a procession of people until someone believed in them. Einstein was four years old before he could speak and seven before he could read. Isaac Newton did poorly in grade school. A newspaper editor fired Walt Disney because he had "no good ideas." Leo Tolstoy flunked out of college, and Wernher von Braun failed ninth grade algebra. Haydn gave up ever making a musician of Beethoven, who seemed a slow and plodding young man with no apparent talent—except a belief in music. Thank God, someone saw something in these people and had courage enough to believe in them and draw out what might have remained dormant forever. That's a scary thought.

On May 24, 1965, a thirteen-and-a-half-foot boat slipped out of the marina at Falmouth, Massachusetts. Its destination? England. It would be the smallest craft ever to make the voyage. Its name? *Tinkerbelle.* Its pilot? Robert Manry, a copy editor for the

Cleveland Plain Dealer, who felt ten years sitting at his desk were enough boredom, so he took a leave of absence to fulfill a dream. Manry was afraid not of the ocean, but of the people who would try to talk him out of the trip. He didn't share it with many, just a few relatives and his wife, Virginia, who was a true believer.

He spent sleepless nights trying to cross shipping lanes without getting run over and sunk. Weeks at sea caused his food to become tasteless, and loneliness, that age-old monster of the deep, led to terrifying hallucinations. His rudder broke three times. Storms swept him overboard, and had it not been for the rope he had knotted around his waist, he would have been lost. Finally, after seventy-eight days alone at sea, he sailed into Falmouth, England.

During those nights at the tiller, he fantasized about what he would do once he arrived. He expected to check into a hotel, eat dinner alone, then see if the Associated Press might be interested in his story. Was he in for a surprise! Word of his approach had spread far and wide. To his amazement, three hundred vessels with horns blasting escorted *Tinkerbelle* into port. Forty thousand people stood screaming and cheering him to shore. Robert Manry, copy editor turned dreamer, became an overnight hero.

His story has been told around the world. But Robert couldn't have done it alone. Standing on the dock was an even greater hero—his wife, Virginia. Refusing to be rigid when Robert's dream was taking shape, she allowed him freedom to pursue his dream. She was his motivator. Without Virginia's belief in Robert there would be no story to tell.

Who are the people who believe in you? And don't cop out on this one by saying, "Well, God believes in me." Sometimes we need someone with skin on to incarnate the truth to us. Finding motivators takes time, but the very best way to ensure you will have motivators is to be a motivator to someone else. The better question might be, Who are the people you are stepping onto the court with? As Coach Cheeks did with Natalie, who are you locking arms with to help make beautiful music with their lives?

The Fundamentals of Friendship

Karen Weihs of George Washington University Medical Center in Washington, D.C., reported in 2001 new evidence that cancer survival is linked to family and friends. Her study of ninety patients with breast cancer showed that the size of a woman's circle of friends and extended family affected survival as much as the severity of her disease at diagnosis. She discovered that a network of supportive persons cut the risk of recurrence and death by fully 60 percent over seven years.

No one who dreams of living well dares to stand alone for long. Trees grow in forests, grass grows in fields and great people develop great friendships. Lewis had Clark, Laurel had Hardy, the Lone Ranger had Tonto, Marshal Dillon had Chester, Tom had Jerry, Fred had Barney, and Batman had Robin. Think of the remarkable friendships in the Bible: Moses had Aaron, David had Jonathan, Paul had Barnabas, and Jesus had His disciples. The Scriptures advise, "A righteous man is cautious in friendship" (Prov. 12:26 NIV). But that does not mean that he forgoes them. It just means he knows the qualities he's looking for in the people he asks into his life.

Likability

The first fundamental of friendship is likability. It's hard to be friends with a person you don't like. I've tried to convince couples planning on marriage of the importance of the likability factor. Love is necessary, but like is essential. As strange as it may sound, like can turn into love, but love seldom turns into like. From these couples, I have heard a thousand times, "I love him, but I don't like him."

Why do you like some people over others? Consider a tuning fork. Strike a tuning fork and it will begin to vibrate at a certain pitch. Bring another tuning fork beside it, and it will vibrate in harmony with the struck tuning fork. This effect is called harmonic resonance. This is how likability works. Theologian Elton

Trueblood spoke about this subject: "What is most rewarding is doing something that really matters with congenial colleagues who share with us the firm conviction it needs to be done."

Likability in friendship is a synonym for compatibility. We gravitate toward the people who have the same values and visions. This doesn't mean we have to agree on everything or even see eye to eye on all things. My best friend is my wife, Paula. Other than our core convictions and passion for authentic faith, we are very different. Our personalities are different; she's an extrovert, and I'm an introvert. Our energy levels are different. She functions very well on one hour of sleep while I need eight hours or more if I can get them. Many things about us are opposite, but we do indeed attract. I love her, but I also like her. I respect her, and maybe that's the key to likability. Find someone you admire and respect, form a friendship, and never let it go.

People with likability wear a facial expression that says, "Hello, I'm energetic, I'm fully engaged in the art of living, and I'm open for business." They don't send signals telegraphing, "I'm hacked off at the world and you better not ask what's wrong with me because I'm just looking for somebody to go off on." Likable people do not wear their problems on their sleeves or walk around with a chip on their shoulders.

You won't be friends with someone you don't like, which is not the same thing as saying you need to be alike to attract. You don't need the same temperaments and personalities to like a person. I don't even think it's important to like all the same things. If you think about it, if you were the same and liked all the same things, one of you would be unnecessary. Likability means you share the same values, and you admire the same virtues. You see some or all of both in the other person, but there's enough tension in the relationship to make it interesting and enough harmony to make it sing.

Confidentiality

I came across this description of friendship not long ago: "If you can refrain from complaining when you are ignored, if you can eat the same food every day and be grateful, if you can forgive those who take their frustrations out on you, if you have absolutely no prejudice against color, creed, politics, or religion, if you can forgive every time you're hurt, and if you can keep every secret no matter what, then you will be almost as good a friend as your dog." Who doesn't dare hope that these qualities can be found in a few close friends? I don't care how much you love your pet; it's not enough to talk to your dog. You were made for loving, long-term relationships with other living human beings with the capacity for true communion, human compassion, and the ability to speak. You long to clean out the closets of your soul by offloading your stuff to a trusted friend who is capable of keeping his mind open and his mouth shut. Hold onto the friend who uses his words as carefully as a surgeon with a scalpel; they are rare.

Taking another person into your confidence is risky business. The Bible cautions, "A gossip betrays a confidence, but a trustworthy man keeps a secret" (Prov. 11:13 NIV). If you have shared a deep secret with someone in the past, it's more than a little likely that you've been burned. Some people just can't be trusted with confidential material. That's why employers require employees to sign a confidentiality agreement. But that doesn't do away with the need to have friends in your life to whom you can say anything and not have to worry about whether they are going to run for the door or the telephone at the end of the conversation.

We are told to confess our sins to each other so that we may be healed (James 5:16). Confession is an act of healing not only with man to God, but also with man to man. It is therapeutic to sit across from another person you trust and say, "This is what I struggled with. This is what I've done, or this is what I'm feeling," without fear it will go any farther. You need someone who will hear it, receive it, and accept it without judgment and sometimes without comment. Sometimes all we need to get by is a sympathetic ear, an emphatic nod, and a closed mouth.

Loyalty

Some phrases you need to hear audibly to understand intelligently. One of those is the four-word statement: "I am with you." If you say, "I'm with *you?*" with the emphasis on the last word *you* and said as a question, it's negative. If you place the emphasis on the third word, *with,* then you are saying that not only am I with you in proximity, but I pledge my loyalty to you in principle. It's all in where you place the emphasis, isn't it? The same is true with loyal friends.

Loyalty in friendship is not denying a friend's weaknesses or shortcomings, but it is refusing to place the emphasis there. I agree with this proverb: "Treat your friends as you do your pictures, and place them in their best light." That's the kind of friends we need because we all know there is enough weirdness in each of us to render us unlovable.

Solomon clearly stated, "A friend loves at all times" (Prov. 17:17 NIV). I define *loyalty* as a commitment between two people never to say or receive anything negative about the other person until it is first said to that person. The commitment to say nothing negative is your assurance, "I've got your back." You can relax, knowing I will be positive. The commitment to receive nothing negative is your assurance that I will not allow other people to say negative things about you in my presence, and if they do, I'll make sure they come straight to you. Loyalty is not passive. It defends and protects the one it loves.

I had a buddy, who I thought was a loyal friend, come to me and say, "I need you to forgive me for all the negative things I've said about you." At first I was taken aback, but I countered, "Are you serious about seeking my forgiveness?" He said, "Yes, very much so. I feel so bad about what I've done, and I need to know you forgive me." I said, "Then go and ask the forgiveness of each person you've hurt by hurting me and then come back and we'll talk about forgiveness." I've never seen him or heard from him again. You see, he took our friendship lightly. He thought he could use the easy way to make right what he had done wrong.

Never betray loyalty because a few careless words can cause a world of hurt and kill a friendship.

Honesty

Honesty is not saying everything you think or feel at the moment you think or feel it. American psychologist and philosopher William James explained, "The art of being wise is the art of knowing what to overlook." Applying that principle to friendship means knowing what to say and when to say it. Truth can be a dangerous thing if not handled with care. You are taught in the Scriptures to speak the truth in love. That's why you cannot speak truth into a person's life overnight. Many have tried to fast-track friendship, but it only tends to alienate. You can speak truth into my life over time because it takes time to build trust.

It took me only two or three miscues to realize my wife wasn't interested in my fashion sense when she asked me how she looked in her dress. She wanted affirmation, not information.

The role of honesty in friendship is to build each other up, not rip each other apart. It is not an excuse for venting your frustrations or clearing your conscience. Some people use honesty as an excuse for being rude and crude. I've learned to duck when someone says, "I just call 'em as I see 'em." Or my all-time favorite is, "I'm only saying this because I love you, but . . ." This is almost always followed up by the verbal equivalent of a whack upside the head with an aluminum baseball bat.

The purpose of honesty is to promote trust: "Wounds from a friend can be trusted, but an enemy multiplies kisses" (Prov. 27:6 NIV). You need this type of friend most when you are confronted with a defining moment or a life-changing decision.

When I was dreaming of starting a church targeted to people who didn't want to go to church, I was plenty scared. Not only was the idea on the cutting edge at the time, but I wasn't at all sure I had the right stuff for the job. For wise counsel I turned to a trusted confidant. Butch and I couldn't have been more unalike. He was a right-brained engineer who likes everything in its place and a place for everything. But he was a loyal friend whose opinion I had learned to trust. I let Butch in on my dream, and then I asked, "Butch, can I do this? Be honest." He said without hesitation, "You can do it. If anybody can do it, you can do it. As a matter of fact, the more I think about it, you were made for this." Because I trusted him to be honest with me, I was able to trust that he was being honest with me. I followed his counsel and took the risk, and my life was changed forever for the better because of it.

Mercy

Aristotle observed that, "no one loves the man whom he fears." That is certainly true when applied to friendship. That's why one of the fundamentals of friendship is mercy. Mercy takes away the fear of judgment and replaces it with the force of grace. How many times did I get in deeper trouble as a kid because I was afraid of humiliation and rejection? Who wants to drag around a load of guilt and shame? But I'll bear it all and hide it all until I find a safe place to dump it all. Mercy understands. Mercy weeps. Mercy embraces and endures.

Friends who are strong enough to extend mercy are rare, but they are the people whose influence you are always open to because they love you most when you deserve it least. I don't know about you, but I can wake up in the morning with a reeking case of the "stupids" that can last all day, so an easily offended friend isn't going to help me very much. Think about it. No one gets up saying, "I'm going out today and see just how big a ditch I can drive my life into." No, it's when I do dumb things, which is on a fairly regular basis, that I need a friend who can look past my faults and see my need.

Before you get the idea that mercy is soft on sin, think again. The Bible stresses that "if someone is caught in a sin, you who are spiritual should restore him gently" (Gal. 6:1 NIV). A good friend of mine invited me to a major recording session he was conducting with a string section. There were thirty to thirty-five people on the sound stage with violins, violas, stand-up bass, and other stringed instruments I did not recognize. They played through the piece once, then stopped abruptly. I never heard so much whining and moaning in all my life. One said, "My seat's too high." Another said, "My headset hurts my ears." On the other side some said, "It's too loud in my ears," "It's cold," or "It's too hot over here." I was thinking, *I know kids who don't behave this badly in kindergarten.* Knowing artists have a reputation for being temperamental, I was anxious to see if my buddy was going to read the riot act to this group of gifted, high-priced whiners.

I watched my friend orchestrate these gifted egos back in focus and on task. He did it by listening to the complaints without judgment, recognizing what was legitimate and what was not. He changed what he could and negotiated what he couldn't. He was patient and empathetic, yet firm and focused. Like a rider on a horse, he held the reins, but not too tightly. Oh, to be that way, to be able to go into an environment where your presence simply exudes grace and mercy.

Good people do really dumb things, left to their own devices. You probably have, too. That's why you need someone who knows when to cut you some slack.

You're not going to make me better by condemning me. Call me a sinner, and I'll try not to disappoint you. Tell me I'm a jerk, and I'll be a jerk. Show me mercy, and redemption is at hand. Call me higher with grace and mercy, and I'll kill myself getting up there.

Mercy is shown in the words we use. The Bible reminds us that, "he who loves a pure heart and whose speech is gracious will have the king for his friend" (Prov. 22:11 NIV).

God specializes in redeeming and restoring people who are messed up beyond recognition. And I've seen their lives come out so splendidly, so beautifully. This is how God treats those who come to Him in faith, and this is how we show our friends we know God.

Tenacity

Every fundamental of friendship (likability, confidentiality, loyalty, honesty, and mercy) hinges on the tenacity of friendship. A true friend will not give up on you. In the movie *Runaway Bride* with Richard Gere and Julia Roberts, you learn something important about women: they want to be pursued. Who knew? There's no manual for this. There's no pamphlet. There's no Web address. Women want to be pursued. And you know what? In our way, we men do too. Some of the greatest friendships in my life have been with people who have hunted me down and have said, "No, you will not ignore me. No, we're going to make this right." Not giving up. Not walking away. We need to be loved most when we deserve it least.

This was illustrated well in an article I read about two friends in Southern California. Anne Hjelle and Debbi Nicholls were friends who were mountain biking on a wilderness trail near Mission Viejo, California, when a 110-pound mountain lion sprang from the brush, pounced on Anne's back, and dragged her off by the head. Nicholls screamed for help and grabbed Hjelle's legs, trying to free her and engaging in a desperate tug-of-war with the cat, while other cyclists threw rocks at the cat until it fled.

Jacke Van Woerkom, who was riding behind Hjelle and Nicholls, later spoke to Nicholls at the hospital.

> "She had some blood on her face. She definitely showed signs of a major struggle," Van Woerkom said. "She was shaking, trembling. She said, 'I was not going to let go. I was not going to let go.'" [Nicholls] described the tenacity of the cat, saying, "This guy [the cat] would not let go. He had a hold of her face. . . ." But the tenacity of the cat was overcome by the faithfulness of a friend. She continued, "I just told her, 'I'm never letting go.'"[2]

Debbi Nicholls gives new meaning to the verse, "A friend loves at all times, and a brother is born for adversity" (Prov. 17:17 NIV).

The Ultimate Friend

The truth is that friends, even the best ones, will fail you eventually. And for that harsh reality God gives this promise: "A man of many companions may come to ruin, but there is a friend who sticks closer than a brother" (Prov. 18:24 NIV).

Speaking to His disciples, Jesus said,

> Greater love has no one than this, that he lay down his life for his friends. You are my friends if you do what I command. I no longer call you servants, because a servant does not know his master's business. Instead, I have called you friends, for everything that I learned from my Father I have made known to you. You did not choose me, but I chose you and appointed you to go and bear fruit—fruit that will last. (John 15:13–16 NIV)

This is revealing stuff. How radical to think that God calls me His "friend"! What kind of friendship is that? In my case it has been fairly one-sided. I'm not happy with that arrangement, and there are times I feel the yoke and light burden of Jesus' presence, but mainly my friendship with God has been characterized by my calls for help. For years I felt bad about that. I thought God wanted me to grow stronger so I wouldn't need to cry out for help so much. Boy, was that dumb! I realize it's the very opposite of what He seeks. Maturity is not measured by the infrequency of my cry for help from God. It is measured by the time between my recognition of my helplessness and my request for help. The closer together these two things are, the greater the maturity and the sweeter the intimacy.

Ask God for help. He will not delay or disappoint. Don't wait. Don't try to fix it on your own. He's not too busy. He is motivated, but He wants to be invited. Call on Him, and let your experience be the same as that of David, who said, "You give me your shield of victory, and your right hand sustains me; you stoop down to make me great" (Ps. 18:35 NIV).

Doing your best will be messy at times and aggravating at others, but there is no other way to live and be happy. Without models, mentors, and motivators around you the wheels will come off eventually. You will forget the words to the national anthem in front of a waiting world or the equivalent thereof. The One who stands with you then will be the One you choose to stand with now. No one excels in life alone.

Commitment #4

EXCELLING WHILE I CAN

*Whether these are the worst
of times or the best of
times, they are the
only times
we have.*

—Art Buchwald

10

I Will Treat Time as Life

*Time is the coin of your life. It is the only coin you have, and only you
can determine how it will be spent. Be careful lest you let
other people spend it for you.*
—CARL SANDBURG

When the call came to speak in south Florida for a week during February, it wasn't hard to say yes. It would be a great time to escape the last bitter cold days of winter. It would also give me time to finish the manuscript of this book since the deadline was upon me. After a teaching session held at a posh country club, I struck up a conversation with a local pastor. He had lived in southwest Florida for more than twenty-five years. I asked him to describe the town where he lived and worked. I was intrigued because it had become a favorite destination for almost every age group looking for surf and sun. He thought a second and said, "We are the place where the young people come to play and the old people come to die." There was sadness in his voice, which sounded more like resignation than bragging.

That statement struck me as an accurate assessment of the attitudes of a lot of people. A growing number of people in our affluent culture value their treasures more than their time. This attitude is spreading like a virus across our social landscape. But can any of us afford such a shortsighted philosophy in light of the emptiness and darkness that seem to be descending on our tiny planet? Writer, theorist Erich Fromm noted, "We are a society of notoriously unhappy people—people who are glad when we have killed the time we are trying so hard to save." But is that all my time is worth? Am I just another nameless, faceless consumer who helps form a demographic so companies can target-market me? Can playing and puttering around to forget you're waiting to die give life either meaning or dignity? No, life is too precious to waste prowling around outlet malls hunting for the newest velvet Elvis or the next "all you can eat" buffet.

Life, at its longest, is short. But as brief as it is, God promises,

> There is a right time for everything:
> A time to be born;
> A time to die;
> A time to plant;
> A time to harvest;
> A time to kill;
> A time to heal;
> A time to destroy;
> A time to rebuild;
> A time to cry;
> A time to laugh;
> A time to grieve;
> A time to dance. (Eccles. 3:1–4 TLB)

I have stood at the bedsides of hundreds of people during their last hours, and all wanted more time at the end. But you get only one life, and if you are smart, one's enough.

Time is a strange thing. We say it's precious. We talk about making the most of it. We claim there is never enough of it, and we wish we had more of it. We personify it by saying, "It flies, it crawls, it's on our side, or it's against us." We equate it with money. We experience the best of it and the worst of it. We quantify events and relationships with it. We consume books, tapes, and seminars that teach us how to manage it. We buy expensive gadgets that promise to help us better organize it. Around the world and throughout the ages, we have developed a million different ways to measure it. And then we turn around and use time to measure our lives. On just about every tombstone, you can determine the number of years a person lived by subtracting the birthday from the death date. But is that the best measurement of a life? The length of a life says little about the impact of that life or the legacy it leaves behind.

Excellence in life is not about outrunning competition, but about outlasting the clutter accumulating as we live. Because you have lived so long and have gotten up after so many good nights' rest, it's easy to be lured into a false sense of immortality. Consider the wisdom contained in these lines:

> Just a tiny little minute only sixty seconds in it
> Forced upon me. Can't refuse it.
> Didn't seek it, didn't choose it,
> I must suffer if I lose it,
> Give account if I abuse it.
> Just a tiny little minute,
> but eternity is in it.

When I was young, with what I thought was time to burn, I was passionate about getting ahead and proving myself. I found it hard to be compassionate and too easy to be ruthless with people who dared impede my progress. After all, I was in a hurry, and I was obsessed with getting to the place called success. As I've lived, I've learned four lessons that only time and experience could have taught. I've learned I should be passionate about God, compassionate with people, patient with myself, and ruthless with my time. This is the divine order of things, which brings my life into alignment. But I have to make these distinctions every day to fight off the friction of a life out of alignment.

The time I spend stoking my passion for God is an investment. It is doing today in time what I'll gladly do for all eternity: loving the Lord my God with all my heart and with all my soul and with all my strength and with all my mind (Luke 10:27). This is what we were made for. God created us relational beings. He didn't want robots, and He didn't need more angels. In His essence He is a relational God. Just after He created the animals and before He created man, God said, "Let us make man in our image" (Gen. 1:26 NIV). Theologians call this "let us" the divine plural.

God was not alone before the creation of human beings. He has always existed in community. We call this relationship the Trinity. God reveals Himself in three distinct persons. He is God the Father, God the Son, and God the Spirit. He is one in essence and nature, existing as three persons. In this we see a unity in diversity living in loving community.

Loving God leads me into community with God the Father, God the Son, and God the Spirit. It also prepares me for community with other imperfect people who, just like me, long to be loved. A passion for God that doesn't make me compassionate with people falls short because the evidence of my love for God is my love for people. Loving God results in loving "your neighbor as yourself" (Luke 10:27 NIV).

The reason we don't love our neighbors is that we don't love ourselves. We don't love ourselves because we don't really understand how much we are already loved. Loving God is easy most of the time and hard some of the time. Being compassionate with people is easy some of the time and hard most of the time. But being patient with myself isn't easy any of the time, and it's hard most of the time. As a matter of fact, I wonder at times if I might not be the most screwed up guy God ever made. I find comfort in Paul's cry of frustration when he screamed, "What a wretched man I am! Who will rescue me?" (Rom. 7:24 NIV). I also find solace in the confession of King David: "O God, according to your unfailing love . . . according to your great compassion blot out my transgressions" (Ps. 51:1 NIV). And I take courage when Jesus recommissioned Peter after his bitter denial: "Feed my sheep" (John 21:17 NIV).

The real breakthrough for me came the day I realized I couldn't do the first three (be passionate about God, compassionate with people, and patient with myself) if I was unwilling to be ruthless with my time. Growing in my passion for God, living in loving relationships with people, and maintaining a strong inner life are not urgent matters. They are important; that's why you must ruthlessly take the time to do them. Activity for activity's sake is at a premium in our culture. I saw a bumper sticker the other day that read, "Christ is coming; look busy." And busy we are, spending thirty or forty of our best years getting enough stuff so we can retire. *Retirement,* for the majority it seems, is just a euphemism for "waiting to die."

I use the word *ruthless* on purpose. Time is life. If you are going to make the most of your life, you will guard your time as carefully as you do your money. You wouldn't give your ATM or credit card along with your PIN to everyone who wanted it, would you? Then why do you feel compelled to say yes to people who want to dominate or waste your time on their agenda? I heard a speaker say, "The past is history; the future is a mystery; this moment is a gift. That's why we call it the present." I resonate with that statement, but there seems to be a conspiracy afoot aimed at making me miserable in the present, fixated on the past, and dreading the future. Maybe that's why the Scriptures issue this warning: "So be careful how you act; these are difficult days. Don't be fools; be wise" (Eph. 5:15 TLB).

We're usually ruthless with people and compassionate with our time. When someone asks you, "May I have some of your time?" she is really asking for a chunk of your life. Be ruthless with time because you have a limited amount, and when it's gone, you want to look back, with no regrets, on how you spent it.

The Truth About Time

Time is a gift, a precious, one-shot, never-to-return-or-be-relived gift. Do you get up in the morning and say, "Good Lord, it's morning"? Or do you get up and say, "Good morning, Lord"? Do you rise and shine, or do you rise and whine? If you embrace time as life, then maybe you should open your eyes in the morning and shout, "This is the day the LORD has made; let us rejoice and be glad in it" (Ps. 118:24 NIV)!

Since time is life and life is a gift from God, the greatest Giver, wasting it is as black a sin as there is. I cringe when I hear people say, "I'm just killing time," or "I've got some time to waste." When is there ever enough time to kill or waste? It was Thoreau who said, "You cannot kill time without injury to eternity." Wasting time is like committing slow suicide where dreams die, love languishes, and souls shrivel.

Read this sobering statement from the half brother of Jesus: "Anyone, then, who knows the good he ought to do and doesn't do it, sins" (James 4:17 NIV). How about this bit of wisdom from Paul: "Make the most of every opportunity you have for doing good. Don't act thoughtlessly, but try to find out and do whatever the Lord wants you to" (Eph. 5:16–17 TLB)?

Wasting time worrying about things you can't control is like flushing money down a toilet. Wasting time fretting over the past diminishes what your life could be right now or at the very least what it may yet become. Wasting time regretting the sins you've already confessed shows you're not serious about being forgiven or you're not confident that God is faithful enough to forgive when asked. Wasting time worrying about the people you think are thinking about you is feeding a false sense of self-importance. Wasting time trying to get even is like drinking poison and hoping the other person gets sick. Wasting time thinking about giving somebody a piece of your mind is a childish misuse of your brainpower.

Wasting your time is wasting your life. It is a sin to waste your life worrying and fretting over stuff you can't control or may never happen. It is childish to waste another day being mad, getting angry, getting even, engaging in gossip, placing the blame, or shaming yourself. You don't have enough time to engage in trying to please everyone or throwing it away by living from one crisis to the next.

Contrary to what you've been told, you can't save time or

make time. You can invest it in something noble and needed, thereby multiplying its value. Wasting time is wasting life, and we have gotten too good at both.

I am a member of the first generation to be raised by television. Today, that has evolved to video games, the Internet, travel, sports, and a long string of good, time-consuming, mind-numbing activities. We allow other people to waste our time by letting them set our agendas. As a result, we are the most worried and anxious we've ever been. The tyranny of the urgent has made us a miserable class of people who have the money to finance a life of endless distractions and mediocre activities that can never make us happy or whole.

Life is a gift, wasting it is a sin, and not everyone has the same amount. My mother is eighty-one plus and going strong, but my dad died at sixty-seven and my brother at forty-nine. My father's death was the first time I lost someone close to me. It hit me hard with a double whammy because it was too soon and he was too young. On the one hand, he was my dad, and I didn't want to give him up. There is never a good time to say good-bye to the ones we love, but my father was at the peak of his life. He was in incredible physical condition. He didn't carry an ounce of fat on his body, he was happy, and he whistled while he worked. He was a great guy, having the best time of his life! After he died, I used to get mad when I saw other men, who looked to be about his age, walking around enjoying life. I resented other guys who had their fathers. I thought, *Why should they have their dad, but I don't have mine? It's not fair.* You know what? It isn't fair, but it's life.

To illustrate the brevity of life, Jesus told this story:

The ground of a certain rich man produced a good crop. He thought to himself, "What shall I do? I have no place to store my crops." Then he said, "This is what I'll do. I will tear down my barns and build bigger ones, and there I will store all my grain and my goods. And I'll say to myself, 'You have plenty of good things laid up for many years.

Take life easy; eat, drink and be merry.'" But God said to him, "You fool! This very night your life will be demanded from you. Then who will get what you have prepared for yourself?" This is how it will be with anyone who stores up things for himself but is not rich toward God. (Luke 12:16–21 NIV)

What's Jesus trying to tell you today? Is He saying it's wrong to work to earn to buy stuff? No, I don't think He's saying there's anything wrong with having stuff, but there is everything wrong with stuff having you! Money is a great servant, but a wretched master! The obsessive pursuit of it blinds you to the things that matter. Loving God and people shouldn't be postponed to a better time when you'll have a bigger bank account and more discretionary time. Right here, right now, is the time to do what you'll be glad you did when your time on life's stage has come to a close. I've heard people say, tongue in cheek, "I can't get sick tomorrow. My schedule's too full." I read a *Calvin and Hobbes* cartoon that said, "God put me on earth to accomplish certain things. Right now, I'm so far behind, I'll never die." I'm not sure it works that way. Life is a gift, and to waste it worrying about the future or fretting about the past hurts only you.

Imagine there is a bank that credits your account each morning with $86,400, but carries over no balance from one day to the next and allows no cash-on-hand balance. Every evening you lose whatever you failed to use that day. What would you do? Draw out and spend every cent, every day, of course! Well, you have such a bank; it's your time. Every morning God gives you 86,400 seconds. Every night you lose whatever you have failed to put to good use. It carries over no balance. It allows no overdraft. Each day it opens a new account for you. Each night it burns the records of the day before. If you fail to use the day's deposit, the loss is yours. There is no going back. There is no drawing against the tomorrow. You must live in the present on today's deposit. Invest it so that you will get from it the utmost in health, happiness, and success! The clock is running, so make the most of today by savoring the miracle and magic of this place and time. If you think about it, you can go anyplace starting from where you are right now. Will the destination be a dead end or a wide and expansive freeway? It's up to you.

When Emily Webb, in Thornton Wilder's play *Our Town*, comes back from the dead to the town of her childhood and finds her mother and father and all her long-dead acquaintances still alive and the town and its environs the same as when she was a child, she begs to go back to the grave. The sheer beauty and wonder of it all—every sight and sound, every tender grace of things, every gesture of love and devotion—are overwhelming. It is too much for her to bear, for she had never realized the miracle of her life when she was living it. That is the regrettable thing about being human, isn't it? We don't know what we've got until it's gone. We neglect our health getting wealth. Then we spend all our wealth trying to regain our health again. This is dumb, but we get smarter the second we see time as life. It is a precious gift from a loving God, and it is a big deal how we spend it.

Why can we human beings be so smart about some things and be as dumb as a stick about others? Time seems to be one of the things we don't get smart about until we're looking back in regret. For example, to realize the value of one year, ask a student who has failed his finals and has to repeat the same classes again next year. To realize the value of a single month ask a young mother who has given birth to a premature baby whose survival is touch and go. To realize the value of one week, ask the harried editor of a weekly newspaper whose deadlines are coming due at the same time. To realize the value of one day, ask a daily wage earner who has ten kids to feed and not a dime to waste. To realize the value of one hour, ask a love-struck girl who is waiting to be reunited with her beau at a train station after a long separation. To realize the value of one minute, ask the beau who missed his train on the way back to see his beloved. To realize the value of one second, ask a young woman who just missed a speeding car that ran a red light at the intersection she went through (the very thing that happened to me the day I wrote this). To realize the value of one millisec-

ond, ask the person who won a silver medal in the Olympics instead of the gold he had been training for all of his life.

Time waits for no one. It doesn't care if you're having a bad
hair day, and it doesn't have sympathy because you stayed up par-
tying the night before. It cannot hold on, slow down, back up, or
come back here. It won't obey your command to "wait a minute"
or "let me catch my breath." It is moving ahead without regard to
your plans or priorities. It isn't against you or for you. And as the
Bible says 457 times in the King James Version, time "came to
pass"; it didn't come to stay.

There is an ancient story about three demons who were
arguing over the best way to destroy the Christian mission in
the world. The first demon says, "Let's tell all the Christians
there is no heaven. Take away the reward incentive, and the
mission will collapse." The second demon says, "Let's tell all
the Christians there is no hell. Take away the fear of punishment, and the mission will collapse." The third demon says,
"There is one better way. Let's tell all the Christians there is no
hurry," and all three immediately say, "That's it! All we have to
do is tell them there's no hurry, and the whole Christian enterprise will collapse."

I've heard people say, "It's my life. I'll do anything I want to
with it. And besides, what's the hurry? I'll get the 'God thing' covered." And you know what? They're exactly right. They can do
exactly what they please, but there will be a test at the end. The
Bible states, "Man is destined to die once, and after that to face
judgment" (Heb. 9:27 NIV). You are not accountable to me, your
parents, or your family, but you are responsible to God for what
you do. That, my fellow traveler, you cannot avoid.

At first blush this may sound like bad news, but it's not bad
news to those who love Him. It's the best news you could hear.
It means you live before an audience of One. Your mama won't
be your judge. You are not even your own judge. You have one
judge, and believe it or not, He is easy to please! God is much easier than your mother-in-law or your boss. Far easier than the people you work with. He wants from you only your heart and your

trust. The Bible points to this truth: "Without faith it is impossible to please God" (Heb. 11:6 NIV).

I still grieve my father's death. I believe I'm going to see him in heaven, but I still miss him. There was a time I could reach out and touch him. Part of my grief is in knowing I didn't take the time to be with him while I could. I justified it by telling him how busy I was, and he responded by telling me how busy he was. Neither of us knew how little time we had left. If we did, no doubt we would have done things differently.

When the people you love die, you feel robbed. You're tempted to blame God and become bitter. But God has warned us that there's a time to be born and a time to die. When people close to you die, go ahead and cry out to God, "Why?" He understands and pities you. He knows better than anyone how frail and weak you are. Knowing a thing in your head and experiencing it in real life are two very different things. When you grieve most, you need to cling to His promises the most. But understand, He has already told you there is a time to be born and there is a right moment to die.

To treat time as life, remember that time is a gift, wasting it is a sin, all of us don't have the same amount, and there will be a test at the end. That having been said, how do you get ruthless with your time practically? A great place to start is to understand the difference between time management and life leadership.

Life Leadership vs. Time Management

Treating time as life is less about time management and more about life leadership. It is true that with the rise of PDAs, electronic calendars, meeting planners, and hybrid devices like the Blackberry and pocket PC/cell phone, we can manage time more efficiently. There are also seminars that teach methods aimed at helping us get more done in less time. These are good things, but they are secondary to the real issue. Time as life is about taking leadership of your life first and taking control of your time second. The first is a process; the second is a system.

Focusing on time management alone means you can fit more into your already crowded life. It turns up the treadmill speed, but it can't assure you that you're on the right one. Those who show they can manage time well are usually rewarded with more to do. After all, as the old saying goes, if you want something done, give it to a busy person.

Life leadership, in contrast, is focused on living effectively, not just efficiently. Time management is more about a linear system with checks and controls. Life leadership is more a process, which changes and grows as you do. You may be terribly efficient at doing things that don't matter, but that just gets you to the dead end more quickly. You want your life to matter (that's effectiveness) the most (that's efficiency) while you can. To manage time as life, decide what matters, determine your contribution, define your tasks, date your days, and discipline your personality.

Decide What Matters

Only you can decide what matters most to you. And when you dare to be definite about what you believe and let it inform what you do, you have taken leadership of your life. If you take this first step seriously, I say, "Congratulations!" because most people don't.

I also want to say, "Get ready." Get ready for things to change, and get ready to be challenged. The minute you take seriously the scriptural mandate, "Seek first his kingdom and his righteousness, and all these things will be given to you as well" (Matt. 6:33 NIV), expect opposition. Satan will oppose this shift because he loses his grip on your life. He will attempt to distract and discourage all those who dare to make seeking the kingdom of God on earth a core value and a top priority.

The kingdom of God, simply put, is the rule and reign of Jesus Christ (God the Son) on the earth. It is a kingdom where the motivation is love and the mission is freedom. The Commander of this righteous army is the One who

> is the image of the invisible God, the firstborn over all creation. For by him all things were created: things in

heaven and on earth, visible and invisible, whether thrones or powers or rulers or authorities; all things were created by him and for him. He is before all things, and in him all things hold together. And he is the head of the body, the church; he is the beginning and the firstborn from among the dead, so that in everything he might have the supremacy. (Col. 1:15–18 NIV)

Declaring your allegiance to Jesus is deciding that His agenda is your marching order. What matters to Him matters to you. Jesus was crystal clear about His motivation and mission: "The Son of Man came to seek and to save what was lost" (Luke 19:10 NIV). The bottom line here is, love matters more than loot, people matter more than power, and grace matters more than greed.

Determine Your Contribution

Once you decide what matters, you can think about what your contribution will be. In Chapter 4, I identified the four levels of living: survival, security, success, and significance. The first three levels are concerned with what you get, but the fourth is about what you give. What will you contribute to the advancement of God's kingdom while you're here? Think about what you want to be remembered for. Are you investing your time, talents, and treasure in ways that help other people?

Make an assessment of where you are in relation to what you believe matters most. Then decide where you want to be in the future. To do that requires you to put down on paper what you believe your calling in life to be. Look at the jobs you've had, add up the successes, weigh in the failures, and factor in the affirmations that others have made about your abilities. What are you good at? What gifts, talents, and skills have you developed over the years of your working life? There's a pattern beginning to show, and if you step back and look, you'll see hints of your contribution already surfacing. Factor these into whatever makes you come alive with energy and great joy, and start putting pen to paper. Write and rewrite. Arrange and rearrange. Take some things off; then add some. Do this until you have a clear and compelling vision and mission statement.

Define Your Tasks

Once you've decided what matters and determined what your contribution should be, define what tasks you need to be doing. After you've done this, your life will take on an alignment that cuts down on friction and sharpens your focus. Doing what you were made to do with the time you have is treating time as life. It's a good thing because as Solomon said, "Reverence for God adds hours to each day; so how can the wicked expect a long, good life?" (Prov. 10:27 TLB).

Maybe the greatest benefit of identifying what you do is to clear off your list all the things you don't do. When you decide what matters, you can check off a whole world of things that don't matter, and you never have to feel guilty about not doing them. When you're clear about the contribution you want your life to make and the legacy you want to leave, you're narrowing the focus of your life from a spotlight to a laser.

Date Your Days

The first three steps find their everyday expression when you date your days. It is true that "what gets dated gets done." When you attach a date to a task that is meaningful to you, good things happen.

Excellence isn't possible in the abstract. It must be made concrete, and that's what having the courage to plan your life and work your plan does. Excelling while I can means doing today's work today. A good friend gave me this piece of advice, "Find out what only you can do in your organization or family, then do only that and let everything else just float by."

Discipline Your Personality

Paul, the great missionary and world-changer, asserted, "I do not run like a man running aimlessly; I do not fight like a man beating the air. No, I beat my body and make it my slave so that after

I have preached to others, I myself will not be disqualified for the prize" (1 Cor. 9:26–27 NIV). He's telling us to take charge of our lives. You do this by training your mind, will, and emotions during the minutes of calm so that you can perform and endure in the moments of stress. Much as a world-class athlete does, do the important work in private so you can do the best work in public.

The important things in life have no lights, no sirens, to let us know they're being neglected. They wait. The difference between the urgent and the important is that important things will wait. Your kids will wait. Right? Your spouse will wait. Your health will wait. I mean, you feel pretty good right now, don't you? You'll take care of yourself later, won't you? You can for a while. We justify postponing the important by assuring ourselves, and those around us, that it's only temporary. Right now it's urgent that I pour my life into chasing the brass ring of success, but it's only temporary. I'm in a period where I'm neglecting my family, my health, my friends, and even my faith, but it's only for a little while. When I get through this intense period of urgent things, I'm going to bring balance back into my spiritual life and my family. After all, I'm doing this for my children. I want to buy my wife and kids what I never had. I've seen so many men and women live the lie of urgent things to the destruction of the important things. Wake up, my friend, and realize your family would rather have your presence than your presents.

Being ruthless with your time means you're not going to let other people tell you how to spend it. You take leadership of your life. You have decided what matters, and you have determined what your contribution is going to be. You've defined your tasks, dated your days, and disciplined your personality.

Today Is "Someday"

Theodore Roosevelt said, "Nine-tenths of wisdom consists in being wise in time." I agree, but I also admit the temptation to put off until tomorrow what I don't absolutely have to do today is as strong on me as the gravitational pull of the earth is on a ten-ton boulder. This propensity to put off until tomorrow what I should be doing today, right here, right now, is expressed in what is maybe the most dangerous word in all the English language—*someday.*

How many times have I said that word as a justification to waste time—therefore, life? Someday I'll be the father I've always intended to be. Someday I'll quit complaining and learn to be grateful. Someday I'll get in shape. Someday I'll slow down and start enjoying my children and grandchildren. Someday I'll get really serious about prayer. Someday I'll study the Bible seriously. Someday I'm going to get organized. Someday I'll take more risks. Someday I'll be more generous. Someday I'm going to learn how to play a musical instrument.

You can waste your whole life waiting for someday: someday when I graduate, someday when I get a job, someday when I get married, someday when we have kids, someday when the kids move away, someday when I retire. Someday I'll stop waiting and start living.

Today is someday. Today is the day "to present yourself to God as one approved, a workman who does not need to be ashamed" (2 Tim. 2:15 NIV). Don't surrender your brain. Think! Study! Today is the time to ask God, "Show me, O LORD, my life's end and the number of my days; let me know how fleeting is my life" (Ps. 39:4 NIV). God gives you a sense of urgency to count each day as though it could be your last.

Today is the day to begin trusting God for great things. Today is the day to take seriously God's promise of provision and protection. Every time I read Eugene Peterson's paraphrase of Jesus' invitation to trust God's love for me, I want to shout, "Yea, God!"

Has anyone by fussing in front of the mirror ever gotten taller by so much as an inch? All this time and money wasted on fashion—do you think it makes that much difference? Instead of looking at the fashions, walk out into the fields and look at the wildflowers. They never primp or shop, but have you seen color and design quite like it? The ten best-dressed men and women in the country look shabby alongside them. If God gives such attention to the appearance of wildflowers—most of which are never even seen—don't you think he will attend to you, take pride in you, do his best for you? What I'm trying to do here is to get you to relax, to not be so preoccupied with *getting*, so you can respond to God's *giving*. People who don't know God and the way he works fuss over these things, but you know both God and how he works. Steep your life in God-reality, God-initiative, God-provisions. Don't worry about missing out. You'll find all your everyday human concerns will be met. (Matt. 6:27–33 THE MESSAGE)

Today is a teachable moment. What is God saying to you as you read this book? What divine opportunity has He planned in the people you're meeting and the places you're going? You are not a human being in search of a spiritual experience. You are a spiritual being having a human experience.

Recharge

As you journey through this life, take the time to rest and recharge your spiritual and emotional batteries. Jesus said, "Come to me and I will give you rest—all of you who work so hard beneath a heavy yoke. Wear my yoke—for it fits perfectly" (Matt. 11:28–29 TLB). The yoke was made so the wiser and stronger ox would bear the greatest weight. It was fitted so oxen could work all day without its chafing and rubbing their skin raw. The younger ox could carry some of the burden, but just enough to learn and grow and mature. What a beautiful metaphor Jesus used! Jesus said, "I'll bear the burden, and here's what I want you to do. Just get in the yoke with Me and I will give you rest, and our time together will recharge your life."

I've heard people say, "I'm afraid to take this 'Jesus as my Lord and Savior' thing too seriously for fear of what might happen if I do." My response is, "Don't you think God can do at least as good as you've done? Do you think He could do any worse than you've done?" You need time to recharge your spiritual, emotional, and physical batteries. This is God's will for you. You say, "I want to be a hard-charging, get-it-done, storm-the-gates-of-hell-with-a-water-gun-type person."

How about the example of Elijah? He was a storm-the-gates kind of guy. But this amazing man needed rest. Listen to this: "All at once an angel touched [Elijah] and said, 'Get up and eat.' . . . He ate and drank and then lay down again. The angel of the LORD came back a second time and touched him and said, 'Get up and eat, for the journey is too much for you.' So he got up and ate and drank" (1 Kings 19:5–8 NIV). What did it do? It strengthened him for the forty-day trip he was about to take. If Elijah needed time to recharge and rest, you do too. It's like taking the time to sharpen your ax. You'll get more done with less stress.

Reconnect

I ran into some good friends at a restaurant not long ago. They had their sweet little granddaughter with them. She was about three or four years old. She was sitting on her mama's knee, and I asked her, "Who's that?" pointing to her grandfather. She said, "That's Pawpaw." And then I looked at her grandmother and asked, "Who's that?" She looked at her, and she said, "Oh! That's Darlin'." Are you at a place in your life where, when you think about what God thinks about you, you hear Him say, "Oh! That's Darlin'"? If you aren't, you should. If you aren't, you need to reconnect. To hear Him say what He thinks of you, point to the angels and say, "Oh, there's My Darlin'. I'm so proud of him."

> I looked upon a farm one day.
> That once I used to own;
> The barn had fallen to the ground.

The fields were overgrown.
The house in which my children grew.
Where we had lived for years—
I turned to see it broken down.
And brushed aside the tears.
I looked upon my soul one day.
To find it too had grown
With thorns and nettles everywhere.
The seeds neglect had sown.
The years had passed while I had cared
For things of lesser worth:
The things of Heaven I let go
When minding things of Earth.

—THEODORE W. BRENNAN

11

I Will Develop a Sustainable Pace

⌒

Do not hurry, do not rest.
—Johann Wolfgang von Goethe

The late columnist Herb Caen wrote in the *San Francisco Chronicle*, "Every morning in Africa, a gazelle wakes up knowing it must run faster than the fastest lion or die. Every morning a lion wakes up knowing it must outrun the slowest gazelle or starve. It doesn't matter whether you are a lion or a gazelle, when the sun comes up, you'd better be running!" Running is not an option on the African plain or in the American fast lane. It's not the actual running that kills most of us; it's running at a pace we can't sustain and were never created for in the first place. As Paul said, "Let us run with patience the particular race that God has set before us" (Heb. 12:1 TLB). The race God sets in front of you, which leads to the finish line and the winner's circle, is paved with patience.

A recent television documentary pointed out that the cheetah survives on the African plain by running down its prey. The big cat can sprint seventy miles per hour, but its one liability is that it cannot sustain the speed for long. Within its long, sleek body is a disproportionately small heart, which causes the cheetah to tire quickly. Unless the cheetah catches its prey in the first burst of speed, it must abandon the chase. I am afraid I've known way too many people just like that. They've grabbed for all the gusto they could get with all the gumption they had only to fade within reach of the prize for lack of heart. Like the cheetah, to survive and thrive, we must develop a sustainable pace for the heart we have.

Too many of us live with oversized ambitions and undersized hearts. We speed into projects with unbounded energy. But for the lack of heart, we fizzle before we finish. We vow to start faster and run longer next time, when what we need is not more speed but more staying power. Motion and busyness, no matter how well intentioned, yield little unless we allow God to strengthen "with might by his Spirit in the inner man" (Eph. 3:16 KJV).

I don't think we can overestimate the price we pay for our overworked and overstressed lives. For example, our most notorious industrial accidents in recent years—*Exxon Valdez,* Three Mile Island, Chernobyl, the fatal navigational error of Korean Air Flight 007—all occurred in the middle of the night. When the USS *Vincennes* shot down an Iranian A300 Airbus killing all 290 people aboard, fatigue-stressed operators in the cruiser's high-tech Combat Information Center misinterpreted radar data and repeatedly told their captain the jet was descending as if to attack when, in fact, the airliner remained on a normal flight path.

In the *Challenger* space shuttle disaster, key NASA officials made the ill-fated decision to go ahead with the launch after working twenty hours straight and getting only two to three hours of sleep the night before. Their error in judgment cost the lives of seven astronauts and nearly killed the U.S. space program.

No one can sustain an all-out, pedal-to-the-metal, going-Mach-two-with-your-hair-on-fire pace for long. God created your body and brain to sustain high levels of concentrated output for only brief periods of time. You need rest to recover and recharge. If you don't exercise, your muscles will atrophy. Put yourself under too much strain, and the stress can kill you. Too much food and you will become lethargic and obese, but too little and you waste away. Your heart gets strong as you stress it moderately, but go too far and you do irreversible damage. You need periods of focused productivity as well as periods of retreat and renewal.

Love fuels my heart, joy strengthens it, peace calms it, and hope anchors it. But the quality of patience develops my pea-sized heart into the heart of a champion. Patience is to the heart committed to excellence what strong legs are to a sprinter and a great pair of lungs is to a marathoner committed to run hard and finish well.

Patience is a fruit of the God-empowered, Christ-led, Spirit-controlled life. It infuses into the redeemed heart a confident calm based on the certain knowledge that God rules, Christ reigns, and the Spirit orchestrates the affairs of life. These truths turn into more than mere religious abstractions in the crucible of real life where most people grow faint of heart long before they become feeble in body or brain.

Like a lot of other people in the South, I was raised in a church culture. Church was where I first learned to define my worth with the word *do.* It was there I learned that God loved me when I was good, but He loved me even more when I was "very good." If your worth is based on doing good deeds, and God's favor was gained by doing a lot of them, it is easy to understand why the quality of patience wasn't very high on my list. I needed to get busy getting on the good side of an ill-tempered Deity.

I grew up believing God had little to no patience with sin-ners like me. I was warned each Sunday that God might rain down His judgment on my childish indiscretions and indecent thoughts any minute. I didn't see patience as a virtue at home or school either. What I heard was "hurry up," "don't be late," "don't doodle, dare, or dream." Children are better "seen than heard." "Shut up." "Don't ask so many questions." "You're always in the way." "Go upstairs and watch TV." And my all-time favorite, "Who do you think you are, the king of England?" Not much pa-tience painted on the canvas of those memories.

I learned patience was something you prayed for when you didn't know what else to do. How could I have known patience was one of the greatest attributes of God Himself? I didn't read this verse until I was in college: "The Lord is not slow in keeping his promise, as some understand slowness. He is patient with you,

not wanting anyone to perish, but everyone to come to repen-
tance" (2 Pet. 3:9 NIV). It was a shock to the brain, but a thrill to
the heart when I heard God was patient. The fact I was still living was proof positive that He was. Why hadn't I figured that out
earlier? If you're going to develop a sustainable pace in the race
you're running, you're going to need God's patience and plenty
of your own.

What is patience? One of my first misconceptions was that to
be patient was to risk being lazy. Boy, was I ever wrong. Some of
the hardest work you will ever do is to exercise your patience
when everything in you wants to run away, strike back, or get
even.

A teenaged boy begged his dad to buy him some barbells so
he could build up his body to impress the girls. The dad hesitated,
the son nagged, so he relented and at least agreed to check out a
set at the local fitness store. "Please, Dad," pleaded the son, "I
promise I'll use 'em every day." "I don't know," said the dad, "it's
really a commitment on your part." "Please, Dad?" said the son.
"They're not cheap either," the father said. "I promise I'll use 'em
every day and I'll put 'em away every time. Please, Dad, I promise. You'll see." The son won his dad over. The father paid for the
equipment and headed for the door. After a few steps, he heard
his son behind him say, "What! You mean I have to carry them to
the car?" Thus is the essence of laziness. The Bible describes it this
way: "Laziness lets the roof leak, and soon the rafters begin to rot"
(Eccles. 10:18 TLB), and someone else carries the weights to the
car.

Patience is not idleness. This is the biggest fear that most of
us type A personalities have when we think about patience. It is
hard for us proactive, high-energy overachievers, who want to fix
everything, please everyone, and be just the best at everything, to
slow down and be still for anyone. For the world-changers among
us, having patience sounds too much like waiting. And to wait is
to let the world pass us by. It may be true that the early bird gets
the worm, but when did we start believing worms were worth
getting up early for?

Patience is not passivity. It is not an excuse for just letting things happen to us as they will. It is a welcome alternative to the frantic, forced lifestyle that's turning us into a society of people in a hurry to no place of particular significance. A national survey discovered that if you're looking for a parking place in the average mall, it's going to take thirty-two seconds. If you find a parking space someone is pulling out of, and he knows you're waiting for him to pull out, it will cost forty-one seconds. If you sit there and honk, it will take you sixty-three seconds. Place us behind the wheel of a car, and patience is passé. From behind the wheel of a two-ton SUV, we want to exert our power, not exercise our patience.

Some people think *patience* is just another word for *resignation*. They resign themselves to being unhappy or unfulfilled. They say, "It's not going to get any better," or "There is nothing you can do about it." When I hear some people say sadly, "Yes, it's bad, but I'm just trusting the Lord!" I don't know who to feel sorrier for: them or the Lord. It's tempting to hide our resentment behind religious resignations.

Patience is a godly virtue. It gives us perspective so "we can rejoice, too, when we run into problems and trials, for we know that they are good for us—they help us learn to be patient" (Rom. 5:3 TLB). I didn't sign up to hear that. I signed up to have money in the bank, authority over the devil, and a problem-free ride. But that kind of Christianity creates a big-bodied, small-hearted, perpetually put-off person.

Seven Steps to S.T.A.M.I.N.A.

A synonym for *patience* is the word *stamina*. Stamina is the capacity to perform well over time under pressure. It is both the strength of patience and the patience of strength. Athletes spend the better part of their training regimens developing it, a robust and resilient economy requires it, and to a marriage, family, or friendship, it's like rebar buried deep within, withstanding whatever weight it's required to carry. It stands the stresses and strains of hurt feelings, broken promises, and the daily grind. With it the ant "stores its provisions in summer and gathers its food at harvest" (Prov. 6:8 NIV). But without it a cheetah, who can run with bursts of speed up to seventy miles an hour, fades a hair's breadth from its breakfast because its undersized heart can't sustain the pace its body can produce.

Arguably the greatest display of stamina ever recorded was the night that Jesus spent before His betrayal in the Garden of Gethsemane. He went there to pray and wait. It was a dark night of the soul when all the plans and pains of eternity were compressed onto one man's shoulders. He took with Him His closest friends on earth, Peter, James, and John. He left them to watch and pray, saying, "My soul is crushed with horror and sadness to the point of death . . . stay here . . . stay awake with me" (Matt. 26:38 TLB). What they ended up missing, because "the spirit is willing, but the body is weak" (Matt. 26:41 NIV), we ended up being mesmerized by. During that time, we are allowed a unique and awe-inspiring glimpse into Jesus' two natures, His humanity and divinity. As the Son of man, He begged, "May this cup be taken from me." As the Son of God, He prayed, "Yet not as I will, but as you will" (Matt. 26:39 NIV).

Jesus faced the most difficult moment of His short life abandoned and alone. He faced the crisis of decision, and He prevailed. Everything that had come before and everything just ahead hinged on that moment. Did He have the stamina to finish what He had started? Yes. He walked His talk and carried His cross so He could die my death, pardon my sin, and secure my soul. In the cradle the angels announced, "It has begun," and on the cross He cried, "It is finished!" He was buried in a borrowed tomb, resurrected on the third day, seen among men and women, and ascended to heaven where at this very moment, He "is at the right hand of God and is also interceding for us" (Rom. 8:34 NIV).

How do we work into our lives today what Christ has already worked out for us in time and eternity? How do we develop a sustainable pace right up to the finish line of our race? Let's use the word *stamina* as an acrostic to consider some practical habits that will strengthen your heart and hands. The first three are vertical disciplines whose purpose is to get you to press deeper into the person and promises of God. The second three are more horizontal disciplines aimed at helping you "work out your salvation with fear and trembling" (Phil. 2:12 NIV). The last step is the result of mastering both the vertical and the horizontal dimensions of your faith.

Surrender to God's Motives

When I was growing up, it was my mother's job to get me to do the things I didn't want to do, but were good for me. She was the disciplinarian in our house. When she cracked the whip, so to speak, my brother and I jumped. Of all the whippings I got and lectures I endured, nothing screws up my face or speeds up my heart more than the memory of Mother making me eat Brussels sprouts. Even today, my skin crawls at just the smell of them. What are they anyway? They appear to be baby cabbages, but they smell like skunk spray. I gagged on the first one, and it went downhill from there. Mother kept saying, "They're good for you." It wasn't that I doubted her; I just couldn't stand the taste. Every time they showed up on the dinner table there was war. Mother insisted I eat one, and I agreed I would eat no more than one. Why do things that are good for you taste so awful and look so gross? To this day, when I hear something's good for me, I can't help thinking it's going to hurt, taste bad, or cost a lot.

There are more than a few times I think we see God that way. He commands us to do certain things, even though we shy away from them, assuring us they are good for us. The Bible gives us one of those "it's good for you" prescriptions when it says, "We can rejoice, too, when we run into problems and trials for we know that they are good for us—they help us learn to be patient. And patience develops strength of character in us and helps us trust God more each time we use it until finally our hope and faith are strong and steady" (Rom 5:3–4 TLB).

We read these and other "good for you" promises with a little hesitation and suspicion until we come to the place where we once and for all surrender to the proposition that God's motives toward us can be trusted. Before you can face the rigors and routines of life well, you must settle this question for yourself. That's why only firsthand faith (see Chapter 5) has any power to sustain excellence and expectation over time. Firsthand faith means you have decided to trust God's heart even when you can't trace His hand. God moves toward you motivated by love. He is not out to "get you" or "catch you" or "burn you"; He is out to love you, lift you, and liberate you.

Surrendering to God's motives means facing the future with the conviction that God has a purpose for everything you're going through. Even though you might not see it or understand it now, you can trust Him. Winston Churchill said, "It is a mistake to look too far ahead. Only one link in the chain of destiny can be handled at a time." When Paul prayed for his "thorn in the flesh" to be removed, God responded, "No. But I am with you; that is all you need. My power shows up best in weak people" (2 Cor. 12:9 TLB). Which translates into "trust Me; I know what's best for you." Is your patience that patient?

Satan wants you to believe that God loves you in proportion to your performance. The only exercise he promotes is jumping to conclusions. That was his tactical approach to Adam and Eve. He didn't challenge God's mandate; he just questioned God's motive. He said to Eve, "God knows that when you eat of it your eyes will be opened, and you will be like God" (Gen. 3:5 NIV). You think God cares for you, but what He is really trying to do is to keep you down. You're more powerful and privileged than you thought. God doesn't want you to find out that you would do fine without Him. After all, this is a big world, and how is God going to rule the world and give two hoots about you at the same time? These are the lies Satan still tells because they're the ones we still believe.

Shakespeare wrote, "One may smile, and smile, and be a villain!" I don't know about you, but I get up these days and I look at the TV and wonder about whom to believe. I can't tell the good guys from the bad guys. It was so much easier when they

wore black or white hats. There was a day when wounded people fell down and bled, which made them easier to find and fix.
But today is the day of the walking wounded where the pain of
the past and the dread of the future can be medicated and masked
by a thousand different drugs of choice. Some are illegal; most are
not. But all are lethal, given enough time and neglect.

I want to fix this fouled up world, but I feel powerless. I used
to hate that feeling. But I've come to welcome it, allowing it to
drive me deeper into the heart of God. As long as I feel capable
of fixing you, me, my world, I will avoid the one thing above all
things that is good for me—trusting God's love for me. Don't rush
over this point, for it is key and it will keep on hindering your
race until you settle it. Patience begins with the confession that
while I can't always trace God's hand; I always trust His heart.

Trust God's Methods

Some of the most gifted trapeze artists in the world are members
of the family called the Flying Roudellas. During a Q and A time
at an exhibition, they were asked how the catcher always seemed
to know where the flyers were, even while hanging upside down.
They explained by revealing the special relationship between flyer
and catcher on the trapeze.

The flyer's job is to let go, and the catcher's job is to catch the
flyer once he does. As the flyer swings high above the crowd on
the trapeze, the moment comes when he must let go. He arcs out
into the air, remaining as still as possible, waiting for the strong
hands of the catcher to pluck him from the air. They placed particular emphasis on the fact that "the flyer must never try to catch
the catcher."[1] The flyer must wait suspended in midair with absolute trust that the catcher will catch him. The same is true in
your relationship with God. Can you guess who the flyer is and
who is the catcher? Don't you wish you could reverse those
roles—at least once in a while?

Trusting God's methods is possible only for the believer who
has first surrendered to God's motives. And even then it is a challenge for stubborn people like me. I say stubborn because even

when all the evidence points to the fact that God has a perfect record as a catcher, I still try to tell God how to do His job. I grow weary of waiting suspended in the midair madness of daily life waiting for God to catch me. Just a few times I'd like to be the catcher. But alas, I confess I do not do well at hanging upside down for long. Hey, I find it a challenge just to keep my balance on solid ground.

For those flyers smart enough to let go and wait for God, their reward is knowing firsthand "what a wonderful God we have! How great are his wisdom and knowledge and riches! How impossible it is for us to understand his decisions and his methods!" (Rom. 11:33 TLB).

God's ways are not my ways. Trying to figure out how God is going to catch me is futile and fruitless. I never look more childish than when I get mad and pout, threatening to withhold my love if He doesn't do things my way right away. How much strength is wasted fighting the very One who fought all the demons of hell to love me? When will I joyfully confess, "As you do not know the path of the wind, or how the body is formed in a mother's womb, so you cannot understand the work of God, the Maker of all things" (Eccles. 11:5 NIV)?

Sometimes people ask me, "What is God saying to you these days?" And I respond, "God is saying to me today what He said to me the night He abducted me as a seventeen-year-old college freshman from my one-room apartment, 'Do you trust Me?'" What sweeter sound could any mere mortal hear as he flies through the air with the greatest of "dis-ease," but to hear the Catcher say, "Let go, wait, and I'll catch you. Trust Me"?

Accept God's Timing

French reformer Saint Vincent de Paul said, "All comes at the proper time to him who knows how to wait." I have never been very good at waiting. Maybe that's why I've underestimated its value to a life well lived. I want what I want when I want it, and I don't think I should have to wait for it. I think that stems from being born a control freak raised in a small town.

Growing up in a small town has its advantages, such as knowing everybody, feeling safe, and being in a grounded environment. But it also has its annoying disadvantages. Like when I'd see something on TV or in a magazine, and I'd go to Newberry's Five and Dime or to Ely's Drugs or to Slinkers Jewelry and ask for the item only to hear, "We don't keep that in stock, but we can order it for you." "How long will it take?" I'd ask. And they'd say, "Two weeks." Why did everything always take two weeks? For a while my only goal in life was to grow up and move to wherever it was you didn't have to order everything you wanted and wait two weeks.

Waiting is inevitable. You might as well get good at it because it is required everywhere you go. Even with a ticket, you will wait in line at the movies, a concert, or a ball game. Even with an appointment, you will wait at the dentist's and doctor's offices. As a matter of fact, there is no chance of not waiting because they've named an entire room after what you'll be doing most of—waiting.

The third step in developing stamina is accepting God's timing, which will include knowing when to wait, when to watch, and when to wade in. With God timing is crucial. The right thing done at the wrong time is the wrong thing. If you doubt that, try bringing your wife flowers the day after her birthday. The right thing done at the right time for the wrong reason is a sad thing. But the right thing done at the right time for the right reason is a bona fide God thing.

The Bible assures us that "he has made everything beautiful in its time. He has also set eternity in the hearts of men; yet they cannot fathom what God has done from beginning to end" (Eccles. 3:11 NIV). God can see the beginning and the end, all at the same time—as well as the middle and every point in between. Our line of sight is limited. We live our lives as if we're walking the streets of downtown Chicago. We see the sidewalk in front of us, the people who surround us, and the concrete canyons that swallow us. The sights can be breathtaking, but they'll always be boxy. We can't see the larger context of the city, and if we stay among the tall buildings long enough, we will be tempted to define the entire city by what it feels like to walk around the base of the Sears building. God has a God's-eye view. He sees it all without distraction.

Accepting God's timing is trusting that He has us where we are, as we are, for a purpose to be revealed in His time. Waiting is not a liability with God; it is an asset. We learn from Scripture that "when we were utterly helpless, with no way of escape, Christ came at just the right time and died for us sinners who had no use for him" (Rom. 5:6 TLB). Author Oswald Chambers said, "God engineers our circumstances as he did those of his Son; all we have to do is to follow where he places us." The majority of us are busy trying to place ourselves. God alters things while we wait for Him. He came at the right time. He has great timing; never early, but never later. He's not "just in time," He's "just on time."

Memories of Mercy

The first three steps are vertical habits or ways in which your attitudes are formed by your relationship with God. These second three are more horizontal in nature, which means they are the practical applications of the first three perspectives.

Memory is a gift from God. You choose whether it's a curse or a blessing. To develop a sustainable pace, use your memory to recall the tender mercies you've received at the mighty hand of God. Doing this will help tame the temptation to feel as though God is either picking on you or has forgotten you altogether. It will also be invaluable if you ever develop an inflated view of what you deserve or what God owes you.

One of the best illustrations of this in the entire Bible is the story that Jesus told of the Pharisee and the publican:

> Two men went up to the temple to pray, one a Pharisee and the other a tax collector. The Pharisee stood up and prayed about himself: "God, I thank you that I am not like

other men—robbers, evildoers, adulterers—or even like this
tax collector. I fast twice a week and give a tenth of all I
get." But the tax collector stood at a distance. He would
not even look up to heaven, but beat his breast and said,
"God, have mercy on me, a sinner." I tell you that this
man, rather than the other, went home justified before
God. For everyone who exalts himself will be humbled,
and he who humbles himself will be exalted. (Luke
18:10–14 NIV)

Believe me, the Pharisee spirit is alive and well, and the publican
mind-set is just as rare today as it was in the first century.

Anytime we set out to remind God of our good deeds and
great sacrifices, we're revealing our Pharisee DNA. But anytime
we bow our knees and confess our needs, that we are utterly un-
done and unlovable outside His mercy and grace, we show signs
that the publican still lives within us too.

Mercy and grace are not the same things. They are the opposite sides of one coin—God's love. Mercy happens when God
withholds from me what I deserve. I've actually heard people say
over the years, "All I want is what I deserve." Are you sure you do?
I'm sure I don't. I want and need mercy for the thickheaded,
hard-hearted, stiff-necked things I've done and continue, I'm sad
to say, to do.

Grace happens when God gives me what I do not deserve
and cannot earn. Not in a thousand tries or a thousand lifetimes
can we merit God's mercy and grace. He is not obligated to give
them, though we are damned if He doesn't. We need mercy to
stay God's judgment for what we've already done and God's grace
to atone for the sin stains on our souls that no amount of good
works can scrub clean. No wonder believers have sung the old
spiritual "Amazing Grace" with such gumption and gusto over
the years: "Amazing grace! How sweet the sound that saved a
wretch like me." You know the word *wretch* is a little strong, isn't
it? Doesn't it attack my self-esteem? Yeah, I think it does, and I

think it's supposed to. It certainly offends the Pharisee in me. But that's the very point, isn't it? The Pharisee in me needs a little slapping around, and the "publican" in me needs more nourishment. That's where memories of mercy come in.

I suffer from a selective memory. I tend to remember all the things that God hasn't done and forget all the things that He has. I need to be reminded that the Lord I love and worship with all my heart, mind, soul, and strength came as a servant. He humbled Himself. The Bible is clear:

> Your attitude should be the same as that of Christ Jesus:
> Who, being in very nature God,
>   did not consider equality with God something to be
>   grasped,
> but made himself nothing,
>   taking the very nature of a servant,
>   being made in human likeness.
> And being found in appearance as a man,
>   he humbled himself and became obedient to death—
>   even death on a cross!" (Phil. 2:5–8 NIV)

We live in a culture that loves to lift up and litigate the cause of human rights. And in the context of man's duty to man, I'm right there with them. My faith demands me to do to others as I would have them do to me (Luke 6:31). But let's not confuse that with man's obligation to God. The truth is, we have a moral obligation to God for which we do not have the moral capacity. Much like the cheetah, we start out fast only to find we don't have the heart for a sustained effort at earning our way back into the good graces of God.

The grateful admission that God has not treated me as my sins deserve is an act of worship that makes every day precious and every blessing priceless. For those with fresh memories of mercy, every day is a good day, and any day above dirt is a privilege. Waking up is a privilege; getting up is a privilege; going to work is a privilege; loving my wife and kids is a privilege. Getting up and breathing in and out all day is a miracle. How could we ever hope for so much and how dare we ask for more? "Lord, have mercy," and our lives are testaments that He still does.

Inventory of God's Goodness

David proclaimed, "The steps of good men are directed by the Lord. He delights in each step they take. If they fall it isn't fatal, for the Lord holds them with his hand. I have been young and now I am old. And in all my years I have never seen the Lord forsake a man who loves him" (Ps. 37:23–25 TLB). His conclusion after having trusted God's motives and methods was that God is faithful. It wasn't how he was "supposed" to feel about God, but didn't. It was what he actually came to believe after a lifetime of walking hand in hand with God. From being in his lowly shepherd's station to defeating Goliath to running from Saul to uniting a divided nation to carrying on his shameful behavior with Bathsheba, David had real reasons to trust God's motives and methods. You, too, if you've walked with God any length of time, can see a pattern of God's faithfulness. I'm not talking about the way He worked with David, but how personal His faithfulness has been to you. If you look closely, you'll see a personalized pattern for the way God leads your life from one level to the next, from one assignment to the next.

At the beginning of every year, I sit down and put pen to paper. I write down in detail all God has done for me the past year. Large and small, it all goes down on paper. The list is always a long one. And when I'm tempted to pout and pooch out my lip at God, get a little anxious and upset and want to give somebody a piece of my mind, and ask, "God, where are You?" I open that book and go through that list. And all of a sudden, it's just like the fog has cleared off a mountain road—I can see. This is reality. All my fuming, fussing, and foaming is not reality. I have an inventory of God's goodness. No one can ever talk me out of my faith because I have too much history with God.

Network of "Get It" People

I meet people everywhere I go whose lives are like spinning tops bouncing from one relationship to the next, one job to the next, one marriage to the next, and it's not because they're bad people. It's because they don't have the right kind of people in their lives who "get it." They may know people who are "with it," but they've yet to find the people who understand that relationships are more important than partnerships. No one can stand long without networking. And I'm talking not about the kind of networking done for success, but about the kind done for significance. You need people in your life who are willing to catch you when you fall, answer you when you call, and carry you when you're wounded.

"Get it" people run in when others run out. They are here not to see through you, but to see you through. They believe building up is better than tearing down. They still see gossiping as a sin for which God has little patience. They have felt the bitter sting of slander and sleaze; therefore, they have the capacity for compassion when the arrows are aimed at you. These people have been testing the fires of adversity and have learned how to turn them into an advantage. They can be trusted because they have been tested. The Bible describes them this way:

> Is there any such thing as Christians cheering each other up? Do you love me enough to want to help me? Does it mean anything to you that we are brothers in the Lord, sharing the same Spirit? Are your hearts tender and sympathetic at all? Then make me truly happy by loving each other and agreeing wholeheartedly with each other, working together with one heart and mind and purpose. Don't be selfish; don't live to make a good impression on others. Be humble, thinking of others as better than yourself. (Phil. 2:1–3 TLB)

Do you have a network, a group of girls, or a band of brothers with whom you can work with one heart and mind and purpose? Can you name the encouragers in your life who help you hang tough and stay clean? Remember, eagles don't flock to bars or around workroom water coolers waylaying coworkers with venomous gossip.

People who are "with it" and "with you" are the safe people to whom you can vent your hurt and anger that otherwise might stay bottled up inside. And surely you know whatever brokenness you bury in your heart will come out at the worst possible moment in the most embarrassing ways. Your "get it" friends will, just by their listening, nonjudgmental ear, save you today from burning bridges you might need to walk back across tomorrow.

For example, over the years, I've had my share of critics. Some of them have been so devoted, they've felt inspired to write me nasty letters dripping with sarcasm and just plain meanness. And being ever so much the patient, understanding overreactor I am, I have felt the corresponding need to answer them. On more than one occasion after investing countless hours crafting a clever and witty rebuttal, I have had the good sense to show my diatribe to my wife, Paula. She would read it and say, "It's all true. Your arguments are lucid and convincing, and it is easy to see you are a uniquely gifted wordsmith. You have painted your opponent into a verbal corner from which there is no honorable retreat." Then she would hand it back to me and say, "Tear it up or burn it. If you send it, you will win the battle, but you'll start a war not worth winning." Thank God, she "gets it."

Do you have any good, gutsy people in your network who have the gumption and grace to be honest in a way you can receive it? You won't last long living on your righteous indignation.

A Long-look Ability

William Shakespeare wrote, "How poor are they that have not patience! What wound did ever heal but by degrees?" A constant curse of our culture is our craving for the quick fix and the fast buck. We want everything fixed *now*, financed *now*, or fun *now*

without much regard to what those choices will do to our futures. It's nothing new really, but I doubt we have been as good at
it as we are now.

We live in a time of instant everything. If there is any waiting
involved, we walk away. If we have to wait an extra second at a
stoplight, we lay on the horn. We have microwave meals, fast food,
quick print shops, eyeglasses made in an hour, ten-minute oil
changes, and overnight delivery from almost anyplace in the
world. We hardly ever hear of the antiquated and arcane concept
of delayed gratification anymore. If you want sex, why wait to find
and form a loving relationship with another flawed person when
you can fire up the Internet and in a few minutes be engaged in
cybersex with a flawless beauty who will never know you, touch
you, or make any demands of you? If you want a better body, why
waste all that time exercising or curbing your appetite when you
can make an appointment to get your nips and tucks done in a
day? Why wait for anything when you can order it, phone for it,
or download it over the Internet? And while I'll be one of the first
to admit I do like downloading music with iTunes and ordering
hard-to-find books using Amazon.com, the stakes I'm talking
about are much greater than getting my Starbucks venti, no-foam,
no-fat, hazelnut latte at the drive-through window because I can't
wait the extra four minutes it would take to go in and risk actual
social interaction. What are we doing with all this extra time and
happiness we've been able to finance, courtesy of credit cards?

Somebody needs to blow the lid off this scam. With all we've
spent and all we've given away, we are not happier, healthier, and
wealthier (where it really counts), and we're certainly not wiser.
We're a well-funded generation of children reliving the vices of
our parents, only we're better armed and adroit at covering our
tracks. We're mad and getting madder. We're tired and getting
more tired every day. We're getting nowhere faster, and we're arriving more fearful, frustrated, and hacked off than ever. I say it's
got to stop somewhere. I say it stops right here and right now
with you and me. No more life from the bottom shelf.

Real life—where real people live and real futures are at

stake—moves at a different pace and rhythm. Because God created us persons and not refrigerators, we grow strong not overnight, but over time. When we're hurt, we can't go online and download a virus fix—we're not plug and play. Excelling while you can means developing a sustainable pace, which means that some things take time. God takes time. Relationships take time. Integrity takes time. Quality takes time. Intimacy takes time. The best things in life take time, and they take trust. That's really what this whole discussion has been about. Trusting God with the time He needs to heal us, help us, and get us home safely. These are the key ingredients of what I call long-look ability.

How many lives have been wrecked taking a shortcut to a place not worth going in the first place? How many wounded hearts have gone undetected? How many hurts have gone unhealed? How many hopes have gone unrealized all because of the availability of a narcotic, a drug, or a magic pill that covered up the symptoms and masked the pain until a soul was lost and only a shell remained?

I've seen this reality in the lives of people who chose a pace and path in life that they never had a chance of sustaining. Like the cheetah, they had a body that could put up with the abuse of fast-lane living, but they didn't have the heart for it. Although I have cried over the loss of so many lives, none has, still to this day, caused me more regret or reflection than the death of my brother at the age of forty-nine.

My brother didn't start drinking to end up dying from it. Like a lot of guys our age, he considered drinking beer a rite of passage, a sign you were cool. I'm sure he wouldn't have downed the first one if he thought for a second it would become a constant companion over the next thirty years. And since we were never close (I use that as an excuse), I never knew what deep hurt and loneliness he was medicating with stronger, stiffer drinks. I do remember vividly the day it dawned on me that he was in trouble. It was a family gathering at my parents' house, not long after my dad's death. Several of us were on the patio when my brother came up to me reeking of alcohol. He began to cry and ask forgiveness for the jerk (he used a different word) he had been. Before I could respond, his wife ushered him away. That's the last family function he would attend—ever.

We saw each other less and less after that. I assumed he was drinking more and more. I remember the day my mother called to inform me that what they thought was the flu was really cirrhosis of the liver. When I visited my big brother in the hospital, he was jaundiced and gaunt. The only hope was a liver transplant, but in his condition even that was tenuous. After a few months of false hopes and a slow wasting away, he was gone.

Standing over his grave, I thought, *How in the world did we get here?* Addictions happen to "other people's" families, but not mine. Up until that moment I had felt sympathy with people caught in addictions, but I didn't feel empathy. How could I? Now I got it loud and clear. Finally, I understood for myself that no one sets out to get hooked on alcohol, drugs, or a thousand different drugs of choice. My brother wasn't a bad person. Had he been able to take the "long look" of where that first drink would lead, there is no doubt in my mind he would have steered clear.

I'm telling you this very personal story to get you to trust me when I beg you to take a long look at the choices you have made and are making. Are you living at a sustainable pace? Are you developing the habits that will sustain you through the seasons and stages of life, or are you on the path that leads to an early death and a wasted life?

Ask God for a wake-up call, right here and now. Beg Him to heal the pain, forgive the sin, and give you a new, bigger, better heart to live well, love well, and finish strong. Pray for the power to trust His motives and methods, though trusting comes hard and patience comes even harder. Remember the cheetah when you are tempted to take on too much and run too fast for too long. Sustained excellence is possible only for those who surrender to God's motives, trust His methods, and accept His timing.

12

I Will Finish Well

◦—

To be somebody you must last.
—RUTH GORDON

It was a hot and muggy Tuesday morning, July 20, 1993, in the White House Rose Garden. It was a special event held so that President Clinton could announce his choice for the new director of the FBI. Vincent Foster, a childhood friend of the president, returned to his White House Counsel's office, took care of some legal business, and talked to the president on the phone while he ate lunch that day at his desk. It appeared to be just another day in the life of this acclaimed Arkansas lawyer living his dream of working beside his friend in the most prestigious office in the world at the pinnacle of power.

A little after one o'clock, Foster left his office, drove his Honda Accord down the streets of Washington, D.C., to an out-of-the-way national park on a bluff overlooking the Potomac River. With an antique .38 caliber revolver in one hand, he walked across an open field, stopped beside an old rusty cannon, raised the gun to his head, and for reasons unknown then and now, ended his life. When President Clinton heard the news, he said, "It would be wrong to define a life like Vincent Foster's in terms only of how it ended." And while in one sense he might have been right, the truth is, Vincent Foster will always be remembered not by where he started his life or even the great achievements he made along the way, but by how he chose to end it. And no matter how sincere and loving the efforts of Foster's friends, family, and colleagues may be to place the emphasis on how he lived, the way he ended his life will always overshadow whatever contributions he may have made.

In this book we have looked in great detail at the four basic commitments of personal excellence. To master all of these and to fail at this one basic truth would be tragic. A life well lived requires both a good start and a strong finish. It's the truth of the child's fable of the tortoise and the hare brought into real life. The race is made up of crossing the finish line as well as leaving the starting gate. It does little good to sprint away at the beginning and have nothing left for a strong finish. It would be like a marathon runner who covered the entire 26-mile course in record time, but who sat down and refused to finish the last 385 yards. The Scriptures urge us to "not get tired of doing what is right, for after a while we will reap a harvest of blessing if we don't get discouraged and give up" (Gal. 6:9 TLB).

The quality of your life is judged not just by how well you start, but by how well you finish. That's why they give out the trophies at the finish line, not the starting gate. How many people can you name who started well with a burst of speed and it appeared for a while at least they were going to outrun, outperform, and outdo everyone around them, but something went wrong along the way? The wheels started coming off their lives in the fast lane. And for a while they seemed to be on the fast track to the good life, but they ended up stuck on the side of the road trying to recall a better place and time in simpler, safer circumstances. I have met too many people whose conversation is about what they did ten or twenty-plus years ago in the good old days. They live in the past, longing for a place and time when the pace was slower and the price of gas was eighteen cents a gallon. If the memories of your past are more vivid and vital than your plans for the future, then you're dead in the water. It's hard to move ahead while looking back.

The Real World

Garrison Keillor, popular radio host of National Public Radio's *Prairie Home Companion*, signs off each of his programs with this quote: "That's the news from Lake Wobegon, where all the women are strong, all the men are good looking, and all the children are above average." Things would be much easier if we lived in a perfect place, but we don't, and we're not going to in this life at least.

In a perfect world life would be easy. Married people would stay married and live happily ever after. Children would grow up loved and never entertain one thought of abandonment or shed one tear of abuse. In a perfect world people would keep their word, and written contracts would be unnecessary. In a perfect world a person's many years of faithful service to a company would be given first consideration when talks of cutbacks and downsizing start becoming a part of the lunchtime scuttlebutt. In a perfect world everyone would be treated with dignity and respect regardless of the color of skin or the origin of ancestors. In a perfect world we wouldn't need police officers, lawyers, speed limits, surveillance cameras, or razor wire. In a perfect world everyone would be honest and honorable; we wouldn't need locks on our doors, mace in our pockets, or war on our minds. But—and this is a big, big but—we don't live in a perfect world.

You and I live in the real world. It's not the world we wanted, but it's the one we got. It's not the one God made, but the one marred by sin, hate, greed, and war. It is a world in which we look for a police officer to feel safe, lean on lawyers to get justice, and long for ways to shed the sadness of suffering. It is a world in which you'd better be armed to the teeth and insured to the hilt. It is a world in which one wrong turn can get you sued and one wrong word can get you shot. I found this letter from an injured worker to his insurance company:

Dear Sirs,

I'm writing this in response to your request for additional information. For block 3 of the accident report form, I put, "Losing my presence of mind," as the cause of the accident. You said in your letter that I should explain more fully, and I trust that the following details will be sufficient.

I'm a bricklayer by trade, and on the day of the accident, I was working alone on the roof of a ten-story building. When I had completed my work, I discovered I had about 500 pounds of brick left over. Rather than carry them down by hand, I decided to lower them to the ground in a barrel by using a pulley, which fortunately was attached to the side of the building at the tenth floor.

Securing the rope at the ground level, I went to the roof, loaded the 500 pounds of brick and went down, back to the ground, and untied the rope holding it tightly to assure a slow descent of the 500 pounds of brick.

You will note, in block 11 of the accident reporting form, that I weigh approximately 200 pounds. Due to my surprise at being jerked off the ground so suddenly, I lost my presence of mind and forgot to let go of the rope. Needless to say, I proceeded at a rapid rate, up the side of the building. In the vicinity of the fifth floor, I met the barrel coming down. This explains the fractured skull and broken collarbone. I continued my rapid ascent, not stopping until the fingers of my right hand were two knuckles deep into the pulley. Fortunately, by that time, I had regained my presence of mind and was able to hold tightly to the rope in spite of the pain.

At approximately the same time, however, the barrel of bricks hit the ground and the bottom fell out of the barrel. Devoid of the weight of the bricks, the barrel now weighed approximately 30 pounds. I refer you again to my weight in block 11 of the accident reporting form. As you might imagine, I began a rapid descent, down the side of the building. In the vicinity of the fifth floor, I met the barrel coming up again. This accounts for the two fractured ankles and the lacerations on my legs and lower body. The second encounter with the barrel slowed me down enough to lessen my injuries when I fell onto the pile of bricks and, fortunately, only three vertebrae were cracked. I am sorry to report, however, that, as I lay on the bricks, in pain, unable to stand, watching the barrel ten stories above me, I again lost my presence of mind and let go of the rope.

As absurd as this situation may sound, I assure you that stranger things happen every day. And when they do, it can be a real test of grit and guts not to lose your presence of mind and let go of the rope.

In the real world it can be hard to know when to hold on to the rope for dear life and when holding on to the rope is more about being bullheaded than brave hearted. When do you know when to get a helmet and when to get another rope? It can be challenging, given the stuff you run into on the road to a great finish.

For example, in the real world you will face disappointing delays. Have you noticed that just about everything takes longer than you planned and costs more than you budgeted? Paula and I built the house we live in now. It's a great house, but it took forever to build. Although the contractor had detailed plans to work from, some of the subcontractors did things the way it seemed best to them. I remember doing a walk-through one night after the air-conditioning people had just finished running the ductwork. I noticed they had placed a major air return duct in what was supposed to be the upstairs linen closet. I couldn't believe they would do such a thing on purpose. Everything halted until we could get them back to the house. We showed them that according to the plans, the air return vent went on the other side of the house. Their only excuse was that from where the main unit sat, it made better sense to them to put it in the closet. I was livid. How dare they change the entire design and hold up the progress because it didn't make sense to them? The result was, they had to send a crew, tear out the ductwork, and reinstall it according to the specifications. I steamed, "Why couldn't they have done that in the first place?"

A house that was supposed to take seven months to build took well over a year because of the delays caused by incompetence and laziness. More than a few times I wanted to let go of the rope and stay where we were. After all, we lived in a perfectly good house, and I liked it there. Thanks to the foresight of my wife, who told me the finished product would be worth the frustration, we persisted. The house was finished per specification, and we love it. It is a perfect house for us. I'm writing this chapter sitting in my very first at-home office. Delays happen, but they need not send us off course and out of the race.

In the real world you will also face demoralizing dead ends. It could be a marriage that began with promise for happiness, but things happened and it ended. Divorce is a dead end no one plans for. It could be a job, career, or business venture you commit time and energy in preparation for, but you come to a dead end and the only thing left to do is to close the ailing business or opt out of a dead-end job. Dead ends need not be the end. Every ending, when God is in it, is really a new beginning. Every closed door with God results in an open window for those who know to look for it.

In the real world you will face repeated roadblocks. Some of them will arise out of the hazards that happen in an imperfect world. The only thing sure about the road ahead is that it will have potholes and breaks in the pavement you can't anticipate until you're on them. It's what you do when you come upon them that makes the difference.

Sometimes a roadblock turns into a serious setback, and you'll have to revert to excelling with what you have (which won't seem like much at the time) where you are (which can look like a desert). These are the conditions along the path in the real world, and all of us face them. No one is immune.

In *Good to Great,* Jim Collins writes about Admiral Jim Stockdale, who was captured in the Vietnam War. He was the highest-ranking United States military officer in the Hanoi Hilton, a prisoner-of-war camp. Stockdale was tortured more than twenty times during his imprisonment from 1965 to 1973. He lived out the war with no certainty he would ever see his family again.

He shouldered the burden of command, doing everything he could to save as many men as he could, while fighting an internal war against his captors and their attempts to use prisoners for propaganda. At one point, he beat himself with a stool and cut himself with a razor, deliberately disfiguring himself, so he could not be put on videotape as an example of a "well-treated" prisoner. Knowing the discovery would mean more torture and perhaps death, he exchanged secret intelligence information with his wife through their letters.

When Collins got the chance to meet Stockdale, who now walks with a limp from the repeated torture, he asked him how he held on despite the uncertainty of his fate and the brutality of his captors. Stockdale responded, "I never lost faith in the end of the story. I never doubted not only that I would get out, but also that I would prevail in the end and turn the experience into the defining event of my life, which, in retrospect, I would not trade."

Stories like Stockdale's are powerful because they teach us to hold on and not let go of hope, even when the future looks bleak and foreboding. More than one person has defied the odds by hanging on a little while longer, because who knows what God might have waiting just around the next corner?

The Quitter's Cycle

I wish I could say stories like Admiral Stockdale's are as common as they are powerful, but my experience tells me they are not. As a matter of fact, for every story of someone who prevailed in the face of adversity, there are thousands more of those who quit the marriage, quit school, quit the job, quit the dream, and saddest of all quit on themselves and God. And each time someone gives up and walks away, it gets easier the next time and the next time and the next time. I have noticed there is a sort of quitter's cycle.

The cycle starts out when people have a dream, a hope, a goal, or a purpose. At first they're excited to have found something worth giving themselves to. I saw a commercial for a high-speed cable service that featured a cute little girl about the age of eight or nine. She wore oversized horn-rimmed glasses. Staring into a computer in a search for bugs, she says, "Bugs are my life." Then it shows the pictures she's found of different kinds of insects. The camera suddenly comes in for a tight shot on her face. She props her chin in her hand, looks deep into the camera, and says, "I'm very passionate."

Let's say you're that little girl and you've found your passion. But you start only dabbling at your dream, nothing serious. You get in just enough to see how the water might be. The problem with dabbling is that dabblers never really throw their full weight into anything. It's like the way that some kids try to get into the swimming pool the first day of summer. They walk to the edge, dip the tip of a big toe in the water, jerk it out, and run away screaming, "Oh, that's tooo coooold!" They run back and sit down without committing themselves to enjoy the water for which they've waited all winter.

A lot of people try to live their lives by dabbling a little in this and a little in that—never jumping into anything with both feet for fear the water is too cold for their taste. And when all you do is dabble at your dreams, the result can be only disappointment. That's pretty much where dabblers live: walking around the edges with a sad little pout, dishing out the endless reasons they have not been able to finish well at anything they've ever started. If you take them seriously, you would think God must not like them very much, for they seem to be the epicenter of a series of misfortunes. But after you've lived a little, you come to adopt a view more like that of Socrates, who said, "If all our misfortunes were laid in one common heap, whence everyone must take an equal portion, most people would be contented to take their own and depart."

The dilemma is the decision: "Do I let go of the rope, or do I press on?" Do I continue to plow and cultivate the life and opportunities that God has placed before me? The alternative to prevailing until the harvest comes is to let go of all I hold dear, giving in to discouragement and despair. The choice, at times, is not as simple as it sounds and certainly never free of pain.

A lot of people will tell you that if you really love God and God really loves you, life is going to be easy; if you were more committed, you wouldn't be having all of your problems. I don't know any person with a strong, firsthand faith in God who hasn't gone through periods of disappointment, but during those disappointments, firsthand faith grows strongest.

We dream. We dabble. We grow disappointed. We face the dilemma of letting go of the rope, and we feel demoralized. Demoralized people say, "I don't care," and mean it. There are many times we say, "I don't care," when we're trying to get people's attention. But when you say, "I don't care," and you really mean it, you're in trouble. All that's left is to disengage and drift. And when you're drifting, you're a sitting duck because only dead things drift downstream. You're open for almost anything that comes into your life that can be incredibly self-destructive. The pioneer and founder of the Methodist Church, John Wesley, said, "Men, never despair, but if you do work on in despair."

Right now you (or someone you know) may be saying or thinking, "God, I've tried to do the right thing, the God thing, but I'm discouraged and about to let go of the rope. I was told if I loved You and trusted You, things would work out my way. I was told if I was committed enough and dedicated enough and good enough, I would be immune to most of this stuff." The truth is, life with God is not an easier life, a better quality life, but it is one worth whatever you have to go through to finish well. So if you let go of the ropes that tie you to the life of God, you will end up fanning out, flaming out, fouling out, and fizzling out.

Who wants to be remembered as the friend who fanned out? This term is used in baseball to describe a batter swinging and missing all three pitches. An example of fanning out in the Bible is a guy by the name of Mark. Barnabas took him along on the first missionary journey that he and Paul conducted. For reasons unknown, Mark quit in the middle of the trip. His failure angered Paul to the point that when "Barnabas wanted to take John, also called Mark, with them, . . . Paul did not think it wise to take him, because he had deserted them in Pamphylia and had not continued with them in the work. They had such a sharp disagreement that they parted company" (Acts 15:37–39 NIV). You don't want to be remembered as a failure.

There's a big difference between failing, which is what Mark did when he tucked tail and ran home, and becoming a failure. On his first "up to bat" John Mark fanned out, but he did not let go of the rope entirely because at the end of Paul's life, while writing to his young protégé Timothy, he said, "Get Mark and bring him with you, because he is helpful to me" (2 Tim. 4:11 NIV). Mark learned that fanning out need not be final or fatal.

You remember some people because they flamed out. Somewhere along the way they lost their first love. Someone who used to be an on-fire, go-for-the-gold good buddy turned into an absentee friend. When you met, the conversation was peppered with energetic and encouraging words, but now there are only silence and blank stares. Now the person's words betray sarcasm in the spirit, arsenic in the words, and sawdust in the heart. The person looks distant and distracted; over time he drifts from your memory until a chance meeting or conversation with a mutual friend recalls how it used to be and you feel sad all over again. It is the same sadness you can hear in Paul's words: "Demas, because he loved this world, has deserted me" (2 Tim. 4:10 NIV).

Never take the chance of burning up all your spiritual fuel and being forced to live on the fumes. It's dangerous. Better people than you and I have been content to run on empty for too long, and now they sit on the sidelines bruised, bitter, and broken.

Some people foul out because they choose to live life out of bounds. It is sad to see a person who once lived boldly and bravely in the face of compromise but, because of disappointment, fear, or laziness, no longer demands much of herself. It is heartbreaking to see a promising man grow careless and lazy in his daily disciplines. But if you walk around the edges long enough, you're bound to fall off, and if you play with fire long enough, you will get burned. The Scriptures ask, "Can a man hold fire against his chest and not be burned?" (Prov. 6:27 TLB).

Some people just fizzle out. They are the people Jesus warned, "Anyone who lets himself be distracted from the work I plan for him is not fit for the Kingdom of God" (Luke 9:62 TLB). Like the cheetah, for lack of heart, they fall short of their goal. They live in their heads too much while neglecting their roots.

Whenever I'm with my good buddy Brian Prout for any length of time, he will bring up the influence of his mother. He says, "My mother gave me two things, roots and wings." I like that, for I have seen too many people crash and burn because they have wings but no roots. It is sad to see good people who have unique gifts that raise them to a level of success and significance where their underdeveloped hearts can't keep them.

Wings are great, but roots are essential. A plant or tree receives nourishment through the root system. Deep, healthy roots are important all the time, but never as much as during the dry season or when the winds of adversity blow. For example, the sequoia trees of California tower as much as three hundred feet above the ground. Strangely, these giants have unusually shallow root systems that reach out in all directions to capture the greatest amount of surface moisture. Seldom will you see a redwood standing alone because high winds would quickly uproot it. That's why they grow in clusters. Their intertwining roots provide support for one another against the storms. You need wings, but to finish well, you are going to need roots too.

I want to leave a legacy behind when my life is done. To do that, I want to be remembered for finishing well. I want my family, friends, and those whom I've influenced in any way to remember that the end of my journey was my finest hour. But more than anything else, I want to feel my Father's pleasure when He says to me, "Well done, good and faithful servant! You have been faithful with a few things; I will put you in charge of many things. Come and share your master's happiness!" (Matt. 25:23 NIV).

The Five Habits

English poet John Dryden once said, "Habits gather by unseen degrees, as brooks make rivers, rivers run to seas." I want to leave you with the five habits that will keep you growing and vital as long as you're alive and make the rest of your life the best of your life.

1. Wait to Worry

As I noted in Chapter 5, fear will be your constant nemesis. One of fear's favorite offsprings is worry. People who finish well have developed the habit of waiting to worry. As Jesus said, "Do not worry about your life, what you will eat or drink; or about your body, what you will wear. Is not life more important than food, and the body more important than clothes? Look at the birds of the air; they do not sow or reap or store away in barns, and yet your heavenly Father feeds them. Are you not much more valuable than they?" (Matt. 6:25–26 NIV). Jesus predicated the principle of "no worries" on the fact of God's love. This is a lesson dished out in the classroom or the small group, but it is worked out only in the push and shove of a life committed to a higher, nobler quest.

Refuse to focus on what might or might not happen. You have the promises of God to rely on and His presence to rest upon. Be bold and confident. The God who has brought you this far will bring you home safely. Nothing is too hard for God. The future belongs to God. You belong to God. The song of our youth, "He's Got the Whole World in His Hands," will be the shout of our old age. And remember, growing older is a privilege; getting old is a choice. Trusting God for great things will make your life ageless and timeless.

2. Work to Worship

One of my favorite psalms proclaims, "Let everything that has breath praise the LORD. Praise the LORD" (Ps. 150:6 NIV). Praise isn't just something done in a church or a cathedral by a choir or an ensemble. I praise God by sensing Him, then serving Him. Real praise is done during the weekday, not just the weekend.

Work is not a curse. Work is not a burden. Work is not something we spend the best years of our lives doing so we can retire and spend the rest eating food we can no longer digest, visiting sights we can no longer see, and lying on beaches we can no longer walk. Work is my chance to show who God is to me and what He is making of me. Work is worship. It's real praise. It makes this God I worship believable to the people around me.

People who finish well see work as worship. That's the activity for which you were made and from which you need never retire. Contemplate what you were made for as you read this: "We are God's workmanship, created in Christ Jesus to do good works, which God prepared in advance for us to do" (Eph. 2:10 NIV). Or what about this bit of wisdom from the wisest man who ever lived? "Whatever your hand finds to do, do it with all your might, for in the grave, where you are going, there is neither working nor planning nor knowledge nor wisdom" (Eccles. 9:10 NIV).

Meaningful work (a noble cause) is God's gift to you. It fills your days with reasons to work well. How you do the work (a commitment to excellence, integrity, and quality) is your gift of worship. If you sense God without serving Him, then you're not worshiping Him, and that's a tragedy. But if you serve God without sensing His presence or pleasure, that's a drudgery. Maybe that's why we tend to worship our work and play at our worship. To finish well, you must get the priority straight. You don't worship your work, but you work as an act of worship to God and service to humankind.

3. Love to Learn

People who finish well have found the habit of lifelong learning. To be alive is to learn and grow, right? The Bible advises, "Let us stop going over the same old ground again and again, always teaching those first lessons about Christ. Let us go on instead to other things and become mature in our understanding, as strong

Christians ought to be. Surely we don't need to speak further about the foolishness of trying to be saved by being good, or about the necessity of faith in God" (Heb. 6:1 TLB).

Healthy things grow. Growing things change. Changing things create chaos. Chaos threatens comfort and the status quo. The only living things that object to this process are people. Plants don't object to it, trees don't fight it, but people do.

To finish well is to remain open to change. That's where learning comes in because when you learn something new, or discover something you didn't know, suddenly, the world is bigger and filled with endless opportunities, but at the same time it's scarier and out of control. That's why waiting to worry is so powerful. Trusting God for new things, greater things, stretches you and keeps you growing.

4. Stop to Start

Those who finish well also know the value of slowing down, being still, and remaining silent for a time. The Bible assures us that God is at the controls when it says,

> He makes wars cease to the ends of the earth;
> he breaks the bow and shatters the spear,
> he burns the shields with fire.
> "Be still, and know that I am God;
> I will be exalted among the nations,
> I will be exalted in the earth."
> The LORD Almighty is with us;
> the God of Jacob is our fortress.
> (Ps. 46:9–11 NIV)

Ever hear someone refer to life as the "daily grind"? That's a graphic description of how too many of us feel too much of the time. Unlike life in the movies, where there is a thrill a minute, life in the real world has a way of grinding you down. Haven't you had days when you felt some sort of spiritual gravity pulling you down?

Would you like to rise above the daily grind and the downward drag of this very day? Does soaring above the mundane with a spirit of peace, joy, and hope sound good to you? Then sit back, slow down, and get ready to mull over some things that are excellent and awesome.

Take God's Word seriously: "Whatever is true, whatever is noble, whatever is right, whatever is pure, whatever is lovely, whatever is admirable—if anything is excellent or praiseworthy—think about such things" (Phil. 4:8 NIV). The very act of thinking about the wonders performed by your awesome God will lift you above the moment. The secret to soul soaring is to rediscover and reclaim your sense of wonder. The wonder of God provides the faith to lean out and spread your spiritual wings to soar like an eagle far above the small and petty things of life. Living in the light of God's awesome power does for you what wings and engine do for an airplane. The wings provide lift and the engine provides the thrust the plane needs to break free from the law of gravity, which is determined to keep the plane grounded.

Airplanes break the law of gravity because they're designed to, and believe it or not, so are you. You can break free from the downward pull of fear, shame, and doubt. These forces form a type of spiritual gravity that works to keep you grounded. To soar as you were designed, you must put out your wings of faith and believe. That's where wonder plays its part.

Think of the love of God as your lift and the Word of God as your thrust. God provides lift as you "humble [yourself], therefore, under God's mighty hand, that he may *lift you up in due time*. Cast all your anxiety on him because he cares for you" (1 Pet. 5:6–7 NIV, italics added). Your spiritual thrust comes from the promises of God. A vast, inexhaustible source of life-giving lift and thrust is yours in the amazing love of God and awesome promises of God contained in the Scriptures. As David said, "Your promises have been thoroughly tested, and your servant loves them" (Ps. 119:140 NIV).

God's promises are just potential power until you believe them and act upon them. Saint Augustine of Hippo declared,

"No man has a right to lead such a life of contemplation as to forget in his own ease the service due to his neighbor; nor has any man a right to be so immersed in active life as to neglect the contemplation of God." Stopping to regain your sense of wonder and mystery from God must be followed by starting back up again to live in the real world by a new and more glorious reality.

5. Start to Finish

Sir Winston Churchill advised, "Death and sorrow will be the companions of our journey; hardship our garment; constancy and valor our only shield. We must be united, we must be undaunted, and we must be inflexible." I have written an entire book on the problem of quitting called *The Power to Prevail*. A paragraph bears repeating here: "Awards get distributed at the finish line. To be able to persevere, to be able to endure, and move forward—that's winning. It's not where you start or even how you start that matters, but how you cross the finish line. Don't be remembered for what you quit because you are weak, but rather what you endured because you are strong."[1]

We are a growing generation of people who are forever gathering around the starting gate. As a result, we're getting good at starts, but lousy at finishes. It has been one of the top reasons that people fail at life. But all good things do come to an end, and the goal is to finish what we start. I long to be able to reflect on my life, as the apostle Paul did over his, and say without fear or regret, "I have fought the good fight, I have finished the race, I have kept the faith" (2 Tim. 4:7 NIV). Maybe that's why I have never dared to pray for an easier life, but I have prayed to be made a better, stronger person. I find nothing attractive in praying for tasks equal to my personal power, but I have assaulted the throne of God's grace for powers equal to an excellent, noble, difference-making task.

In Ronald Reagan's first inaugural address on January 20, 1981, he made reference to the simple white grave markers in Arlington National Memorial Cemetery:

Under one such marker lies a young man—Martin Treptow—who left his job in a small town barber shop in 1917 to go to France with the famed Rainbow Division. There, on the western front, he was killed trying to carry a message between battalions under heavy artillery fire.

His diary was found on his body. On the flyleaf under the heading, "My Pledge," he had written these words: "America must win this war. Therefore, I will work, I will save, I will sacrifice, I will endure, I will fight cheerfully and do my utmost, as if the issue of the whole struggle depended on me alone."

I want that to be my legacy. I reject the easy way and the path of least resistance. Electricity may move through a circuit with the easiest route. Rivers always travel around a mountain because it is easier than going through one. Frequently, people are like that too. It is easier to sit in front of the television set than to care for a neighbor's needs. It is easier to get angry at your mate and let that anger smolder over the course of time rather than sitting down and working through the problem. Thumbing through a *Reader's Digest* is much easier than having a time of personal Bible study. And so we find that we humans are prone to take the path of least resistance. But there is one difference between us and electricity and rivers. They will never have to give an account of what they have done. We will. Thus, perhaps we should incline ourselves to take the path of greatest persistence. This means committing to finish your quest on this earth more in love with Jesus Christ than when you began.

Choose to keep learning right up to the day they carry you out. Continue to make plans right up to the end. I talked with a friend several years ago who had just received news that her ninety-four-year-old mother was found dead. I asked her where they found her mother. She said, "They found Mom sitting at her desk hammering out a new set of ten-year goals, which included a company she wanted to start, a book she wanted to write, and a planned trip around the world—alone." I thought, *That's finish-*

ing well. Never stop living and making a difference. Live each day so that when the last one comes, you will leave behind a legacy, an ultimate contribution.

Committed to Excellence

Thank you for taking this journey with me. My mission has been to honor Jesus Christ by helping you excel in every area of your life. I hope these core commitments will cause you to make the most of your one and only life so that, in the words of Henry Wadsworth Longfellow,

> Lives of great men all remind us
>   We can make our lives sublime,
> And departing, leave behind us
>   Footprints on the sands of time.

Make of your life something excellent. Excel in your love for God and people. Excel in your everyday efforts so that they may be considered worship before the One who has given you life. And as the end of the journey in this life comes one day, you will be prepared for the journey that is ready to begin in the next life where "no eye has seen, no ear has heard, no mind has conceived what God has prepared for those who love him" (1 Cor. 2:9 NIV).

When I think of finishing well, I think about others who have already finished their race. Country legend Johnny Cash was right when he sang, just a few months before his death, "Everyone goes away in the end." As you get closer to the shore of the next world than you are to this one, keep in mind the perspective given to us by poet and author Henry van Dyke:

> I am standing upon the seashore. A ship at my side spreads
> her white sails to the morning breeze and starts for the
> blue ocean. She is the object of beauty and strength. I stand
> and watch her until at length she hangs like a speck of

white cloud just where the sea and sky come to mingle with each other. Then someone at my side says: "There, she is gone!" "Gone where?" Gone from my sight. That is all. She is just as large in mast and hull and spar as she was when she left my side and she is just as able to bear her load of living freight to her destined port. Her diminished size is in me, not in her. And just at the moment when someone at my side says, "There, she is gone!" there are other eyes watching her coming, and other voices ready to take up the glad shout: "Here she comes!"

Never let the labels, libels, and limitations that others try to project onto you deter or discourage you from being the best you, you can be. Refuse to listen to the experts—who themselves may be mired in mediocrity—tell you what you can and cannot do. Trust God's opinion of who you are and what you can achieve. Commit your life to excellence, then you can be assured you will have lived well, loved well, and left behind you an enduring legacy.

Notes

Introduction
1. Mitch Albom, *The Five People You Meet in Heaven* (Hyperion, 2003), p. 104.

Chapter 1
1. Religion News Services, "Book Probes Post–Sept. 11 Spirituality," by Douglas Todd, August 27, 2002.
2. Max Lucado, *Applause of Heaven* (Word, 1999), p. 175.
3. Rubel Shelly, "Starting Today"; in *Men of Integrity* (May/June 2003).
4. Frank Tillapaugh, *Unleashing Your Potential* (Gospel Light Publications, 1988), p. 82.
5. Brennan Manning, *The Ragamuffin Gospel* (Multnomah Books, 1990), pp. 116–17.

Chapter 2
1. Frederick Buechner, *Telling the Truth* (Harper & Row, 1977), p. 70.

Chapter 3
1. Max Lucado, *Applause of Heaven* (Word, 1999), p. 154.
2. Jim Loehr and Tony Schwartz, *The Power of Full Engagement* (Free Press, 2003), pp. 8–9.

Chapter 5
1. Brennan Manning, *The Ragamuffin Gospel* (Multnomah Books, 1990), p. 118.

Chapter 6
1. Bernard Goldberg, *Bias* (Perennial, 2002), p. 90.

Chapter 7
1. Sting, *Broken Music* (Bantam Books, 2003), p. 14.

Chapter 9
1. Lee Strobel, *God's Outrageous Claims* (Zondervan, 1998), p. 118.
2. *USA Today,* January 9, 2004.

Chapter 11
1. See Henri J. M. Nouwen, *Sabbatical Journey* (Crossroad, 2000).

Chapter 12
1. David Foster, *The Power to Prevail* (Warner Faith, 2003), pp. 128–29.

How to get in touch with Dr. Foster

David Foster is the founding and senior pastor of
Bellevue Community Church in Nashville, Tennessee
(www.BellevueCommunityChurch.com).

He hosts a popular radio talk show *Making Life Work*.
He and his wife, Paula, are highly respected teachers
of "Married and Loving It" and "The Power of Positive
Parenting" seminars across the country.

To get information on other books, seminars, or teaching series,
or to contact him, check out his Web site at
www.fosteringhope.com.

WITHDRAWN

AUG 29 2005

ELKHART PUBLIC LIBRARY

Elkhart, Indiana

DEMCO